SGGS6001

Family Care and Social Capital: Transitions in Informal Care

Patrick Barrett • Beatrice Hale • Mary Butler

Family Care and Social Capital: Transitions in Informal Care

 Springer

Patrick Barrett
School of Social Sciences
University of Waikato
Hamilton, New Zealand

Beatrice Hale
Independent Researcher
Dunedin, New Zealand

Mary Butler
School of Occupational Therapy
Otago Polytechnic
Dunedin, New Zealand

ISBN 978-94-007-6871-0   ISBN 978-94-007-6872-7 (eBook)
DOI 10.1007/978-94-007-6872-7
Springer Dordrecht Heidelberg New York London

Library of Congress Control Number: 2013942814

Printed on acid-free paper

Springer is part of Springer Science+Business Media (www.springer.com)

Foreword

When I first became involved in the carers movement more than 20 years ago there was very little literature available either for carers themselves or for those interested in caring in its wider social context. Since then, not only has the movement itself grown hugely so that carers and caring are recognised in many parts of the world, but the range of literature has grown too. There are many guides for carers and many academic studies, both very welcome to those who are caring and to those who are interested in helping them. This book, though, occupies a unique place and I am delighted and honoured to be asked to write a foreword.

This work will be of great value to those who work directly with carers and to those studying the caring process, both in terms of relationships between individuals, their history, obligations and developments, as well as in the wider context of social policy. Carers too will find it most useful, no matter what their individual situation since their voice is strong throughout.

As someone who has seen the development of the carers movement since the days when the word was frequently mis-spelled as 'career', I am especially pleased that the book emphasises the importance of achieving complete recognition for the role of carers and the growth of a common identity around the shared role of care giving. My work as a campaigner for carers led to me being created a 'Peer of the Realm' with the opportunity to contribute to making legislation in the British Parliament. In that role I see clearly that the power of the carers movement worldwide will drive policy and will ensure that carers everywhere are given the recognition and the rights that they so richly deserve.

House of Lords, Palace of Westminster,   Baroness [Jill] Pitkeathley
London, UK
July 2012

Acknowledgements

This book has been written with the assistance of numerous kind and good people, and there are many we would like to acknowledge. Patrick acknowledges the generosity of the many research participants, their families and their carers who have shared their experiences of giving and receiving care. Together we acknowledge friendly colleagues who have listened patiently, helped with discussions, and shaped ideas by their questions and comments. Among these, Beatrice wishes to acknowledge the generosity of carers, especially those in the early carers' groups, and particularly the mentorship of Professor A.J. Campbell, whom she describes as 'geriatrician extraordinaire', and the assistance from anthropologists, the late Peter Wilson, and Ian Frazer. Members of the local New Zealand Association of Gerontology group gave valuable feedback in research seminars. The Otago University Library and the Bill Robertson Library are exceptional in their collections and their helpfulness. Correspondents from New Zealand, Canada, Scandinavia and the United Kingdom must also be mentioned for their willingness to discuss and assist, both face-to-face at conferences and through email discussions.

Mary would like to mention leaders from within the disability community, both carers and people with disability, for examples of how to live a good life under difficult circumstance. In particular: Cathy Mathews (Brain Injury Association), Lawrence Chok (Inclusion Aotearoa), Jan Moss (Complex Carers Group), Sharon Cooke (individualised funding pioneer), Jean and Stuart Burnett (payment of family carers campaign). She is grateful for 2 years of lively debate about care and disability as a member of the Ministry of Health National Reference Group for co-developing a new model for supporting people with disability. The Donald Beasley Institute for the study of intellectual disability was a consistent source of support, particularly the late Dr. Anne Bray and her successor as director, Dr. Brigit Mirfin-Veitch. The Bioethics Center at Otago University provided a safe haven to have intellectually stimulating conversations about care. Professor Grant Gillett and postgraduate students helped to make connections to the wider ethics literature.

This conversation has flowed into the School of Occupational Therapy, through the patience of Dr. Linda Robertson and Sian Griffiths. Parthasarathi Rajagopalachari has been a constant source of guidance about how care informs the 'grihastha' (householder) spiritual path.

Finally, and not least, as always we acknowledge our families who have lived with this book until completion.

Contents

Introduction

Family Care and Social Capital: Transitions in Informal Care

Family Care and Social Capital: Transitions in Informal Care is intended to be read by those working with family and other informal carers and by family caregivers themselves. This includes various health and social care professionals, including doctors and medical students, social workers, occupational therapists, field officers, and others working with people with disabilities and their caregivers. We organise our review and discussion of issues in family and informal care around some of the important situations where this occurs: the care of babies and children, care for adults with acquired disability, care for family members with intellectual, physical and mental disabilities, care for older people, and care occurring across multiple generations. It is not possible to include all caregiving situations; nevertheless, what we offer is an approach by which to consider other caring circumstances, such as where there are mental health issues or in palliative care situations.

With improvements in medical knowledge and treatment practices, an increasing number of people with complex and multiple needs have increased longevity. This has occurred alongside the implementation of policies of deinstitutionalisation and a shift towards community care. In this context, informal and family carers play an increasingly important role. Today, family carers face ever more complex caring situations, intermittently or continuously, either as direct hands-on carers or as support carers.

Many become informal caregivers following the birth of child with disabilities, as a result of developmental delays, or mental or physical health problems; others will move into the role after a family member experiences a traumatic health event or following a later diagnosis. Such carers go on to take a greater or lesser part in caregiving. Carers for older people tend to be either spouses or adult children who take on caring following, for example, the debilities of strokes or Parkinson's disease, or the slow progression of Alzheimer's disease. Within these larger categories are other groups with their own distinctive vulnerabilities – there is an emerging awareness of the needs of young carers of parents and grandparents, and grandparent carers of young children, and a growing interest in migrant and distant caregiving.

Caregiving invokes emotions of love or affection, of duty, and of mutual support, and is usually seen as part of being a member of a family or living in a close relationship. As such, we have to ask, why are we considering informal caregiving as a distinctive role? Should it be seen simply as an extension of a family or neighbourly relationship and, therefore, embedded in that relationship? From our personal experience, from working with family and informal caregivers, and also our own research in this area, we see family and informal caregiving as much more than that. Caregiving is indeed an expression of nurturing and support, but in situations of multiple and complex needs, family members or neighbours can be called on to care in ways that are non-normative. Consequently, life course processes for caregivers are framed or constrained by their caregiving role. It is important to give attention to such caregiving given that it has a significant impact on the lives of carers, affecting their physical and mental health, their social connectedness, and their material security. We suggest these need to be acknowledged and that such caregiving be given greater social recognition. Recognition may take various forms: support through community arrangements that make it easy to care; societal recognition through an acknowledgment that this is a special role; political recognition in terms of policy measures to support the work of care; and recognition of the health of both of the care-recipient and the caregiver.

Informal and family caregiving is portrayed variously as ranging from being a 'burden' to being a positive 'transformative experience'. Zarit et al. (1980, 1986) emphasised the 'burden' of care to demonstrate the extent of the work involved and the consequent strain on caregivers. Others, notably Scorgie and Sobsey (2000) and Scorgie et al. (2004), have focused on the transformative experience for caregivers in a positive sense. If we focus on the experience of carer burden, we see informal caregiving in terms of its workload and other demands, and in terms of the consequences for families and for individuals, in terms of physical costs, social constraint, and in terms of barriers to participation in paid employment. Becoming an informal caregiver, however, can also lead to the development of a specialised knowledge and skill in the area of care, and be associated with personal growth. Both perspectives offer insight into the experience of care and both are evident in the accounts of caregiving that follow.

Informal and family care is emphatically a type of labour and, as such, work for which there is a case for formal recognition through social policy support. This question is increasingly the subject of debate in many countries. Successive courts in New Zealand have recently ruled that family and informal caregiving does actually merit payment but the formal policy response of government has yet to be confirmed.

Aside from debates about payment for family caregivers, in each of the following chapters we sketch out different forms of practical support which we interpret as an indication of the wider environment of social capital. The notion of social capital represents the potential social resources for positive support – the bonds through which families and communities express mutual support and the bridges which link families and communities with formal organisational forms of support. Social capital does imply informal social networks and the contribution they make within families and communities. It also captures the way informal caregivers build their own capacity to care as they acquire specialised knowledge and skills, and the spill-over effects of this. We observe many instances where informal caregivers extend their advocacy for the person they care for to broader community-wide activities, through their membership of disability support networks, and through their advocacy and involvement with formal care, health and education organisations.

The experiences of the caregivers in different stages of the life course show that there are considerable commonalities, and we propose that such commonalities can be seen as a community of care practice. Carers are unified by a dynamic that encompasses their movement through similar transition experiences, such as the moment of assuming responsibility, the development of care-related skill and knowledge, interaction with formal health and welfare professionals, and various phases of separation and possible relinquishment. These commonalities are experienced across different types of disability, relationship to the person with disability or societal attitudes to disability. In this sense the community of care practice can be identified as a unique culture in its own right. An appreciation of this shared experience reinforces the case for appropriate policies of recognition and support.

Chapter Outline

Chapter 1: Family Care and Social Capital

There is a growing scholarly interest in family and informal caregiving. Chapter 1 introduces this field of study and makes a case for giving greater recognition to family caregiver needs. It reviews the broad approaches to the study of informal caregiving and traces how the carer movement has developed alongside the emergence of new and critical insights from the disability movement. We recognise informal and family care as complex work deserving greater recognition, and make a case for bringing the voices of informal caregivers to the policy-making table.

Chapter 2: Informal Care in Social Context: An Expression of Social Relationships

In this chapter we seek to locate informal care within the context of social networks and broader care systems. Informal family care cannot be explained by the ordinary logic of self-interest, but instead exemplifies the inclination to place the care needs of other family or community members above one's own interests. The level of informal care provided is an indication of a community's social capital. While social capital is a slippery concept, it may be taken as an indicator of 'the ability of actors to [provide and] secure benefits by virtue of membership in social networks or other

social structures' (Portes 1998, p. 6). Having laid out a rationale for the closer examination of informal care today, we draw attention first to the value of the care given by
using Bourdieu's concept of social capital to examine resources and skills brought by
expert practitioners of care in various areas of disability. Furthermore this brings
together the field of caring studies with disability studies by examining the response
of people with disability to the care that is given. The discussion on the centrality of
informal care and its place in the concept of social capital will conclude with a reflection on the importance of public policy which facilitates family care and reinforces
environments where the capacity to provide such care is enhanced, not undermined.

Chapter 3: The Dynamic Experience of Caregiving

The focus here is on outlining a rite of passage framework for uncovering the
transition experiences of individuals as they adopt the role and responsibilities of an
informal caregiver. The framework implies a beginning point of change, a period
of confusion and instability, and passage towards a new point of stability and reconnection. This approach has been used elsewhere (Hale et al. 2010) in our analysis of
the transition into supported independence in later life, and facilitates a detailed
analysis of the experiences of change through a key life transition – in this instance,
that of becoming a caregiver. Focussing on the three stages provides for the analysis
of the complex changes faced by the caregiver, these occurring within broader
socially constructed contexts which define the nature of family relationships and
responsibilities, as well as the policy measures to support those relationships and
responsibilities. Our approach to the analysis of transitions in the experience of
caring, which allows for attention to be given to key moments of need, and use of the
concept of social capital to comment on the way various social and collectively
provided resources create environments which influence the capacities for care, we
believe makes a contribution to understanding family and informal care.

Chapter 4: Informal Caring and Early Childhood

We begin our focus on the everyday experience of caregiving by examining the
issues of caring for young children with congenital conditions or impairments from
early childhood injuries. Caring for people in this life stage, especially by parents,
presents distinctive challenges. We follow through the stages of separation, liminality
and the notion of reconnection(s) to highlight the immediacy of the carer experiences.
Our ideas about reconnection are discussed, in terms of outreach and the wider
social recognition of the new role and identity.

We refer to examples of the experience of carers to reveal the practical, personal,
emotional and social dimensions of their lives. Cases emphasise the need to

(1) appreciate the practical supports required for caregivers, be they actual services or information; (2) understand the personal and emotional challenges associated with caring in this context – grief, sadness, fear for the child's future, feelings of inadequacy, feelings of isolation; (3) understand the social situation – gender issues, the home environment, the social networks, the introduction of health and allied professionals; and (4) appreciate the financial and employment implications for caregivers. We recognise the learning and knowledge acquired by family carers as they grow in their expertise. The chapter will conclude by considering the types of supports necessary to facilitate effective caring in these contexts.

Chapter 5: Caring for Family Members with a Lifelong Disability

In this chapter we move the discussion to care for adolescents and adults with lifelong disabilities. Caregivers in this situation are confronted daily with the ongoing dependency of the person with disability and, for parents, this can lead to a state of continuous parenthood. Caring across the life course, however, can lead to the development of expertise in care practice, in working with professionals, and in advocacy for the person with disability and for others in similar situations. As they develop in this way, we can begin to see lifelong caregivers as making an important contribution to social capital. The chapter will conclude by considering the types of supports necessary to facilitate effective caring in these contexts.

Chapter 6: Caring for Adults with Acquired Disabilities

Caring for an adult who has acquired a disability or developed a major disease or illness provides another context of informal care work. The care relationship must be negotiated as the boundaries of the disability are gradually ascertained. In this chapter, we reflect on the way the vulnerability of the person with disability is shared with the primary informal caregiver. We give greater focus, therefore, to the person with disability as a way of recognising that as they achieve 'reconnection', so too does the caregiver. This provides the context for a discussion of creating authentic lives for both caregiver and cared-for. Ethical issues which can arise within this relationship have been exemplified by the feminist movement, which has given a nuanced analysis of the possibility for exploitation within this form of care. In terms of the disability movement itself, most of the dialogue about care comes from those who have acquired a disability and this dialogue highlights ethical flashpoints. The chapter concludes by considering the types of supports necessary to facilitate effective caring in these contexts.

Chapter 7: Caring for Older People

As the population ages, a growing amount of the additional care needed will come from informal caregivers. This chapter reviews the experience of caring for an elderly spouse, partner or parent. The focus is on the transition into becoming a primary informal caregiver for a spouse or aged parent and the implications for the caregiver. We use the rites of passage framework more explicitly than in other chapters to illustrate the phases of separation, liminality and reconnection, and we examine these in terms of the temporal, spatial and relational dimensions. We conclude by reflecting on what it means to be reconnected as a caregiver in this caregiving situation.

Chapter 8: Caring Across the Generations

This chapter focuses on carers who are themselves vulnerable in particular ways – young carers and older carers. There has been growing awareness of a group of young people who play a critical role in caring for parents, grandparents or siblings. Young carers face particular challenges as they carry responsibility for the care of another while negotiating the demands of adolescence, schooling and the transition into adulthood. Caregiving at this age presents a variety of developmental challenges. At the other end of the life course are grandparent carers. Here, too, there is a growing awareness of a group of people who face particular challenges from a caregiving role. Many fully substitute for the role of parents and become exclusive caregivers for, usually, their grandchildren. We focus on the experience of taking up this role and reflect on the consequences.

Chapter 9: Recognising and Supporting Informal Care

We conclude the arguments in the book by reviewing the commonalities of the different caregiving situations. This includes outlining the particular insights obtained by analysing the caregiver experience at key transition points. By framing the experiences of caregiving as a series of transitions, and by relating these to the changing needs of the person in need of care, we draw attention to both the experience of the caregiver and the particular needs they face at key junctures.

Doing so provides a basis for recognising the increasingly critical role of family and informal caregivers in supporting people within the community. It also provides a basis for considering the specific supports that can be provided to individual caregivers by health professionals and other sectors within the social service network. Further, it leads to consideration of broader policy measures to build society's capacity, or social capital, to support such care. We bring together our preceding observations about how to support effectively family caregivers, and we make a case for policy settings which facilitate greater recognition of the informal care sector and the critical role it plays in meeting contemporary demands for health and social care. We recommend the informal care sector be supported through a variety of policy instruments and that efforts be made to carefully integrate the activities of governments with those of families in the care of those most in need.

References

Hale, B., Barrett P., & Gauld, R. (2010). *The age of supported independence*. Dordrecht: Springer.

Portes, A. (1998). Social capital: Its origins and applications in modern sociology. *Annual Review of Sociology, 24*, 1–24.

Scorgie, K., & Sobsey, D. (2000). Transformational outcomes associated with parenting children who have disabilities. *Mental Retardation, 38*, 195–206.

Scorgie, K., Wilgosh, L., & Sobsey, D. (2004). The experience of transformation in parents of children with disabilities: Theoretical considerations. *Developmental Disabilities Bulletin, 32*(1), 84–110.

Zarit, S. H., Reever, K. E., & Bach-Peterson, J. (1980). Relatives of the impaired elderly: Correlates of feelings of burden. *The Gerontologist, 20*(6), 649–655.

Zarit, S. H., Todd, P. A., & Zarit, J. M. (1986). Subjective burden of husbands and wives as caregivers: A longitudinal study. *The Gerontologist, 26*(3), 260–266.

Chapter 1
Family Care and Social Capital

1.1 Introduction

The book that follows draws on our research and experience in working with family caregivers, both professionally and personally. We also draw on insights from contemporary research into informal care, along with relevant case studies and vignettes, to offer a theoretically informed account of the experience of informal caregiving. Our purpose is to highlight what we see as critical issues faced by informal caregivers, and in so doing provide a guide for people working in the area of disability and care.

There is a growing scholarly interest in family and informal caregiving corresponding to a paradigm shift in ways of thinking about how to care for people with multiple and complex needs who live in the community. The period of institutionalisation was marked by the disempowerment of family carers who were given the message that the care they provided was not as good as professional care for their loved ones. For example, disability, especially serious disability, was seen as requiring the skills of a professional (Dubrow 1965). Following the period of de-institutionalisation, many of the same attitudes about the necessity for professional skill remained intact within the formal care sector where, even among the most enlightened formal care providers, there has been a tendency to 'capture' people with disability and work with them outside the family context in order to help them achieve their goals. From the 1980s, however, there has been a growing recognition of the importance of a host of family, friends or neighbours who as non-professional caregivers have performed a wide range of tasks in support of the person in need. These carers have demonstrated that they could achieve positive outcomes that would not otherwise have been attainable. Many people with disability, for example, have been raised to have lives that were not possible in an era when non-regularised, family care was something to be shunned and hidden.

Such family care can be seen as an expression of the available social capital. This is the first of several ways we refer to the concept of social capital in this text (see Chap. 2 for a fuller account). We see social capital as a resource for people with

P. Barrett et al., *Family Care and Social Capital: Transitions in Informal Care*,
DOI 10.1007/978-94-007-6872-7_1, © Springer Science+Business Media Dordrecht 2014

complex needs who live in the community. Finding ways of nurturing and expanding such resources within families and neighbourhoods has potential to enhance the lives of both those in need of care and those who provide care. In the chapters that follow, we examine the nuances of what social capital means in a variety of contexts of family and informal care, and in a range of common caregiving situations across the life course. From this overview, we identify shared experiences of caregivers in these situations and we discuss these with the intention of enhancing formal care practice and care policy.

We are aware that how we describe the practicalities of caring reflects our view of the world. We also see theory as having potential to provide for 'flashes of insight' (Turner 1969) which not only illuminates individual circumstances, and identifies commonalities across different situations, but which can also inform both practitioners and policy makers.

Clarification of terminology and definitions is essential, especially in this area of care where there are common terms but a variety of different meanings and references. To care 'about' someone refers to emotions of affection. To care for someone refers to the act of providing support, help, and assistance. Care within families and communities, and by paid care workers, is both an affect and an action. The term carer is often used for members of a family who provide care, while caregiver often refers to the formal paid nurse or aide. We use both terms, carer and caregiver, to refer to family members, friends or neighbours who provide care. When we refer to paid caregivers, we use the terms care workers or formal caregivers. When we refer to the people requiring care, we use various terms that indicate the person within the particular care situation, such as a loved one, a child or person with a disability, care-recipient, or an older person with an acquired disability, these different situations being the topics of Chaps. 4, 5, 6, 7 and 8. To describe the actions of carers or caregivers, we use the term informal or family care. Informal or family care refers to care or support, including physical and practical assistance for the activities of daily living, that has a major impact on the lives of the people offering the support, be they parents, spouses, adult children or friends and neighbours.

1.2 Making Informal Care Visible

Informal and family care continues to be taken for granted as an expression of family and neighbourly affection, responsibility and duty. Elizabeth Roberts' comment in an oral history study of caring that 'relatives were cared for because it was assumed that was what one did' (Cook 2007, p. 6), captures the taken-for-granted nature of informal care – it is 'what one does.' The 'one' has, however, typically been female and the caregiving typically seen as an extension of the domestic work role. The consequences for women of such assumptions began to be recognised and questioned in the 1960s by, for example, the Reverend Mary Webster, a Congregational minister who had given up her work to care for her parents, and who, on the death of her parents, reflected on the disadvantages, not least financial, that her sense of filial obligation and love had created for her (Cook 2007, p. 8). Her reflections resulted in the cause of women like herself being publicised on a large scale and in the establishment of the National Council for the Single Woman and her Dependants in 1965. She outlined a need to:

> draw the attention of Government and Opposition to the difficulties that confront single women when they have to care for dependants, and urges that steps should be taken to consider and alleviate their difficulties through social policy and legislation (Cook 2007, p. 12).

The Reverend Mary Webster's situation involved caring for an older dependent. Such a role is increasingly required of both the single and the married today, given the widespread policy of ageing in place. As Lim and Zebrack (2004) suggest, caring for an ill or disabled family member is becoming an expected part of family life. This is all the more so given that families today are also dealing with the consequences of the change from institutional care to home care for younger people with disabilities. Families have become more, rather than less, involved in caring for members with impairments across the life course, whether they live in the family home or outside of it. This introduces new social roles into accepted normative stages of the family life course, and these raise new challenges for individuals. Such challenges revolve around the demands of the care responsibilities and other accepted life stage roles, tensions around the competing demands of paid employment and family work, and issues of carer 'burden'.

This, therefore, touches on the opportunity costs of family caregiving and in so doing introduces a second way in which we refer to the notion of social capital and its significance for informal care. Social capital can also be thought of as those individual or family resources that are depleted or leached through association with those with multiple or complex needs. Many of the critical issues in informal caregiving stem from the fact that caregivers can come to share in the reduced circumstances of the person with complex needs. In effect, the complex need can become the circumstance for reducing the social capital of the whole family group. A gendered perspective of social capital recognises that this loss tends to be inordinately felt by female caregivers. How we negotiate these has important implications for the wellbeing of the cared-for person as well as their family members.

In initiating the recognition of care, the Reverend Mary Webster created greater public visibility of informal caregiving and its consequences for those family members providing the care. Informal caregiving is beginning to be recognised, socially and politically, as making a critical contribution within the social services of welfare states. It continues to be the backbone of care provision in many countries. Our intention here is to contribute to that growing recognition by providing an account of a range of common caregiving situations and, hopefully, an understanding with which to engage in debates about the greater recognition of and support for family carers.

Growing awareness of the significant demographic and social trends in the late twentieth and early twenty-first century and the implications for the demand for and supply of care have bolstered the lobbying initiatives of the likes of Mary Webster and those of the care movement in signalling the importance of informal care and the needs of informal caregivers (Dalley 1988). Structural and numerical population ageing are increasingly recognised as indicators of a growing demand for care, particularly informal care, given the greater needs of older-old people for help and support (Walker et al. 1995; Pool 2007).

The significance of informal care in meeting the needs of an older population is all the more important given falling birth-rates in most OECD countries, meaning there will be fewer adult children to care for older people. Further, the tendency for greater longevity of people with chronic illnesses and disabilities in tandem with declining rates of residential living is leading to more care being provided in the community as either support in the family home or supported living elsewhere. Social trends in the form of changing family structures, higher labour force partici-pation by middle-aged women, the emergence of 'sandwich' generation caregivers, and the geographical dispersal of families all affect the potential supply of care within families. In response to demographic and social trends, therefore, there is growing interest in the meaning of informal and formal care, its costs to families and to the wider society, how it might be supported, and the ideal arrangements of social service systems to meet growing needs in a way that complements family and informal caregivers (Fine 2007; Phillips 2007; Arksey and Glendinning 2007).

This highlights a third sense in which social capital will be discussed – the social capital which informal caregivers represent to society as a whole. Caregivers have long recognised the significant savings that their labour represents, when the alter-native would once have been welfare or institutional care for those they care for. Therefore care labour represents a resource to society.

1.2.1 Recognising Caregiver Need

Cook's (2007, p. 6) review of the history of the carers' movement states that 'the carer's role as we now understand it was not fully articulated until the 1980s.' While there has been growth in formal care services over the past 40 years, informal care remains the preferred option for people with chronic illness and disability, most of whom have been found to prefer families to provide care (Marin et al. 2009, p. 14). Informal care is preferred because it is seen as an ordinary expression of love, help and support within families and among neighbours. But such care can also be described as extraordinary, given that it goes beyond normal or usual care within the family life course (Biegel et al. 1991). Caring for a family member with a chronic illness or disability presents distinctive challenges.

The manner in which this can push a family to the edge of endurance has often been kept as a private matter. Affluent as well as poor families can find themselves overwhelmed with the responsibilities of care. It is easy to ignore the extraordinary stresses faced by families when they lack sufficient resources, financial, social, phys-ical or emotional. Occasionally a family does have the resources to draw attention to its plight, and is willing to do so, as in the case of the Kelso family where the father was a CEO and the mother an activist for disabled people (as reported in Kittay 2002,

p. 269). They were able to use their accumulated resources and their personal networks to draw attention to the difficulties they faced, and their story illustrates how un-ordinary their caregiving demands were. They made the front page of newspapers when they abandoned their multiply disabled and medically fragile young son in a hospital during the Christmas holidays, when relief caregivers were in very short supply. The care demands meant they were unable to live an ordinary life.

This example also highlights the fourth sense in which social capital is referred to here. The capacity to advocate both individually and politically can be seen as in indication of social capital resources available to a family. The Kelso family was affluent, and had acquired a political *savoir faire* which gave them leverage within the political spectrum to draw attention to their plight.

Informal caregiving is therefore both ordinary and extraordinary. It implies an ongoing need, and an ongoing commitment by the caregiver beyond the usual family care situation. It can be seen as an extension of family or neighbourly duty, one that has important consequences for care-recipients and caregivers. It is of concern that within this relationship, carers' needs tend to be unacknowledged, and this is what Mary Webster highlighted. She demonstrated that both the person in need of care and the family caregiver are vulnerable to poor and negative outcomes. The caregiver actually comes to share the dependency of the person cared for, during the lifetime of the cared-for person and afterwards. In fact, Kittay (2002) suggests that the greater the need of the cared-for person, the greater the risk to the caregiver. Both the cared-for person and the caregiver are vulnerable.

There are many reasons why carers may need support from health care and welfare professionals, not least because of the physical and emotional challenges of caregiving, but also the challenges within the care relationship and the human tendency for it to go awry. Much has been made in the disability movement of the potential for abuse by the caregiver, yet in a care relationship it is not only the care receiver who is in a vulnerable position; caregivers are vulnerable also, and face the risk of being devalued and dominated by those they care for (Fine and Glendinning 2005). The autistic child with difficult behaviour can grow into a large man capable of intimidating the person caring for him. A nuanced perspective of social capital will recognise both the opportunity costs of caring and also the power issues that can arise.

So while informal care today has come to play a critical role in welfare systems, it presents significant risks for individual caregivers in terms of the consequences of carer stress and burden, and significant social, economic and personal costs. Researchers into informal care have, therefore, consistently argued for family caregivers to be better supported (Phillips 2007).

1.3 Informal and Formal Care

Support occurs within the context of the particular configuration of informal care and formal care services. Formal care is delivered 'through extensions to social policy initiatives, these being expressed in different countries through different combinations of state, community and private, for-profit actors' (Fine 2007, p. 138). The extent to which formal care arrangements facilitate or frustrate the abilities of families to provide care to family members is a central theme in research on informal caregiving. The way the linkages between formal and informal caregiving are understood is influenced by the way we conceptualise the contribution of informal care. The contribution of informal care in the care process is conceptualised in a number of ways: as that of an 'informant' in the interaction with formal care workers; as a 'therapy assistant'; as a 'co-client'; as a 'collaborator'; and as a 'director' (Nolan et al. 2001, p. 94). Twigg (1989) describes the possible roles as carers as a 'resource', as 'co-workers', or as 'co-clients'. Each of these perspectives involves positioning the informal caregiver in relation to formal care. While not purely substitutable, what happens in one domain certainly influences the other. The interactions between health and social care professionals with informal carers occurs within the context of policy settings, and such settings are, of course, the outcomes of political, social, cultural and economic environments.

Contemporary reviews of European social care systems have pointed to a number of challenges in creating supportive environments for informal caregivers (Marin et al. 2009). These include issues around the coordination and integration of formal and informal care systems; the vexed issue of financial support; the practical issue of developing sensitive needs-assessment practices; training for carers; organisational support for informal carers; the need for greater recognition of the informal care sector; and the development of shared visions for all stakeholders (Marin et al. 2009, p. 5).

These issues signal the tension in the relationship between informal and formal care. Twigg (1989) characterised that tension in such a way as to suggest informal caregivers were marginalised in the care process when formal care workers were involved: 'carers are on the margins of the social care system ... the 'out-there' against which agencies act.' Further, not only have informal caregivers been marginalised in relation to formal care workers, all too often they are seen as a cheap resource that can be utilised to 'reduce the long-term fiscal costs of care related to potentially avoidable institutionalization and worsening of disabilities' (Singer et al. 2009 p. 97). Nolan et al. (2001) points out that the most common goal in supporting informal caregivers is to maintain them in their role and thus contain caregiving costs. Such a view, he suggests, 'is essentially exploitative and not supportable on moral, ethical or even pragmatic grounds' (Nolan et al. 2001, p. 92). Cummins (2001, p. 83) actually suggests that 'the forces that encourage family care are minimally concerned with family welfare.' To recognise the contribution and significance of informal care is, therefore, not the same as seeing it as a free resource with the potential to compensate for deficiencies in publicly funded care (Marin et al. 2009, p. 14).

With much attention in policy and practice concentrated on ensuring that carers continue in the role, and less interest in why and how they take it up or how they move on afterwards, informal caregiving continues to be poorly understood within formal health and social services, and as a consequence these have been less than responsive to the needs of informal carers. But there is a need to recognise the importance of informed choices in care, the need for adequate support and preparation, ongoing responsive support, and the provision of information, knowledge and skills. At the same time there is potentially great value for professionals in recognising the expertise of carers (Brown et al. 2001, p. 28).

Nolan et al. (2001, pp. 92–93) talks of many carers who 'feel ill-prepared for their role, lacking essential information and basic caring skills,' and describes Askham's call for carer support as interventions which assist carers to: 'take up (or not take up) the caring role; continue in the caring role; give up the caring role.' Kittay (1999, p. 132) comments that such supports should be considered as a matter of justice, and carers should be treated 'as if their work mattered (because it does) and as if they mattered (because they do).' She described as 'nested dependencies' the collection of those supports necessary to sustain the work while considering their well-being as 'doulia.'

Recognising caregivers and people with disability as experts on their own lives can present a profound challenge to professionals and the formal care sector. This is highlighted particularly clearly when arguments are developed against the payment of family carers, as has been evident in the example of the group of New Zealand families taking a case against the Ministry of Health (Human Rights Review Tribunal 2010). The position of the Ministry has reflected first, concerns over cost containment and secondly, a reluctance to recognise the significant work of family members. If attention is paid to what families actually do as caregivers, such arguments against the payment to carers cannot be sustained (Butler 2010). Our argument throughout this book is that caregiving is a significant extension of what families normally do, it is extraordinary, and when it constrains the caregiving family member from leading a normal life, then that caregiving should be considered as work.

In contrast with the view that an active formal care sector weakens the incentives and inventiveness of the informal 'community' sector, we propose that smart policy informed by a grounded knowledge of the needs of carers, particularly at key moments in the caring cycle, enhances the capacity of both sectors to provide quality care for those in need. If informal carers are to be supported effectively and if such care is to be sustained, there is a need for a greater awareness by formal care workers and health and social care professionals of the experiences of carers and the issues they face. The purpose of such awareness is, of course, to support the environments of home and community, so that carers are empowered and able to perform the practical and emotional work of caring in such a way as to facilitate quality care that respects and supports the dignity of cared-for person. Support for caregiving families ought to be aimed at not only reducing stress and ameliorating distress but also at promoting potential positive benefits to the caregiver and care receiver (Singer et al. 2009, p. 98).

1.4 Increasing Scholarly Interest in Informal Care

With the increasing awareness that family and informal carers are the 'lynchpin of community care' (Nolan et al. 2001, p. 91), this topic has begun to receive greater attention from academic and policy-focussed researchers. Care has become, as Williams (2001, p. 470) suggests, an increasingly central concept in social policy:

> Care is a central analytic referent in social policy … care has become increasingly significant in a number of different policy-relevant discourses, for example in the move to a 'mixed economy of care', in community care, in the treatment of children in care, in debates about what constitutes good parenting, in long-term care for older people, and in claims for the recognition of care responsibilities in employment-based 'work-life balance' policies. All focus, in one way or another, on what care means, its uses and abuses, what it costs, how it is supported, how it is delivered, and by whom.

Fine (2007) summarises five broad approaches to the study of care that have emerged from the 1970s – these being 'parallel literatures, each indicative of a coherent, but in many ways quite distinct set of interests and concerns' (p. 140). The divisions represent to some degree occupational divisions. They are:

- The ethic of care debate which sees care primarily as a disposition towards others, a concern for maintaining relationships and nurturing the world around us (Fine 2007, p. 140).
- Care in the social policy tradition which has been concerned with themes of the feminised burden of care, first, in the domestic sphere and more latterly in the field of paid care work. This approach has been informed by the disability activists who have challenged the view that the cared-for are a burden, and the beneficiaries of a one-way process in which they are recipients, to an approach where care is seen within the context of more complex and mutually beneficial interpersonal relationships.
- Care as it has emerged from the caring professions such as nursing which has included, initially, a claim to position nursing as the 'science of caring,' but which more latterly has emphasised 'the importance of communication and understanding … the supervisory tasks of counselling and listening' and less so on the work of physical care tasks (Fine 2007, p. 142).
- Care in the literature on work-life balance positions paid care in opposition to unpaid care and asserts they are not simple equivalents. Caring, 'from nurturance and provision of nutrition, through to domestic cleaning, education and spending leisure time together …is seen in positive … light but as threatened by the nature of contemporary employment' (Fine 2007, p. 143).
- The final approach deals with care within the context of managing 'the demographic transition and the adequacy of resources to care for an ageing population' (Fine 2007, p. 143). In this approach, both paid and unpaid care and the relationship between the two are brought into the equation.

What follows in the subsequent chapters reflects aspects of each of these approaches, although much of our work falls within the social policy and disability approach.

Caregiving is a dynamic process. Individuals move into and out of caregiving at different stages of the life course, and in the same way as the person in need of care will be influenced by his or her life course stage, so too will the needs and experience of the informal caregiver. The dynamic process of moving into a caregiving role, and the dynamic nature of caregiving itself has been captured by researchers who emphasise transitions (Orlowska 1995; Hirst 2002, 2005; Nolan et al. 2001; Bury 1982; Williams 2000; Olaison and Cedersund 2006; Janlov et al. 2006). We outline our approach to capturing this dynamic nature in Chap. 3. We adopt a process-oriented method, examining caregiving experiences by focussing on key stages in the caregiving process, particularly the transition points in terms of initial points of change and disruption, periods of liminality and doubt, and reconnections. Such an approach explores the changing roles of carers through the caring cycle.

1.5   Informal Care and the Disability Movement

The relationship between carers and care-recipients has been a key concern of the disability movement (Kroger 2009). Disability researchers have voiced the criticism that the concept of care has been based on a notion of disabled people as non-autonomous, second-class citizens. This has led to some harsh commentary from the most articulate disability researchers:

> Care … has come to mean not caring about someone but caring for in the sense of taking responsibility for. People who are said to need caring for are assumed to be unable to exert choice and control. One cannot, therefore, have care and empowerment, for it is the ideology and the practice of caring which has led to the perception of disabled people as powerless (Morris 1997, p. 54).

In response to new critical insights that cared-for people are assumed to be powerless, the disability movement has strongly advocated for strategies such as individualised funding in order to challenge such assumptions and achieve choice and control in their care. As part of this they have stressed that informal family care is the worst possible scenario since: 'enforced dependency on a relative or partner is the most exploitative of all forms of so-called care delivered in our society today for it exploits both the carer and the person receiving care' (Morris 1997, p. 56). This position indicates the existence of what has been, and to some extent still is, conflicting interests between the carer and the person with disability (Tabatabainia 2003; Thomas 2007; Tossebro 1998).

The apparent polarity does not appear to be so great when it is remembered that both the disability movement and the carer movement (through its feminist links) both have a strong commitment to emancipatory aims (Watson et al. 2004, p. 341). Williams (2001, p. 483) has suggested that there should be new dialogue between informal carers, formal carers and those who receive care and support. The individualised funding movement, which seemed originally to exacerbate the divisions between caregiving and disability, has increasingly become a way of articulating some of the common aims. Caregivers require some form of recognition for the vulnerability that they share with their disabled family members; people with disability increasingly want to include family care among the range of possible options that are available to them. However, neither party wants to feel that this relationship is marked by the kind of exploitation described by Morris (1997) above. Real choice would be able to include informal care:

> Some people will wish to have their support needs met through personal relationship, which means there will still be family members and friends involved in providing care. However, this must be something that both parties feel they have choice over and, where choices conflict, that they have some scope for negotiation (Parker and Clarke 2002, p. 357).

During this period of confrontation the aversion to the notion that care effectively usurped the choice and control of the cared-for led to the development of a range of alternative concepts, such as 'help' (Shakespeare 2000), 'support' (Finkelstein 1998) or 'assistance.' All of these formulations of care aim to emphasise the contractual element of the relationship that began to arise around questions of individualised or personalised funding. Yet these concepts bring nothing dramatically new in terms of understanding the role and labour involved with care. In practice, these terms have been used as people with disability have moved into the market for employing personal assistants, rather than in relation to informal care. As this relationship has become more commonplace there has been a tendency on the part of disability writers to return to the language of care (Morris 2001; Shakespeare 2006).

1.6   Care as Complex Work

At the root of these struggles over language is a tension about what is considered 'good' care: disability activists, working within a justice paradigm, emphasise choice and control as essential, whereas care scholars highlight the need for creativity and flexibility.

> Disability research emphasizes rights, justice and independence whereas the ethics of care writers want to go beyond individualism and rights-based thinking and underline the collectivism and interdependence of all people (Kroger 2009, p. 406).

Since Hilary Graham (1983) defined care as a 'labour of love,' researchers have identified specific features of two indispensable elements of care: the physical work of caring and the emotional work. According to Kittay (2002, pp. 259–60), a philosopher and herself a mother of a daughter with severe disability, care is 'a labour, attitude and a virtue.' Kittay's comment thus differentiates between the labour involved in care and the kinds of attitude with which it is carried out. She emphasizes the interrelationship between these elements of care in ways that raise questions about the way care has tended to be seen as a boundaried professional task.

> Care is a multifaceted term … a labour, an attitude, and a virtue. As labor, it is the work of maintaining ourselves and others when we are in a condition of need. It is most noticed in its absence, most needed when it can be least reciprocated. As an attitude, caring denotes a positive, affective bond and investment in another's well-being. The labor can be done

without the appropriate attitude. Yet without the attitude of care, the open responsiveness to another that is so essential to understanding what another requires is not possible. That is, the labor unaccompanied by the attitude of care cannot be good care (Kittay 2002, p. 259).

Ruddick (1989) clarified this further in her detailed ethnographic and philosophical exploration of the work of mothers as a specific practice which could be generalised to other caring work. She takes a practicalist perspective, where the practice of care is defined by the demands of the task, the shared goals of carers and the means to achieve these goals. The practice of care is defined by the demands of the person in need of care for protection, nurture and integration into a social network. Each of these elements require specific knowledge, skills and attitudes in order to bring them to fruition. For example, she described the virtues that underpin maternal practice: preservation of the child requires attentive love, humility and cheerfulness; fostering growth requires judgment; and training for social integration requires the capacity to welcome change.

Held (2006) distinguishes between different kinds of care:

> Taking care of a toddler so that he does not hurt himself yet is not unduly fearful is not much like patching up mistrust between colleagues and enabling them to work together. Dressing a wound so that it will not become infected is not much like putting up curtains to make a room attractive and private. Neither are much like arranging for food aid to be delivered to families who need it half a world away. Yet all care involves attentiveness, sensitivity, and responding to needs (p. 39).

The focus on the labour aspects of care has helped to erode some of the conceptual boundaries between formal and informal care. For example, Waerness (1984) has described as 'the rationality of caring,' an approach to care that is marked by flexibility and creativity generated by a real personal connection to the person being cared for. There is some need for such cross-fertilization of ideas. There has been insufficient research carried out on the similar functions performed by informal and formal caregivers, and the support they need, regardless of the caregiving situation or category. Exceptions to the above are Biegel and Schulz's Family Caregiver Applications Series published by Sage in the 1990s, Singer et al.'s work (1996), and a review of the literature on family-centered services across fields (Allen and Peter 1996). Nolan et al. (2001) talk of 'uniting disciplines' and 'providing a shared and reciprocal sense of direction and purpose' (p. 2). Jagger et al. (2001) point out some of the important examples of this kind of cross-disciplinary analysis. They focus on defining functional descriptions of disabilities centred on the concepts of ADL (activities of daily living) and IADL (instrumental activities of daily living). These, they say, cut across categories of disability and point to the level of care that families are required to provide and, by extrapolation, the kinds of support caregivers are likely to need.

While we might frame contemporary care services in terms of participation and empowerment (Wolfensberger 1998), Phillips (2007) portrays these as becoming increasingly formal and bureaucratic. Policy and practice discourses tend to ignore informal caregiver expertise and focus on the discourse of burden and stress, working towards policies of 'respite' and 'support'. Accepting carer expertise, as recommended by Nolan et al. (2001), may not change the focus on burden and the need for respite, but, as Brown et al. (2001, p. 24) indicate, it will redefine the lay and professional relationship, with carer as an 'active agent and analyst of their own experience,' and allow for possibilities of sharing information and skills, and the possibilities of choice of how best to care.

Being an active agent indicates the possibilities of choice, and choices include to not care, to care, with help, to be in the workforce outside the home, and of recognising care at home in terms of work, rather than solely in terms of family duty, love, and affection. All too often carers entering the care relationship feel that there are few or no choices. Featherstone (1980) described this when she likened the moment of choosing to care with the situation of saving someone from drowning. It would be hard to call this a choice, where inaction will result in harm, and action, conversely, has such a peculiarly urgent quality.

The issue of choices touches on the interconnectedness of the choices that are made by both the carer and the disabled person. For those with severe cognitive, communication, intellectual, and/or physical deficits the possibility of being cared for into adulthood by family carers is their best and often only chance of a life with dignity. This was recognised in a U.S court case where Bergstedt, an American, was cared for by his father for 21 years after a swimming accident left him quadriplegic (Ho 2008). When his father became terminally ill, Bergstedt felt that society would 'cast him adrift in a sea of indifference' and force him into a nursing home. The case went to court and eventually Bergstedt was granted the right to die and his respirator was disconnected. It seems that the court acknowledged in this way that his fears were reasonable and that it would be impossible for him to have a reasonable quality of life outside the family setting. The court did not feel able to address the cause of his despair and to help him find an appropriate substitute caregiver. This touches on the fears of many carers of adults with severe disability that the person with disability cannot be adequately cared for after their death. Some of the strongest lobbying for reasonable alternatives to family care comes from families who have had to face this kind of Hobson's Choice. This has led to a strong lobbying from such families for adequate alternatives to family care.

1.7   Bringing the Voices of Informal Caregivers to the Table

By drawing on our research, and on the practical experience of Hale and Butler, we hope to give a voice to those who are typically excluded from consideration. In subsequent chapters, we examine a variety of care situations within the community through the eyes of caregivers to convey how they experience the multiple aspects of the role. This includes recognising the important developmental changes they go through when becoming a caregiver and the impact of the social environment on their caregiving experience. Our focus, then, is not only on the acts of caregiving, but also the changes the caregiver experiences and the way their caring occurs within social context.

A key purpose in our approach is to inform practice and policy and to stimulate a greater awareness in debates about informal care. We do not approach the subject as authorities or experts with the intention of settling policy debates in this area, but with the intention of improving the quality of practice and policy as it relates to informal care and stimulating argumentation and public deliberation. To this end, we are concerned not only with new knowledge and better public policy, although that is undoubtedly a goal, but also with promoting change. We seek to promote a greater awareness of informal care and its importance, and we attempt to inform policy development by bringing the voices of informal carers to the decision table. In this regard, we see our work as supporting the intentions of the various carer organisations, and more broadly in supporting the purposes of the carer movement.

Moreover, in providing information to assist decision makers, we seek to represent a range of interests, arguments and discourses in the analytical process. In doing so, we seek to help decision makers and, more broadly, interested citizens develop alternatives that speak to their own needs and interests. And this is why there is a close link between our approach and the participatory processes that are associated with it. The goal is to provide access to and explanation of information related to informal care to all parties, to empower the public to understand this sector, and to promote serious public discussions – supplying citizens with the knowledge and understanding to make informed choices. In this regard, we see our work as facilitating more democratic decision making in this policy area. We conclude, therefore, with Timonen's (2009) remarks:

> If research can shed light on the ways in which formal and informal caregivers interact, and illuminate the differences and similarities between informal and formal caregiving, policy makers and practitioners will be in a better position to design policies and interventions that support both types of caregivers equally. … The possibilities for enhancing the work and the lives of all caregivers and the quality of care provided to [those] who receive care from multiple sources, are endless (p. 324).

Discussion Suggestions

Do you agree with the idea that a carer comes to share the vulnerability of the care-recipient? If so, can you discuss what this means

In what circumstances might it be appropriate for the state to support family members who act as informal carers?

How might a state intervene to enhance the quality of care provided?

What policy tools does your country have at its disposal?

Further Reading

Cook, T. (2007). *The history of the carers' movement.* London: Carers U.K.

Fine, M. D. (2007). *A caring society? Care and the dilemmas of human service in the 21st century.* Basingstoke: Palgrave Macmillan.

Held, V. (2006). *The ethics of care: Personal, political, and global.* Oxford: Oxford University Press.

Nolan, M., Davies, S., & Grant, G. (2001). *Working with older people and their families.* Buckingham: Open University Press.

Phillips, J. (2007). *Care.* Cambridge: Polity Press.

References

Allen, R. I., & Peter, C. G. (1996). Towards developing standards and measurements for family-centered practice in family-support programs. In G. H. S. Singer, L. E. Powers, & A. L. Olson (Eds.), *Redefining family support: Innovations in public-private partnerships*. Baltimore: Paul H. Brookes.

Arksey, H., & Glendinning, C. (2007). Choice in the context of informal care-giving. *Health & Social Care in the Community, 15*(2), 165–175.

Biegel, D. E., Sales, E., & Schulz, R. (1991). *Family caregiver in chronic illness: Alzheimer's disease, cancer, heart disease, mental illness and stroke* (Family Caregiver Applications Series). Thousand Oaks: Sage.

Brown, J., Nolan, M., & Davies, S. (2001). Who's the expert? Redefining lay and professional relationships. In M. Nolan, S. Davies, & G. Grant (Eds.), *Working with older people and their families*. Buckingham: Open University Press.

Bury, M. (1982). Chronic illness as biographical disruption. *Sociology of Health & Illness, 4*(2), 137–169.

Butler, M. (2010). Care ethics and the payment of family carers: Implications for occupational therapy. *World Federation of Occupational Therapy Bulletin, 62*.

Cook, T. (2007). *The history of the carers' movement*. London: Carers U.K.

Cummins, R. A. (2001). The subjective well-being of people caring for a family member with a severe disability at home: A review. *Journal of Intellectual and Developmental Disability, 26*(1), 83–100.

Dalley, G. (1988). *Ideologies of caring: Rethinking community and collectivism*. London: Centre for Policy on Ageing.

Dubrow, A. L. (1965). Attitudes towards disability. *Journal of Rehabilitation, 31*(4), 25–26.

Featherstone, H. (1980). *A difference in the family*. New York: Basic Books.

Fine, M. D. (2007). *A caring society? Care and the dilemmas of human service in the 21st century*. Basingstoke: Palgrave Macmillan.

Fine, M. D., & Glendinning, C. (2005). Dependence, independence or interdependence? Revisiting the concepts of care and dependency. *Ageing & Society, 25*(4), 601–621.

Finkelstein, V. (1998). *Re-thinking care in a society providing equal opportunities for all*. Discussion paper prepared for the World Health Organisation. Milton Keynes: Open University.

Graham, H. (1983). Caring: A labour of love. In J. Finch & D. Groves (Eds.), *A labour of love: Women, work and caring* (pp. 13–30). London: Routledge & Kegan Paul.

Held, V. (2006). *The ethics of care: Personal, political, and global*. Oxford: Oxford University Press.

Hirst, M. (2002). Transitions to informal care in Great Britain during the 1990s. *Journal of Epidemiology and Community Health, 56*(8), 579–587.

Hirst, M. (2005). Carer distress: A prospective, population-based study. *Social Science & Medicine, 61*(3), 697–708.

Ho, A. (2008). The individualist model of autonomy and the challenge of disability. *Bioethical Inquiry, 5*, 193–207.

Human Rights Review Tribunal. (2010). Atkinson v MOH Reference n. HRRT 33/05. In the matter of a claim under the Human Rights Act 1993 and its amendments.

Jagger, C., Arthur, A. J., Spiers, N., & Clarke, M. (2001). Patterns of onset of disability in activities of daily living with age. *Journal of the American Geriatric Society, 49*(4), 404–409.

Janlov, A., Hallberg, I., & Petersson, K. (2006). Older persons' experience of being assessed for and receiving public home help: Do they have any influence over it? *Health & Social Care in the Community, 14*(1), 26–36.

Kittay, E. F. (1999). *Love's labor: Essays on women, equality and dependency*. London: Routledge.

Kittay, E. F. (2002). When caring is just and justice is caring: Justice and mental retardation. In E. F. Kittay & E. K. Feder (Eds.), *The subject of care: Feminist perspectives on dependency*. Oxford: Rowman & Littlefield.

Kroger, T. (2009). Care research and disability studies: Nothing in common? *Critical Social Policy, 29*, 398–420.

Lim, J., & Zebrack, B. (2004). Caring for family members with chronic physical illness: A critical review of caregiver literature. *Health and Quality of Life Outcomes, 2*, 1–10.

Marin, B., Leichsenring, K., Rodrigues, R., & Huber, M. (2009). *Who cares? Care coordination and cooperation to enhance quality in elderly care in the European Union.* Vienna: European Centre for Social Welfare Policy and Research.

Morris, J. (1997). Care or empowerment? A disability rights perspective. *Social Policy & Administration, 31*(1), 54–60.

Morris, J. (2001). Impairment and disability: Constructing an ethics of care that promotes human rights. *Hypatia, 16*(4), 1–16.

Nolan, M., Davies, S., & Grant, G. (2001). *Working with older people and their families.* Buckingham: Open University Press.

Olaison, A., & Cedersund, E. (2006). Assessment for home care. Negotiating solutions for individual needs. *Journal of Aging Studies, 29*(4), 367–380.

Orlowska, D. (1995). Parental participation in issues concerning their sons and daughters with learning disabilities. *Disability & Society, 10*(4), 437–456.

Parker, G., & Clarke, H. (2002). Making the ends meet: Do carers and disabled people have a common agenda. *Policy & Politics, 30*(3), 347–359.

Phillips, J. (2007). *Care.* Cambridge: Polity Press.

Pool, I. (2007). Demographic dividends: Determinants of development or merely windows of opportunity? *Ageing Horizons, 7*, 28–35.

Ruddick, S. (1989). *Maternal thinking: Towards a politics of peace.* Boston: Beacon Press.

Shakespeare, T. (2000). *Help.* Birmingham: Venture Press.

Shakespeare, T. (2006). *Disability rights and wrongs.* London/New York: Routledge.

Singer, G. H. S., Biegel, D. E., & Ethridge, B. L. (2009). Toward a cross disability view of family caregiving studies. *Journal of Family Social Work, 12*(2), 97–118.

Singer, G., Powers, L., & Olson, A. (1996). *Redefining family support: Innovations in public-private partnerships.* Baltimore: Paul H. Brookes Pub. Co.

Tabatabainia, M. M. (2003). Listening to families' views regarding normalization and deinstutionalization. *Journal of Intellectual and Developmental Disability, 28*(3), 241–259.

Thomas, C. (2007). *Sociologies of disability and illness: Contested ideas in disability studies and medical sociology.* New York: Palgrave MacMillan.

Timonen, V. (2009). Towards an integrative theory of care: Formal and informal intersections. In J. Mancini & K. A. Roberto (Eds.), *Pathways of human development: Explorations of change.* Plymouth: Lexington Books.

Tossebro, J. (1998). Attitudes to deinstitutionalization before and after resettlement; the case of a Scandinavian welfare state. *Journal of Developmental and Physical Disabilities, 10*(1), 55–72.

Turner, V. (1969). *The ritual process.* Harmondsworth: Penguin.

Twigg, J. (1989). Models of carers: How do social care agencies conceptualise their relationship with informal carers? *Journal of Social Policy, 18*(1), 53–66.

Waerness, K. (1984). The rationality of caring. *Economic and Industrial Democracy, 5*, 185–211.

Walker, A. J., Pratt, C., & Eddy, L. (1995). Informal caregiving to aging family members: A critical review. *Family Relations, 44*(4), 402–411.

Watson, N., McKie, L., et al. (2004). (Inter)dependence, needs and care: The potential for disability and feminist theorists to develop an emancipatory model. *Sociology, 38*(2), 331–350.

Williams, S. (2000). Chronic illness as biographical disruption or biographical disruption as chronic illness? Reflections on a core concept. *Sociology of Health & Illness, 22*(1), 40–67.

Williams, F. (2001). In and beyond new labour: Towards a new political ethics of care. *Critical Social Policy, 21*(4), 467–493.

Wolfensberger, W. (1998). *A brief introduction to social role valorization. A higher-order concept for addressing the plight of societally devalued people, and for structuring human services.* Syracuse: Training Institute for Human Service Planning, Leadership & Change Agentry (Syracuse University).

Chapter 2
Informal Care in Context: An Expression of Social Relationships

2.1 Introduction

Care is the activity of looking after someone in need, and the act of providing such care is an expression of connectedness between individuals within families and communities. Informal care, therefore, is an expression of social relationships. In this chapter, we consider the social context of care, drawing on the concept of social capital and its key elements of the social bonds and bridges that provide the setting within which such care is provided. We focus, first, on the theory of social capital, and subsequently on its value in the broader policy context. We conclude the chapter with a brief discussion of some of the criticisms of the concept.

The growing importance of informal care and the recognition of a need for better policies to support informal caregivers implies we need a better appreciation of the experience of informal caregivers. As noted in the Introduction (p. xiv), formal and informal care are very much interdependent, but that interdependence tends to be downplayed when examining one or the other. Instead, much of the writing on caregiving tends to focus on either informal care or formal care. Many caregiving studies have also tended to limit the focus to the dyadic relationships between the family caregiver and the care-recipient, neglecting the broader context that may involve other informal and formal carers. Piercy (1998, p. 109) emphasizes, with regard to obtaining a full picture of care for older family members, there is a need to examine the roles played by 'multiple and extended family members.' Additionally, since much informal care is performed within the privacy of the home or between neighbours, it tends to be underappreciated, despite the growing scholarly and policy attention given to it. It is therefore critical to promote an understanding of the interconnectedness between the formal and informal care sectors, and what each contributes to the care needs of people with disability. In this respect, our purpose is similar to that of the already mentioned carers' movements, inasmuch as it is oriented to giving voice to informal carers.

Informal care needs to be seen in its social context, and in the way the social networks involved in care are integrated (Timonen 2009). Such networks comprise

P. Barrett et al., *Family Care and Social Capital: Transitions in Informal Care*, DOI 10.1007/978-94-007-6872-7_2, © Springer Science+Business Media Dordrecht 2014

those of the cared-for person and their caregivers, the wider community context, and the health and social policy environments within which they are embedded. These policy environments reflect and inform specific cultures of caregiving and the allocation of care responsibilities, and they frame and structure the interactions between informal carers and the formal care sector.

A helpful way of grasping this context is through the notion of social capital. We do so in the way described by Woolcock (2010) in his overview of the 'rise and routinisation' of the concept:

> Essentially contested concepts such as social capital do their work through the fruitful public debates they facilitate, not the clean, unambiguous, consensual path they chart (Woolcock 2010, p. 482).

The concept highlights several issues for fruitful debate. For example, it offers one way of explaining why people with the same level of impairment will go on to have varying levels of disability or other negative, or positive, outcomes. Disability as a construct is today seen as being closely linked with environmental and social factors. It does not inevitably arise from a specific impairment and people with identical conditions may have different outcomes, depending on the supports available to them. Variations of the maxim 'it's not what you know, it's who you know' are found in languages all over the world, and the notion of social capital provides a frame of reference for considering these issues across several planes. The social model of disability implicitly makes this connection, but in focusing on environmental supports, or the lack of them, has underemphasised the myriad supports provided by informal care, through mechanisms of family, friends and community.

While not without its critics, the social capital literature does provide some insight into the way communities are structured, the 'bonds' that link individuals within networks and the 'bridges' that link people across networks. It also draws attention to the nature of the relationship between caregiver and person with disability, and the specific resources in the form of care that are given and received. By drawing on the concept of social capital, we aim to recognise the impact of the broader societal and cultural environments on social networks within which care is provided. Some care policy regimes facilitate strong networks with the capacity to provide quality care through the formal sector, while others might be described as relying more on informal care. Giving attention to the policy context allows for the recognition of the different ways in which countries allocate and support such responsibility between families, the state and private markets for the delivery of care.

2.2 Informal Care in the Context of Social Relationships

Hands-on care almost always involves family members while support and instrumental activities are often undertaken, too, by neighbours and friends, and less socially close connections such as club or church connections. The underlying premise is that there are stable social ties, not necessarily longstanding as Peek and Lin (1999) and van Tilburg (1998) suggest, but of goodwill and commitment. Members of such a network may be asked to increase their commitment either of instrumental or social and emotional support (van Groenou and van Tilburg 1997), and the extent and depth of that support can become designated as care, a set of actions which differ from the usual normative social relationships in everyday life (Walker et al. 1995).

Becoming an informal caregiver places the caregiver in a context that, by definition, entails (an)other person(s). The study of caregiving, therefore, prompts us to think of the caregiver in relation to other individuals. This relationship begins with the care-recipient, but it generally extends to encompass a much wider constellation of other caregivers, formal and informal. Consequently, caregiving places the individual in an inherently 'social' context in relation to the care-recipient, other carers, and social contacts (where these are present), and as such expands the focus from the individual providing care towards the context in which they find themselves. Any attempt to understand caregiving, its antecedents, processes, and consequences, requires us to take into account the broader context that involves at least three separate layers, namely:

1. The care-recipient: his or her personality, life expectations, and reactions to the need for care;
2. The social and family network including formal carers where present: their expectations, level of involvement, and recognition of the contributions made by the primary caregiver;
3. The social care system: expectations, availability, and conditions attached to support; recognition and support of both informal and formal caregivers.

These systems of networks and care, based on close and formal bonds, become institutionalised as a 'network' in which the close social ties are its foundation and support (Keating et al. 2005).

Since informal care is given to single individuals who are connected in some way with the carer, this relationship is troubled from the outset by the fact that there are no boundaries on the potential response (Levinas 1989). Formal care, on the other hand, is society's response to the 'needs of strangers' (Ignatieff 1984) and it is constrained from the outset by utilitarian pressures in the direction of efficiency. Formal care is provided by a range of individuals, with a greater or lesser degree of training and skills from paid carers to health professionals. The degree of formality in the relationship varies considerably, but tends to occur within bureaucratic systems.

While informal care has a lower level of social recognition than paid or professional care, it tends to require a higher level of focus and responsibility across several domains. For example, the degree of responsibility carried by informal carers tends to be constant and without borders, whereas professionals have a more boundaried responsibility. Philosopher Elizabeth Wolgast (1992) used the expression 'artificial personhood,' to explain how membership of a professional organization tends to get in the way of clear acknowledgement of responsibility. It is not possible for informal carers to avoid responsibility in the same way. This is reflected in a temporal relationship that is sustained, whereas the response of the health

Table 2.1 Dimensions of care and the degree of formality/informality of the relationship

		Temporality	Spatiality	Responsibility	Relationship
Degree of formality	Informal	Sustained ⬇	Constrained ⬇	Constant ⬇	Thick ⬇
	Formal paid carer	Episodic ⬇	Permeable ⬇	Intermittent ⬇	Less Thick ⬇
	Formal professional care	Occasional	Mobile	Boundaried	Thin

professional is often occasional. The quality of the relationships is obviously different and Margalit (2002) used the comparison of thick and thin to capture this distinction:

> Thick relations are grounded in attributes such as parent, friend, lover… Thick relations are anchored in a shared past or moored in shared memory. Thin relations, on the other hand, are backed by the attribute of being human. Thin relations rely also on some aspects of being human, such as being a woman or being sick. Thick relations are in general our relations to the near and dear. Thin relations are in general our relations to the stranger and the remote (Margalit 2002, p. 197).

The differences in the temporal and spatial parameters of formal and informal care are compared in the above table. The table also identifies the implications of each form of care for the degree of responsibility that lies with the caregiver, and the implications for the relationship between the caregiver and the cared-for person (Table 2.1).

Informal and continuous caregiving usually depends on a relationship of love, affection, duty and, while other forms of caring exist, such as occasional, or irregular, informal help and social support, these basic components of caregiving create the fundamental 'bond' (Putnam 2000) for the provision of informal care, or 'social care' in Putnam's terms. But informal care and support can extend beyond this intimate relationship to what Keating et al. (2005) have written from their study of social networks and informal care in Canada. They define social capital as potential support and cooperation for mutual benefit that is developed over time through the building of trust and through norms of reciprocity. The possession of social capital makes possible access to a wide range of resources, such as care and support, through contacts with competent others. If we are to understand informal care, we need to understand the nature of such connections and/or the access to them.

2.3   Bridges and Bonds

Social capital does provide a way of understanding aspects of relationships within social networks. With Turner's (1974) reference to theory as a means for obtaining insight, we believe we can draw on these ideas as a way of obtaining a better understanding of informal care within its broader context. The reference to bonds and bridges are one of these ideas. Putnam (2000) described bonding social capital as exclusive in nature, strengthening ties within homogenous, socially-similar groups and enhancing access to internal resources, whereas bridging social capital is inclusive, strengthening ties between heterogeneous, socially diverse groups and enhancing access to external resources. He has also theorised on the greater benefits of bridging social capital, contending that, while bonding social capital is a means to 'getting by', bridging social capital is a means to 'getting ahead'. It seems likely that both forms operate for carers. Bonding social capital describes the relationships that immediately support the person in need, whereas bridging social capital tends to describe the relationships that the carer forms with broader support networks. This resource of bridging social capital may not be available for all informal carers.

Bonding social capital is that which exists between people of equal standing or people in similar situations and similar backgrounds, such as family friends and close neighbours. It refers to intimate relationships within homogenous groups where the needs of members are known. In these networks there is an emotional intensity and the provision of reciprocal services, such as in families where there is a long history together and where there are strong normative obligations to care. Bonding social capital is best suited to providing the social and psychological support for its members to assist in their 'getting by' – or coping with day-to-day activities within their communities.

Bridging social capital refers to more complex, fluctuating social contacts between people from different, more heterogeneous social environments. Bridging social capital is useful in connecting people to external assets, offering access across social networks to other social opportunities or resources. Families alone are less likely to possess these network assets. They are more likely to be non-kin links to community supports. Bridging social capital is a concept that places the focus specifically on the ability to link across networks.

Bridging social capital is rapidly lost when the carer and disabled person are not able to invest in social networks. It is not simply a matter of higher incomes groups having greater access to bridging social capital. Bourdieu (1986) would say that the capacity to communicate in ways that enable bridging social capital is created through systems of training that are embedded deep in social structures. He coined the term habitus to describe the way that culture is transmitted through durable dispositions and practices that are developed in daily life. The habitus is therefore is a form of 'embodied capital' (Bourdieu 1986, p. 48) and it produces an ethos that regulates interactions and bodily practices. It is not a solitary practice, but rather a family, group and class phenomenon, where those who have faced common material conditions learn to act in according with those conditions.

Care networks, in terms of social capital language, are bonding networks. They help in coping with day-to-day life in terms of the performance of care tasks within the home or in the community setting. A strong informal care network assumes families are the basis for support, providing the most responsive, knowledgeable and nuanced care. Yet there are also concerns about their fragility as services are increasingly rationed. Families' abilities to sustain high levels of care and gain access to formal services that might assist their caring are therefore increasingly important. Keating et al. (2005), though, ask whether this might mitigate against connecting to external resources. That is, does access to strong bonding social capital mitigate against connecting to formal care services? Wenger's (1991) suggestion that strong family networks tend to be less open to community-based networks is consistent with this view. This has implications for the types of services and policies that might strengthen bonding social capital and bridging social capital.

2.4 Macro and Micro Perspectives

Social capital theorists distinguish between macro and micro approaches. Macro approaches tend to be concerned with degrees of social integration at the community level and with degrees of civic involvement. Micro approaches focus instead on individual relationships within social networks. Both perspectives are relevant when considering informal care. The macro approach is associated with Putnam's work, which is described as a model of civic involvement and community support. Putnam (2000) focused almost exclusively on formalised civic involvement and maintains that it is possible to develop social capital by joining civic groups. There has been considerable exploration of how large scale investment may effectively mobilise social capital initiatives on the ground. The micro approach is associated with the work of Bourdieu (1986) and focuses on the investments required to activate or mobilise social capital on an individual level. Bourdieu pointed to the fundamental connection between capital and different forms of labour time investment.

Social capital at both the macro and micro level become expressed, or embodied, as care through efforts to produce lasting and useful relationships. The work of creating social capital requires investment of time, energy and competence, in similar ways to the investment of economic capital. While economic capital can give access to many goods and services, without any secondary cost, not all 'services' can be easily or blatantly bought, such as services and resources that fall under the rubric of love and duty, generosity and friendship. Such services and resources can only be obtained through social relationships (or social obligations). Until the moment of need, however, there is usually some degree of uncertainty about whether they can be effectively mobilised.

2.4.1 Micro Approaches

The micro approach focuses on individuals and is concerned with the potential for benefits to accrue to individuals through their membership of and participation in social groups, through the deliberate construction of sociability for the purposes of creating such a resource. Informal care, performed by family members and members of the community, without payment or any binding agreement concerning the provision of such care, is a fundamental resource in maintaining disabled and chronically sick people at home and in the community. This resource is given in the form of labour of the carer. The micro approach to social capital is clearest in the link made by Bourdieu (1986) between social capital and labour:

> The universal equivalent, the measure of all equivalences, is nothing other than labor-time (in the widest sense); and the conservation of social energy through all its conversions is verified if, in each case, one takes into account both the labor-time accumulated in the form of capital and the labor-time needed to transform it from one type into another (p. 54).

From this perspective, social networks are not a natural given, but must be constructed through investment strategies that are oriented to the institutionalisation of group relations, and that become usable as a reliable source of other benefits (Portes 1998, p. 3). Bourdieu's approach implies a deliberate building by individuals of potentially useful relationships, investing one's time and energy to ensure future returns. Bourdieu (1986) defined the social resources that accumulate as:

> the aggregate of the actual or potential resources which are linked to possession of a durable network of more or less institutionalized relationships of mutual acquaintance or recognition (p. 248).

He emphasised the interchangeable nature of different forms of capital and pointed to the fundamental connection between capital and different forms of labour time investment.

The volume of the social capital possessed by a given individual depends on the size of the network of connections he or she can effectively mobilize and on the volume of capital possessed in an individual's own right by each of those to whom that individual is connected. In conceptualising social capital in this way, Bourdieu helps us to see both the actual and the potential resources that may be used for action, and the dynamics that underpin how people access, or are denied access, to these network-based resources.

Ahn and Ostrom (2002) build on this approach and explain that social capital can be seen as a way of understanding the propensity of actors to cooperate through working together to reach particular goals. It is thus an explanation of the way collective action leads to the accumulation of resources. This method of understanding social capital sees it as the way working together in collaborative initiatives has the potential to build up the capacity of the collective.

> Here, social capital is seen as 1) the product of the actors' motivations for forming an association (the values and aspirations that underpin the co-operative relationship); 2) their behaviour (types of association that define how actors co-operate); and 3) their perception of collective issues (cultural beliefs and influences, etc) (Franke 2005, p. 1).

2.4.2 Macro Approaches

Macro, or ecological, approaches to social capital, typically associated with the work of Putnam (2000), tend to focus on themes of shared identity, interests and trust within communities, and the resulting degree of community cooperation. Putnam (2000, p. 19) defined this as the '… connections among individual-social networks and the norms of reciprocity and trustworthiness that arise from them.' He suggested that participation in social groups and activities generates access to social capital. Thus a community which is rich in social capital can be described as socially cohesive, cooperative and caring. In this perspective, social capital is seen as 'both a glue that bonds society together and a lubricant that permits the smooth running of society's interactions' (Smith 1997, p. 170).

The macro approach to understanding social capital focuses on the significance of social integration and social cohesion. It refers to the 'stock' of resources built up over time which encourage mutual consideration and cooperation. It draws attention to the way a community's social, political and cultural institutions express norms of trust and reciprocity, which lead to the conditions for social engagement, mutual support and collective benefit (Putnam 2000).

With regard to informal care, what matters is the way social capital at both the macro and micro level facilitates the generation of resources such as care and support (Portes 1998). It emerges from social ties and is then used by individuals and groups. It reflects the interdependence between individuals and groups within a community, and it has both individual benefits and group benefits (Franke 2005, p. 2).

2.4.3 Social Networks and Social Capital

We cannot, therefore, fully understand informal care without an appreciation of the way in which individuals are located within networks and the way networks are embedded within the broader collective. Another way of saying this is that we cannot understand informal care without an appreciation of the informal and formal institutions which structure the social network context. From a social capital perspective, these social networks are a resource that can be drawn upon for the purposes of securing support. In the Canadian Policy Research Initiative study (Keating et al. 2005, p. 3), social capital was defined as the 'networks of social relations that provide access to needed resources and supports.' Informal care, performed by family members, neighbours or others from within the community, without payment or any formal agreement concerning the provision of such care, is therefore a fundamental resource. In seeking to contextualise the experience of informal care, the concept of social capital as developed by Keating et al. (2005) offers this insight:

> Viewing networks of social ties as a form of capital asset provides a lens for examining how these ties can be invested in and drawn upon in ways that complement other capital assets available to individuals and communities (p. 1).

Social capital is therefore understood as being the aggregate of actual and potential resources from institutionalised relationships within social settings. To say such resources are institutionalised is a means of referring to how they become 'set' or established as a set of social beliefs and practices. That is, an individual's relationships within families and communities are guided by established norms, rules and conventions that inform beliefs and behaviours around informal care. Norms are the shared, internalised prescriptions for behaving in a particular way, these being reinforced by members of a social network. Rules are the accepted directives that are mutually understood and applied (must, must not, may). Conventions refer to accepted ways of doing things. Those norms, rules (formal and informal) and conventions promote ideal social goals, such as the ideal family structure, and social roles and practices within social networks. To say they are institutionalised, in this interpretation, is to say they have become shared concepts, they are implicitly known rather than explicitly laid down.

This is what James (2000, quoted in Irving 2011, p. 24) is referring to when he explains the persistence of certain modes of thinking and being as part of the regular, habitual world:

> an experience of a world seemingly 'shot through with regularities' and 'essentially bound up with the way in which one moment in our experience may lead us towards other moments.'

Such regularities are also evident in the linguistic and social conventions around family and informal care, and they structure different expressions for family and community care in different settings.

2.5   The Dynamics Between Claimant and Donor in Social Capital Exchanges

The micro approach to social capital can usefully remind us of the dynamics between the carer (the donor), the person in need of care (the claimant) and the resources that are exchanged in the caregiving process. It enables us to distinguish between: (a) the possessors of social capital (those making the claim); (b) the sources of social capital (those agreeing to the claim); (c) the resources themselves. All too often the donor and claimant are viewed separately, and this can be like 'watching only a half court during a basketball game' (Bar-Tal et al. 1984). One of the strengths of the micro approach is the fact that it provides a single framework to gain a perspective on resources, donor and claimant. In a sense, it provides a form of triangulation, and a multi-faceted view of the care dynamic.

Focussing on the donor, the claimant, and the resources that are exchanged has the capacity to add a more nuanced perspective of caregiving. It enables us to avoid the tendency to see all social capital transactions as inherently positive, as it is often the case that donors are forced to take on responsibilities that exceed their capacity, leading, for example, to situations of carer burden. Feminist writers have long recognised the possibility of exploitation when resources are euphemised as 'natural', and they have been concerned about the power imbalance between donors and claimants, particularly in situations where claimants have the power. However, sometimes the power of the claimant rests not on their position in society, but on the extent of their need. Kittay (1999) describes the responsive carer as 'transparent' to such needs, where she cannot walk away from an expression of dependency. The notion of such transparency is important to an understanding of how some of those with seemingly low levels of social capital can continue to access resources through their relationship with a competent and committed donor. This person is not self-interested or disinterested (as a participant in the Rawlsian original position), but rather the donor is passionately interested 'but the interest is vested in the well-being of another' (Kittay 1999, p. 51). But the extent of need of the claimant and their vulnerability if they are abandoned may be such that it is beyond the capacity of the donor to provide for it.

There is also the possibility that a potential donor may betray perfectly legitimate claims (Bourdieu 1986) and refuse the claimant what might have been expected in terms of reciprocity. The ambiguity of social capital is that, though it has economic capital at its base in the form of labour time, the subtle economy of time is always in danger of being misrecognised. This loss of social capital is partly alleviated by the concept of 'closure' (Coleman 1988, p. 899), which describes the existence of sufficient ties between a certain number of people to guarantee the observance of norms. Such ties are an investment strategy that requires an unceasing effort of sociability in order to affirm and reaffirm the recognition of exchanges. The situation of caregivers who become socially, financially and legally marginalised through giving (Schofield et al. 1998; Kittay 1999) is an indication of how fragile this 'closure' can be at a community and societal level. The power dynamics associated with a request, and the possibility of betrayal, makes it clear how tortuous the claimant's task can be.

2.6 The Resources of Social Capital

In the policy discourse on social capital, informal care is frequently described as a 'natural resource'. The premise is that disability services are funded and natural supports do not require any further support, because they are readily available and reasonably easy to access. However, we problematize the description of informal carer as a 'natural resource' because the dynamics associated with giving and receiving care can be anything but natural. Bourdieu (2001) recognised the capacity of some claimants to ensure that a particular social order or way of understanding social roles and responsibilities to be posited as natural. It describes, for example, the situation of an elite group which can demand care without even seeming to ask.

> [T]he particularity of the dominant is that they are in a position to ensure that their particular way of being is recognised as universal (Bourdieu 2001, p. 62).

The sense of 'naturalness' associated with care can be understood as a privilege, and not necessarily available to those with low levels of social capital. The person who accesses care is effectively appropriating the labour time of this other. Good care or natural care will then become invisible and the labour of the carer can feel as natural as using the limbs of one's own body. For the claimant, such natural care allows the 'dis-appearance' of the body (Leder 1990) so that the lived body can resume its career as the background of everyday tasks. This is an extraordinary gift on the part of the carer, but that gift is at risk of being subsumed under a cloak of invisibility created by the notion of 'naturalness.'

However, for claimants who do not have access to such high levels of social capital, asking for resources from an unwilling donor may be a source of deep shame. Care is anything but 'natural' in this situation. Those who can, tend to avoid asking for help, and develop adaptive preferences for doing less when they find themselves in a situation where resources do not match their need. This is defined as 'preferences persons form unconsciously that downgrade options that are inaccessible to them' (Elster 1987, p. 119). These preferences can also be made consciously as a way of 'coming to terms with adversity' (Sen 2002, p. 634) and they are the preferences expressed when people have adjusted to a second class status (Nussbaum 2006). Such dynamics are expressed when people refuse to ask for help because it undermines their sense of independence (Boneham and Sixsmith 2006) or makes them feel like a burden (Cousineau et al. 2003, p. 111 in McPherson et al. 2010).

In 1983, Gardner introduced the idea of multiple intelligences which included both interpersonal intelligence (the capacity to understand the intentions, motivations and desires of other people) and intrapersonal intelligence (the capacity to understand oneself, to appreciate one's feelings, fears and motivations). Emotional labour has generally come to be associated with paid employment, yet informal care can require intense practice of both interpersonal and intrapersonal intelligence. The specific competencies of carers were theorised by Ruddick (1989) based on an ethnographic and philosophic account of maternal practice. This was generalised to the work of carers of adults with brain injury by Butler (2010), and it can potentially be extended to describe the work of all carers. This describes care as the labour that goes into producing three specific outcomes: maintaining the substance of the person; fostering that person's growth; and enabling social acceptability.

These benefits of social capital operate at an individual level, but the practice of care also creates social capital within the wider societal context. It was not so long ago that societal expectations meant that the most obvious place for people with disability was within an institution. Families felt pressured into placing their relatives in an institution not only because they felt that the disabled person would get better care than they could give, but also because there were few examples of disabled people living successfully in the community, due to lack of effective supports and a philosophy focused on institutional care. Social capital can therefore describe the change in focus to empowerment within the community, with community support, and the dynamic where it has become not only acceptable, but expected, that families care for the disabled person in the community, as Wolfensberger (1972; Wolfensberger et al. 1996, 1998) insisted. The greater number of people practicing care in this way has led to the development of support groups and the development of channels for the diffusion of knowledge and information. Although individual carers may feel battered and isolated, as a group, carers have achieved considerable benefits for the disabled community. For example, it was the efforts of carers that gradually created the case for integrated mainstream schooling. It has also been carers who have created a variety of work opportunities for severely disabled adults living in the community, from sheltered workshops to the more recent development of micro-enterprises.

2.7 Critics

Theories of social capital are not without criticism. Edwards et al. (2003) for example, argues that social capital is an inadequate tool, both conceptually and empirically. They draw attention to potential problems that derive from the 'in-built static and formulaic ideas about the social fabric, which cannot capture the intricate dynamics of people's relationships within and between families' (Edwards et al. 2003, p. 267). They thus argue that social capital theory has important weaknesses in the way it explains the values that inform social interaction, the actual resources that people generate and acquire through social interaction, and how these might change in society over time. A more general concern is the way a focus on social capital has the potential to instrumentalise aspects of communal life (Scanlon 2003). That is, it can lead to a focus on social bonds in order to exploit them more effectively in the achievement of specific policy goals. The concern is that in doing so, the non-economic social connections between members of communities are seen simply as cost-benefit type market calculations that have the potential to assist a reluctant state to reduce its responsibility for social welfare. Social capitalists of this orientation therefore tend to see the benefits of a strong sense of mutual trust and reciprocity as being a basis for increasing economic efficiency in key areas of government policy. As Edwards et al. (2003) argue, such a view:

> aids the shift in responsibility for 'social inclusion' from economy to society, and from government to individual, informing policies that focus on social behaviour. This reduces the cost to government, since ... social capital provides non-economic solutions to social problems (p. 9).

We do not dispute the criticism that to focus on social capital can be a way of providing support to arguments that governments should economise on social care by using the social ties of social capital. We accept the arguments of Wilkinson and Pickett (2009) who, in 'The Spirit Level', refer to the way there are higher levels of social capital in countries which have lower levels of economic disparity. The active reduction of social inequality, their argument implies, leads to higher levels of social capital, and larger income gaps lead to deteriorations in social capital. Further, economistic approaches to the study of social capital tend to see it through political economy lenses. In so doing, they neglect the 'messiness, unpredictability and intricacies of social life' (Edwards et al. 2003, p. 10). In what follows, we do aim to take account of the intricacies, unpredictability and disarray which can be experienced in care receiving and caregiving. It does provide access to a perspective that takes account of the aggregate of actual and potential resources from 'institutionalised' relationships within social settings.

2.8 The Care Network, the Community and the Policy Contexts

The notion that care is nested within micro, meso and macro levels of influence implies different layers of influence. Keating et al. (2005) have identified these as the personal context, the community context, and the broader policy context. At the micro level, the cared-for person is located alongside and within their social, support and care networks, at the meso level, he or she is located within communities, and at the macro level within the broader policy settings of local, state, national or federal levels of government (Keating et al. 2005).

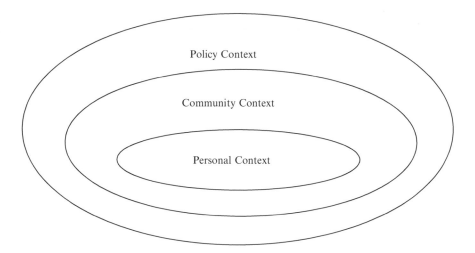

The personal context is the point at which support is provided to the individual. They suggest it can be seen as incorporating social networks, support networks and care networks. Social networks are comprised of the people known to those on need of care and with whom they have strong connections. It is the potential of these support networks to provide care which might be described as the degree of social capital. Social network capital refers to the number of members who are prepared to give assistance and the actual resources they can bring to bear on the situation. However, one of the axioms of social network study is that the 'mere presence of a tie between two people does not equate with the provision of support' (Walker et al. 1993, p. 72). Rather it is the ability to actualise the support potential.

Support networks, by contrast, consist of the actual members of a social network who provide everyday help and support those in need of care. These are the activities such as regular monitoring, emotional support, assistance with instrumental activities of daily living. Members of support networks are those with strong, stable ties with kin and friend relationships (Keating et al. 2004). When support network members are called upon to increase the amount of help and support to a person in need of care, be that instrumental or emotional support, they become members of the care network. Care networks, according to Keating et al. (2005) 'are less diversified and more fragile with higher proportions of close kin than those without chronic health problems' (p. 3).

2.8.1 The Broader Policy Context

> Policies are the more macro values and programs that influence the ways in which communities and networks relate to older adults. By virtue of these influences, the state has a central role in the construction of [care] through the allocation of scarce resources and the transmission of beliefs concerning family care and support. The policy environment itself is complex with public programs existing across levels of government and sectoral domains (Keating et al. 2005, p. 25).

Esping-Andersen's (1990) notion of a welfare state regime accommodates the way social norms inform family care practices, and therefore the way responsibility for care is allocated between the family, the market and the state. This is a way of capturing the broader context of families, social networks and policy settings. It implies the notion that informal care is nested within micro, meso and macro levels of influence. The notion of welfare state regime is an attempt to capture the policy contexts and the broad set of formal and informal structures and processes as they relate to the way different levels of government policy, or even nations, or groups of nations, protect vulnerable citizens and promote wellbeing. The idea of a welfare regime blends many different elements – moral values, social goals, institutional forms and social practices.

In Esping-Andersen's terms, welfare regimes are characterised by different patterns of state, market and family forms of care provision. According to Esping-Andersen (1999, pp. 34–35) a welfare regime is 'the combined, interdependent way is which welfare is produced and allocated between state, market and family.' Welfare regimes reinforce broad political, economic and social interests and ideas, and these tend to follow distinct paths of development. Policies have an ongoing effect in terms of their influence in the way they lead to the preservation of existing ways of doing things, which tend to reproduce or intensify the original care patterns. This happens when social policies for care result in pressure on families to conform to the accepted way of delivering care – the policies both reflecting and reinforcing patterns of care. Social pressures include the influences of policy which determine the allocation of care responsibilities and the types of care deemed to be acceptable. It includes the way formal care organisations are given certain caregiving roles, and the way norms around formal and informal care are developed and sustained through training and education processes.

2.9 Summary

Informal care may be seen as an expression of social capital, this referring to the resources within social networks for mutual support and cooperation. The notion of social capital allows us to take account of the impact of individual strategies which build the capacity of the broader collective, and of the stock of resources that are built up over time. Informal care is an expression of these resources. It is, therefore, fundamentally embedded within the networks of social relationships that give access to needed supports and help. Family members, neighbours and members of the wider community who provide care do so on the basis of the norms of reciprocity and mutual obligation built up within social networks. It is the bonds that exist within longstanding kin relationships and local neighbourhoods, and the bridges that connect people to resources and support across networks. Social networks occur within broader policy contexts, these both reflecting and reinforcing the norms about appropriate responsibility for the provision of care between the family, the community, the market and the state.

Locating informal care within the context of broader health and social policy contexts implies recognising informal and formal caregiving as overlapping domains. Such recognition implies approaching the examination of informal care, as we do in subsequent chapters, in a way that appreciates the following:

1. Care occurs along multiple dimensions (physical, psychological, social), by multiple providers (informal, formal), and in multiple spheres (home, community, institutions);
2. Experiences of caregiving are shaped by a personal context, including earlier life experiences (e.g. relationship quality before caregiving commenced, caregivers' background);
3. Caregiving involves distinct and important developmental experiences;
4. Caregiving experiences are shaped by specific characteristics of and processes in a wide range of inter-connected social settings (both proximal settings of everyday life and distal settings such as the state and its policies);
5. There will be differentiation in care-related experiences across cohort, sex, race and social class groups (see Settersten 2006, p. 4).

Most, if not all, questions that can frame our exploration of informal care can also apply to formal care. In addition to the above, Timonen (2009) proposes that we should understand caregiving as dynamic, something that is subject to change and transformation in the kind and sources of care over time. Our study of caregiving needs to incorporate the care-recipient, the caregiver(s) and their social context(s). She also recommends taking account of the micro and macro levels of social context (family, social network, society, social care, welfare state, political, and cultural levels). The significance of this is, as Timonen (2009, p. 324) states, the pressing need to understand better the way informal care is influenced by formal care in order to strengthen the design of policies and interventions 'to support both types of caregivers.'

Discussion Questions

What are the beliefs in your family about who is the appropriate caregiver for a disabled child or frail elder? Are these beliefs universally shared? If not, then how do others view this situation?

'There are no boundaries on the potential response' in caregiving. Discuss this idea.

How do national health and social policies reinforce beliefs about who is responsible for providing care to family members?

Social capital has been described as both a goal of policy ('our goal is to build social capital') and a tool for policy. What is the difference between the two?

How is social capital related to the experience of informal caregivers? What type of social capital is likely to strengthen informal carers?

Further Reading

Fast, J., Keating, N., Otfinowski, P., & Derksen, L. (2004). Characteristics of family/friend care networks of frail seniors. *Canadian Journal on Aging, 23*(1), 5–19.

Keating, N., Otfinowski, P., Wenger, C., Fast, J., & Derksen, L. (2003). Understanding the caring capacity of informal networks of frail elders. *Ageing and Society, 23*(1), 115–127.

Portes, A. (1998). Social capital: Its origins and applications in modern sociology. *Annual Review of Sociology, 24*, 1–24.

Putnam, R. (2000). *Bowling alone: The collapse and revival of American community*. New York: Simon & Schuster.

Stone, D. (2008). *The Samaritan's Dilemma*. New York: Nation Books.

References

Ahn, T. K., & Ostrom, E. (2002, August 29–September 1). *Social capital and the second-generation theories of collective action: An analytical approach to the forms of social capital*. Annual Meeting of the American Political Science Association, Boston.

Bar-Tal, D., Goldberg, M., & Knaani, A. (1984). Causes of success and failure and their dimensions as a function of SES and gender: A phenomenological analysis. *British Journal of Educational Psychology, 54*(1), 51–61.

Boneham, M., & Sixsmith, J. (2006). The voices of older women in a disadvantaged community: Issues of health and social capital. *Social Science & Medicine, 62*, 269–279.

Bourdieu, P. (1986). The forms of capital. In J. Richardson (Ed.), *Handbook of theory and research for the sociology of education* (pp. 241–258). New York: Greenwood Press.

Bourdieu, P. (2001). *Masculine domination*. Stanford: Stanford University Press.

Butler, M. (2010). Care ethics and the payment of family carers: Implications for occupational therapy. *World Federation of Occupational Therapy Bulletin, 62*(November), 46–52.

Coleman, J. S. (1988). Social capital in the creation of human capital. *The American Journal of Sociology, 94*(Supplement), S95–S120.

Cousineau, N., McDowell, I., Hotz, S., & Hebert, P. (2003). Measuring chronic patients' feelings of being a burden to their caregivers: Development and preliminary validation of a scale. *Medical Care, 41*(1), 110–118.

Edwards, R., Franklin, J., & Holland, H. (2003). *Families and social capital: Exploring the issues*. London: Families and Social Capital ESRC Research Group.

Elster, J. (1987). *Sour grapes: Studies in the subversion of rationality*. Cambridge: Cambridge University Press.

Esping-Andersen, G. (1990). *The three worlds of welfare capitalism*. Cambridge: Polity Press.

Esping-Anderson, G. (1999). *The social foundations of postindustrial economies.* Oxford: Oxford University Press.

Franke, S. (2005). *Measurement of social capital: Reference document for public policy research, development, and evaluation.* PRI Project: Social capital as a public policy tool. http://www.horizons.gc.ca/doclib/Measurement_E.pdf, 17 June 2012.

Gardner, H. (1983). *Frames of mind: The theory of multiple intelligences.* New York: Basic Books.

Ignatieff, M. (1984). *The needs of strangers.* London: Vintage.

Irving, A. (2011). Strange distance: Towards an anthropology of interior dialogue. *Medical Anthropology Quarterly, 25*(1), 22–44.

James, W. (2000). *Pragmatism and other writings.* London: Penguin.

Keating, N., Swindle, J., & Foster, D. (2004). The role of social capital in aging well. *Geneal Social Survey,* Canada. http://www.verterans.gc.ca/pdf/pro_research/social-capital-in-aging-well.pdf

Keating, N., Swindle, J., & Foster, D. (2005). *Social capital as a public policy tool (thematic policy studies).* Ottawa: Policy Research Initiative.

Kittay, E. F. (1999). *Love's labor: Essays on women, equality and dependency.* New York/London: Routledge.

Leder, D. (1990). *The absent body.* Chicago: University of Chicago Press.

Levinas, E. (1989). *Ethics as first philosophy. The Levinas Reader* (S. Hand). Oxford: Blackwell.

Margalit, A. (2002). *The ethics of memory.* Cambridge, MA: Harvard University Press.

McPherson, C., Wilson, K., Chyurlia, L., & Leclerc, C. (2010). The balance of give and take in caregiver-partner relationships; an examination of self-perceived burden, relationship equity, and quality of life from the perspective of care recipients following stroke. *Rehabilitation Psychology, 55*(2), 194–203.

Nussbaum, M. (2006). Capabilities as fundamental entitlements. In A. Kauffman (Ed.), *Capabilities equality: Basic issues and problems* (pp. 44–70). New York: Routledge.

Peek, M., & Lin, N. (1999). Age differences in the effects of network composition on psychological distress. *Social Science & Medicine, 49,* 621–636.

Piercy, K. (1998). Theorizing about family caregiving: The role of responsibility. *Journal of Marriage and Family, 60*(1), 109–118.

Portes, A. (1998). Social capital: Its origins and applications in modern sociology. *Annual Review of Sociology, 24,* 1–24.

Putnam, R. (2000). *Bowling alone: The collapse and revival of American community.* New York: Simon & Schuster.

Ruddick, S. (1989). *Maternal thinking: Towards a politics of peace.* Boston: Beacon Press.

Scanlon, C. (2003, July 19). *The problem with social capital. The age.* Melbourne: John Fairfax Holdings.

Schofield, H., Bloch, S., et al. (Eds.). (1998). *Family caregivers: Disability, illness and ageing.* Sydney: Allen & Unwin.

Sen, A. (2002). *Rationality and freedom.* Cambridge: Belknap Press.

Settersten, R. (2006). Aging and the life course. In R. H. Binstock & L. K. George (Eds.), *Handbook of aging and the social sciences* (pp. 3–19). Amsterdam: Elsevier.

Smith, T. (1997). Factors relating to misanthropy in contemporary American society. *Social Science Research, 26,* 170–196.

Timonen, V. (2009). Toward an integrative theory of care: Formal and informal intersections. In J. Mancini & K. Roberto (Eds.), *Human development and the lifespan: Antecedents, processes and consequences of change.* Plymouth: Lexington.

Turner, V. (1974). *Dramas, fields and metaphors: Symbolic action in human society.* Ithaca: Cornell University Press.

van Groenou, M., & van Tilburg, T. (1997). Changes in the support networks of older adults in The Netherlands. *Journal of Cross-Cultural Gerontology, 12,* 23–44.

van Tilburg, T. (1998). Losing and gaining in old age: Changes in personal network size and social support in a four-year longitudinal study. *Journal of Gerontology: Social Sciences, 53B*(6), S313–S323.

Walker, M., Wasserman, S., & Wellman, B. (1993). Statistical models for social support networks. *Sociological Methods & Research, 22*, 71–98.

Walker, A., Pratt, C., & Eddy, L. (1995). Informal caregiving to aging family members: A critical review. *Family Relations, 44*, 402–411.

Wenger, C. (1991). A network typology: From theory to practice. *Journal of Aging Studies, 5*(2), 147–162.

Wilkinson, R., & Pickett, K. (2009). *The spirit level: Why more equal societies almost always do better*. London: Allen Lane.

Wolfensberger, W. (1972). *The principle of normalization in human services*. Toronto: National Institute on Mental Retardation.

Wolfensberger, W. (1998). *A brief introduction to Social Role Valorization: A high-order concept for addressing the plight of societally devalued people and for structuring human services* (3rd ed.). Syracuse: Training Institute for Human Service Planning/Leadership and Change Agentry (Syracuse University).

Wolfensberger, W., Thomas, S., & Caruso, G. (1996). Some of the universal "good things of life" which the implementation of Social Role Valorization can be expected to make more accessible to devalued people. *SRV/VRS: The International Social Role Valorization Journal/La Revue Interationale de la Valorisation des Roles Sociaux, 2*(2), 12–14.

Wolgast, E. (1992). *Ethics of an artificial person: Lost responsibility in professions and organizations* (Stanford series in philosophy). Stanford: Stanford University Press.

Woolcock, M. (2010). The rise and routinization of social capital, 1988–2008. *Annual Review Political Science, 13*, 469–487.

Chapter 3
The Dynamic Experience of Caring

3.1 Introduction

The human life course is no longer understood as progressing according to a linear model, but is seen as rather more cyclical, with education, work, recreation and caregiving being activities that occur across the whole lifespan, and with transitions into and out of such activities being reversible. Points of transition involve risks and opportunities and these are framed by the context of social capital outlined in the previous chapter. Such transitions are influenced by the availability of support from immediate and wider networks, both formal and informal, and these very much influence the likelihood of achieving favourable outcomes (Davey 2006, p. 26).

The focus of this chapter is on providing a framework for the recognition that the adoption and relinquishment of informal caregiver roles is very much a dynamic experience characterised by upheaval and change. The different care situations, the nature of the need or disability, and its trajectory, all influence how the care role is accepted, how the activity of caring will change over time, and the way in which caring will come to an end. Scholarly accounts of caregiving emphasise this dynamic nature, often as a series of transitions between different stages of caring – broadly, of 'taking it on,' 'working through it' and 'ending' (Wilson 1989). Aneshenal et al. (1995, p. 9) refer to the trajectory of caregiving, taken on expectedly or unexpectedly, as a caregiver 'career,' Montgomery and Koloski (2000, p. 10) refer to change and continuity in the caregiving experience, and Nolan et al. (1995, p. 10) frame their excellent analysis of caregiving around stages of transition. Each of these approaches recognise common experiences among carers – of progress through broadly similar stages through which carers pass, similar changes to living situation, the adoption of similar activities, the encountering of similar emotional terrain, and the learning of related caring skills (see also Wallengren et al. 2008; Pereira and Botelho 2011; Hirst 2005; Power 2010). Even though caregiving is provided in a variety of situations to meet a diversity of needs, it is these similarities in experience that unite carers in various ways, for example, such as becoming members of the various carers' associations, support groups, and internet chat groups.

P. Barrett et al., *Family Care and Social Capital: Transitions in Informal Care*,
DOI 10.1007/978-94-007-6872-7_3, © Springer Science+Business Media Dordrecht 2014

We propose in the following pages that the classic rites of passage framework is a useful analytic tool to capture the dynamic experience of becoming an informal caregiver. This framework helps in teasing apart the process of change and in scrutinising closely the experience of important life transitions in terms of recognising changing social identities. Van Gennep's original concept of three stages, separation, liminality and reconnection, was developed to understand the changes in social status and roles, and the different religious rituals associated with these. As Hockey and James (2003) suggest, though, the model has a much wider applicability, and can be used to understand changes in social role and identity in modern secular contexts. They maintain that:

> According to the analytic model, passage through each of the three phases of the ritual meant that individuals had been detached from their previous social position, processed through an intermediary state which shared the features of neither the previous nor the successive social position, and then had been incorporated into a new set of rules, roles and obligations (Hockey and James 2003, p. 25).

The model thus illuminates the experience of *becoming* a carer and captures both the individual and social aspects of transition. The actual change can be examined spatially, temporally, and in terms of the implications for social relationships of those who make this transition. The framework allows attention to be given to the stage of liminality, an 'in-between' stage characterised by an unsettledness. The third involves reincorporation and reconnection with the wider society, with a new set of rules, roles and responsibilities, raising the question of 'reconnections' and some of the key issues with achieving 'reconnection'.

Van Gennep (1909) developed his original concept to understand the different religious rituals in the cultures he studied, in particular the rituals which marked transitions between different life stages and movement from one role to another. However, we use the concept in a secular sense, and in doing so follow Turner (1969, p. 3) who observes that 'it is not a theorist's whole system which so illuminates but his scattered ideas, his flashes of insights taken out of systemic context.' Other theorists who have applied this concept to secular situations include Teather (1999), Hugman (1999), Hallman (1999) in family caregiving, Hockey and James (1993, 2003) in considering passages through the life course, Twigg (2000) applying a rite of separation to bathing and baths, Frank (2002) observing an incomplete rite of passage in her study of assisted living, and Parks (2003) with her focus on care at home, and Hale et al. (2010) in their work on aged care in the community.

An advantage of the rites of passage framework for this study is in the way in which it recognises the social processes of change, highlighting the disruptions, the changing social roles and obligations, and in emphasizing the need for social reconnection as individuals assume a transformed identity. It also reveals the risk of failing to complete the passage and reach a stage of reconnection or reintegration. Consequently, the value of this framework lies in its recognition of a movement which ends in a different, transformed social status, recognised by the wider society.

Additionally, by subdividing the transition into three stages – separation from the current identity; liminality, the uncertainty brought by change; and the third stage of 'reconnection', the re-entering of the social world in a new life stage – allows for a more detailed examination of the changes that occur. In Janlov et al.'s (2006, p. 334) terms, these transitions are:

> marked by a starting point of change, through a period of instability, discontinuity, confusion and distress to a new beginning or period of stability.

The rite of passage concept is, therefore, a simple heuristic which allows for the scrutiny of change experiences in terms of three broad social processes: separation denotes an initial point of change, or a biographical disruption in Bury's (1982) terms: liminality denotes a state of upheaval, disorder and therefore improvisation and searching; and reconnections, a stage of acceptance and recognition by the wider society.

We suggest there are a number of merits in using this broader approach. First, it recognises that for many informal carers, caring does not come to an end, but, if we accept this stage of reconnections, caregiving can be seen as very much a part of the life that is lived as a parent or spouse. Second, identifying specific times in the caregiving career allows for the close scrutiny of the complex individual and social processes of change, thus providing us with a deeper understanding of those processes. Furthermore, in drawing attention to a stage of reconnection, the framework places the focus on what is needed to ensure informal carers and the people they care for are not socially excluded, but are supported in such a way as to remain connected or become reconnected to the wider society. For carers, this means ensuring the demands of informal care work are not such that they become vulnerable to social and economic disadvantage, such that they lose the capacity to participate in broader aspects of family and social life. We suggest that these insights have potential to inform the nature and content of interventions.

What follows is a more detailed review of the argument that the rites of passage framework is a useful analytical tool to be applied to caregiving, allowing for a better understanding of this life change. We draw on several researchers to demonstrate the applicability of this concept (Janlov et al. 2006; Olaison and Cedersund 2006; Hale 2006). These researches draw attention to the common experiences of change, subdivided into stages of separation, liminality and reconnection. We suggest that caregiver experiences at each stage within this framework can be analysed in more detail by giving attention to the spatial, temporal and relational dimensions of change.

3.2 Separation: The Beginning of Transition

Informal caring is a response to a need of a family member, friend or neighbour. However, with care having shifted into the public sphere (Fine 2006), there are other means of meeting that need. So when someone's increasing need moves them across a threshold then, an exchange with health and allied care professionals is initiated. Although the implications of the process of assessment are under-acknowledged, this is a significant moment in the lives of both the person in need and the informal caregiver (Richards 2000; Olaison and Cedersund 2006; Janlov et al. 2006; Hale et al. 2010). For informal caregivers, it implies movement into a new role and identity, that of caregiver.

Informal caregivers face major change when natural caring situations are transformed into patient–caregiver relations (Efraimsson et al. 2001, p. 813). Bury's (1982) term biographical disruption seems to us to capture the nature of the experience. Becoming an informal caregiver is a dynamic experience. It can occur as a 'drift' or a 'sharply punctuated event,' with subtle changes of relationships, group memberships and social participation, and equally subtle changes in the attitudes of others. What makes this change significant as an experience of separation is the way in which it involves a challenge to the normatively defined role of spouse, parent, child, or neighbour. The anthropologist Van Gennep (1909) characterised separation as an event which detaches the individual from his or her previous social status, and which initiates a course of change that results in the position of individuals being redefined within their particular social and cultural context.

In his research, he identified the events associated with separation as planned rituals that divest individuals of their recognised status, moving them to a new social identity. Rituals identified by Van Gennep (1909) included enforced relocation or physical markings such as body modifications, head shaving, tattooing and scarification. Such events were conducted ceremonially and publicly, and were intended to be a visible stripping from the initiates of their identities to remove them from previous social statuses. These rituals demarcate the line between the old life and the new. In secular terms, similar separation experiences can be identified at the beginning of important life transitions.

In the unceremonial transition into becoming an informal caregiver, we suggest an initial realization of responsibility for care, a personal decision to take it on and that meeting with formal care services or assessors in the development of care plans, where the carer is officially recognised as a part of the arrangements for care, is a defining separation experience. Cameron and Gignac (2008) observe that such experiences comprise that point in time where the primary responsibility of the family member or friend as that of caregiver is clearly recognised and expanded to such an extent that caregiving begins to define identity and life choices. Ducharme et al. (2011), in their study of care for a family member with dementia, capture the significance of this when they refer to the way the inclusion of a spouse, parent, child or neighbour in 'diagnostic disclosures' mark the official entry into the caregiver role. Nolan et al. (2003, pp. 25–26) refer to this as 'the confirming stage,' this being

> a period of transition to the caregiver role during which time caregivers are inevitably faced with new responsibilities. They must learn to cope with the losses and the changes in the relative's behavior that characterize the [need for care] and to plan for future care needs (Ducharme et al. 2011, p. 485).

Needs assessments or diagnoses provide a basis for the formal recognition of needs and brings the caregiver into contact with the formal system, and although there may rightly be debate about the extent to which informal carers are appropriately recognised as they become a part of a care plan, their situation and capacity is usually assessed at this time as well. Care plans, for example for older people remaining home with care, typically take account of what the family, and in particular the primary caregiver, can do. This can be seen as an initial formal recognition of a family caregiver role.

Interactions with formal service personnel can be thought of as a type of institutional conversation in this process of recognition, with the effect that the caregiver learns the accepted philosophy and rationale for the provision of formal support services, such as home care, respite care, or other forms of funded support. This interaction is characterised by the power of the assessor to determine eligibility for formal services, and in these exchanges the informal caregiver has a relative lack of power. Assessors are the gatekeepers of access to formal support and the information required to get that support. The dialogue is controlled by the assessor. She (typically) introduces and closes off the topics examined and the informal caregiver must accept the judgment of the assessor if they are to receive help (Olaison and Cedersund 2006). Care plans which incorporate an assessment of what it is the family member can do are thus developed, and these assessments and plans both reflect and reinforce socially defined expectations of caregiving and might be thought of as a social script of caregiving. The caregiver becomes aware of the particular needs categories recognised by the formal sector and begins to see her or his situation as falling within these. The cared-for person's needs are a defining element, influencing how the caregiver is positioned in relationship with the formal sector, for example, taking full responsibility as in the case of children, or assuming increasing responsibilities in the case of older people. The situation will vary depending on the disability, the level of need, and the degree of autonomy and control which can be exercised by the care-recipient.

What follows is a brief review of what separation main mean for individual caregivers in spatial, temporal and relational terms.

3.2.1   Separation: Spatial Dimensions

Since informal care is typically, but not exclusively, provided in the home or community setting, when someone is perceived as a caregiver, it makes sense to focus on the dynamics of home to understand the caregiving context. Parts of this context are the spatial disruptions which often accompany this transition. The home is an important source of an individual's identity, but the meaning of the home changes when it becomes a place of intensive care work (Hale 2006; Wiles 2003; Twigg 2000).

An important assumption underpinning community care and care at home is that remaining at home allows those in need of care to continue to have access to the ideals of home, the warmth and stability, continuity, independence, security, autonomy, safety and familiarity typically associated with the home. However, to provide care in the home often requires conscious spatial decisions. House modifications and visible assistive devices are material indicators of the changes that occur when one becomes an informal caregiver. New possessions, the accoutrements of care, such as the required assistive devices begin to define the spatial environment. Former meanings and identities associated with home in these situations are threatened or compromised.

Rooms may be given new functions – the public space of a lounge becomes a bedroom; instead of a double bed, there are two single beds; instead of the whole house fully used, there is reduced usable space to a manageable track between the bedroom, bathroom and kitchen. Sleeping arrangements are often reorganised – the living room becomes a bedroom, other rooms are reorganised to accommodate overnight carers; a spouse moves into another bedroom altogether. Grab rails, ramps, raised toilet seats, and special grab poles for getting in and out of bed, as well as aids for assistance to move around the home, increase usable reachable space. Equipment to assist functioning – the presence of a walking frame, a 'talking book', and a white stick; a wheelchair beside the bed, a bedpan on the seat – exemplify the types of actual spatial adjustments that begin to define the rooms of homes where frail or disabled people live (Saarenheimo et al. 2004). The reorganisation and modification of space in the home at this stage is undoubtedly an adaptation strategy designed to compensate for loss and to maintain function, the basic purpose of this being to respond to the need for care.

On the surface, spatial reorganisation to create functional areas and to accommodate the introduction of formal care into the home appears straightforward. But such re-arrangements and improvisations affect caregivers in important ways. The para-phernalia of disability shapes their living spaces and has been found to lead to the caregivers and co-resident family members feeling their living areas are no longer their own. Hale's (2006) research found there was an important sense in which the meaning of home was dictated by the disability needs of the care-recipient, with the home becoming a place *of* care and a place *for* care. One participant from this research commented:

> I used to think my house was not my own but the place was set up like a hospital anyway and I used to have wheelchairs [for my husband], walking frames, seats and bed with frames up the side and lifts, you know, overhead lifts, things over the top, and there was no room to turn around … I had no space, I lost my space (Hale et al. 2010, p. 72).

Another aspect of the spatial dimension is worth mentioning here and it relates to the impact of becoming a caregiver on experiences outside of the home. Informal caregivers become bound by the responsibilities within the home and become spatially trapped or restricted. This need to be present and accessible as a caregiver imposes limits on mobility in such a way as to be an important marker in the caregiver transition experience (Power 2010).

3.2.2   Separation: Temporal Dimensions

The separation experience can also be observed in temporal dimensions, that is in terms of the experience of time. To study the experience of time is to study how people's lives are constructed and framed through their temporal environments. Westenholz (2006) has proposed the notion of 'time identities,' these being socially negotiated and socially constructed subject positions that help people feel secure and enable them to act. Within households, these may be observed in the daily rhythms laid down during a family's life together and this frames day-to-day expectations. Such daily rhythms structure the organisation of the self and the home. The onset of disability and the need for care can be seen as critically transforming these pre-existing ways-of-being in time and place.

Disruption to the daily temporal rhythm is most evident following the sudden onset of the need to become a caregiver, be that a consequence of an accident or disabling condition such as a stroke with its resultant difficulties. Being 'suddenly hit' by the demands of a care situation and a sense of responsibility to meet the need are typical of this experience.

This type of upheaval in a caregiver's life, we suggest, is punctuated by the formal assessment process and often the subsequent involvement of formal caregivers in the home. These experiences introduce a new temporal element into a household. Pereira and Botelho (2011), in their analysis of the experiences of those who suddenly become caregivers, refer to the experience as a loss of control over time and of being thrust into a mode of living for the moment: 'time begins to be built around schedules over which they have little control' (p. 2451).

Caregivers subsequently experience a sudden clash between caregiving responsibilities and their own personal projects (Pereira and Botelho 2011, p. 2452). The immediate demands of the situation dictate how they live their daily lives – their routines, or lack of them. Becoming an informal caregiver involves giving up personal time, and a need for flexibility to respond to the demands of the care situation. Routines need to be redesigned to accommodate spur of the moment demands, forcing cancellations or postponements. For example, in the first days at home following hospital discharge, it is well known that caregivers do not allow time for themselves. Rather, they focus their time on caring for their loved ones, expressing a devotion to providing care to the dependent relative. It is a time of chaos, confusion and little reflection, a time that Bridges (2001, p. 5) associates with feelings of loss and the need to abandon an old way of life or a previous identity: 'we lose or let go our previous perspective, our previous attitudes, our values, our self-image.'

Time is thus experienced by new caregivers as frenzied or seemingly unending, and the early stages of the caregiving experience can be understood as a period of deep anxiety that is related to the loss of control of the present and anxiety about the future. Pereira and Botelho (2011) point out that at this stage of the process, caregivers often feel they have no choice and, frequently, are ambivalent about taking on the caregiving responsibility. Feelings of wanting to help are accompanied by fear about the future. This process reflects Westenholz's (2006) observation that time identities are socially situated and are not static, and in the process of social negotiation the delineation between the individual and the environment changes. The process of social negotiation associated with the transition into becoming a caregiver involves clashes between time identities as the relationship between the informal caregiver, the care-recipient, the household environment, and the formal care services are brought into contact. Continuity in a temporal sense implies an individual maintaining his/her daily rhythm. It refers to personal organization and the maintenance of an acceptable temporal rhythm to the day, the week, or the month (Larson et al. 2008). When that continuity is broken, lived time becomes sporadic and non-homogeneous (Chapman 1997). Time is interrupted and a new disability time is imposed by the need. The ability to maintain personal temporal rhythms is lost.

3.2.3   Separation: Relational Dimensions

Separation experiences associated with becoming a caregiver can also be seen as involving disruption within the social networks of individual carers. We can see this in terms of the care relationship, wider family relationships and personal social relationships, and each of these differ according to the life course stage of the caregiver. The demands associated with becoming a primary caregiver of a child with a disability, for example, lead to disruptions in spousal and other family member relationships. The need to be present as a caregiver limits the ability to get out of the home, or to spend time with other family members within the home. Often other children become substitute caregivers in times of need. With regard to becoming an informal caregiver to people at the other end of the life course, Clare Wenger (2002) has observed that the networks of dependent, home-living disabled older people change from being characterised by attachment to the broader social environment and support networks to become characteristically family dependent or private and restricted. Such networks tend to be smaller and have lower levels of community involvement. Becoming an informal caregiver, therefore, presents demands which lead to the important renegotiation of personal and social relationships.

The notion of relational separation captures changes to family roles that accompany the assumption of caregiving. Once the need for care is such that a commitment to care is triggered, the caregiver is caught up in a process of interaction which has the effect of creating new identities and roles, and these have important implications for the nature of the relationship with the cared-for person. Among married couples, for example, roles can change from 'spouse' to 'care-recipient' or 'caregiver,' with resulting conflicts and confusion. While personal social networks are disrupted, new relationships formed with assessors and formal care workers. Despite this, people who become informal caregivers do face increased risk of social isolation. This results from challenges to mobility given the need to be present as a caregiver, with consequential difficulties in maintaining personal social ties. With problems in being able to come and go from the home, caregivers are no longer able to easily be with friends and this diminishes the ability to sustain social networks (Pereira and Botelho 2011, p. 2451). The result is often loneliness and depression as carers lose the social world in which they had lived.

3.3 Liminality

The rites of passage framework suggests that separation experiences are followed by a period of liminality. According to Van Gennep's (1909) research, a liminar is on the threshold between two different states. Established structures and a sense of the normal order of things are overturned. Our analysis of the reported experiences of people who become informal carers leads us to conclude that they too experience liminality following the assumption of the caregiver role. In fact, most caregiver experiences could well be described as liminal (see Pereiro and Botelho 2011). Reference to disconnectedness, disparities, and chaos, as well as anxieties, concerns, bewilderment (Hale et al. 2010), emphasizes experiences of upheaval, anxiety and fearfulness. Again, such liminal experiences can be teased apart in terms of their spatial, temporal and relational dimensions.

Family carers can be said to be in a liminal position in that they are neither professional caregivers, nor are they passive family members. Their situation is often one of responsibility without authority. They tend to be expected to assume more responsibility for making decisions or in persuading the cared-for person about decisions, but at the same time they report that they are often excluded from decisions that affect the person they care for, or decisions are made without consideration of the implications for them as caregivers.

Within these exchanges, there is a tension between supporting the decisional autonomy and independence of the cared-for person and that of the caregiver. Caregivers take on greater decision responsibility and because of their relationship as a family member often play a role in persuading them, for example, to accept decisions relating to their care or health: this may be persuading them to have an assessment, to visit the doctor, to change or review medication, to go into hospital, to have an operation, or to accept formal help. Family carers are often expected to take responsibility for these decisions, but they have limited authority. They cannot be said to have authority over the cared-for person – this goes against the norms of reciprocity and compassion that are often the motivation for the caring role. They also report little authority over or input into decisions by health and allied professionals. There is little recognition that they have an intimate interest in and knowledge of their situation. And being excluded from such decisions reflects a narrow focus by health professionals that does not take the family or household situation into consideration, only that of the cared-for person. Being excluded can result in carers approaching the care work with limited knowledge of the options available to them. As Hale (2006) found, this can lead to an ambivalent relationship with health care and care professionals, and in feelings of anxiety in carrying out their responsibilities.

3.3.1 Liminality: Spatial Dimensions

Family and informal care implies the cared-for person and the caregiver continue to live in their own home, outside of an institutional context, in a way that avoids the disruption associated with moving into another care space. However, in the same way as residential living to support a person with a disability represents a new 'landscape of care', so too does caring for a person in the home. To support and maintain a disabled or frail family member within the home requires important changes in domestic organisation. Weaver (1999, p. 75) comments in describing the changing home environment with ramps, and other equipment, such as hoists, and housing modifications to accommodate the paraphernalia of disability. She summarises the feelings of many parents:

> it is worth tolerating the invasive nature of the [assessment] procedures because there are some wonderful items available… One piece of equipment can completely change your life and make possible parenting tasks that other families take for granted (p. 75).

Clearly, assistive devices and modifications enable care to be provided.

But as we have observed, when these lead to a reordering of space, meanings associated with the self and the home are challenged. Such reorganisation, we suggest, reframes the meaning of the space, from independent space to a space which indicates dependence on support and makes the disability more visible. It contributes towards reframing the identities of the caregiver and the cared-for person, both to the individuals concerned and to outsiders. While the improvement of the spatial environment to increase functionality is appreciated, as Weaver (1999) has said, such devices draw attention to the disability and are a constant reminder of change. The material possessions of disability devices mark the new social identity and make it visible. So while Turner comments that the removal of material markers of identity were an indication of the passage into a state of liminality, we suggest that the addition of disability aids are markers signal a similar passage.

Caring has a considerable impact on the mobility and routine of the carer, with implications, for example, for their experiences within the home in terms of enjoying friends' visits, or for their experiences outside of the home as part of a local community or in terms of leisure activities. Being an informal caregiver requires constant consideration to questions such as the time of outing, and whether appropriate, convenient and comfortable spaces are available, and the receptiveness of those spaces towards the person being cared for. For example, in situations of caring for children with intellectual disability, Power (2010) writes:

> [P]ublic interaction has specific consequences for mothers taking their children… out, as the actions of the child, the mother and others present make visible the rules of what is considered to be acceptable behaviour and etiquette in public places. … going out in public space can involve considerable layers of negotiation, mediation and management (p. 110).

Being unable to move around freely, therefore, can and does inhibit the personal networks of the carers, not only in terms of leaving the house but also in socialising within the home. The world outside the home also has to be considered in terms of admission to the private home space. While many older people, for example, do welcome the provision of formal care services within the home with relief (Barrett et al. 2005; Hale 2006), for others, the introduction of formal caregivers into the home leads to feelings of disruption and intrusion. When formal care workers are involved in assisting with daily functions such as housework, they move into personally defined areas. Private spaces become public with the entry of health officials and care workers, but handing over such spaces leaves household members feeling that there home is no longer their own.

One further dimension is that of bodily space. Care means for many people the care of the bodies of disabled or frail individuals when those individuals would normally be looking after themselves. Cleaning, grooming, lifting, for example, are aspects of caregiving which must be noted. Body work, as Twigg (2000) described, was often distressing, both for the caregiver and the cared-for person. It can be particularly difficult when adult children are caregivers. Accepted boundaries of personal privacy are broken in washing, toileting and dressing, and this is a source of stress for both carers and recipients.

> And it was something that I had to be aware of, too, that he absolutely hated his daughters having to do anything private with him. He absolutely hated it. … If he'd used the toilet and he couldn't clean himself … he never ever liked his daughters to help (Hale 2006, p. 151).

The norms which inform familial roles and expectations are suspended when there is a requirement for bodily care and management of adults and older adults who normally deal with their own bodies.

3.3.2 Liminality: Temporal Dimensions

Temporal liminality may be understood as ranging from the disordering of, and loss of control over, one's daily life, to longer term temporal questions related to disability and the loss of ability to live an autonomous, independent life. Spatiality and temporality are closely connected. As Power (2010) indicates, caregivers have to consider how far they can go in terms of how long they can leave the person they are caring for, and also, where can they take the person for whom they care, where are the acceptable and accessible places?

For family caregivers, time continually feels as if it has been 'stolen' and life begins to be built around schedules, over which they have little control.

> We lost our personal life… most of it depends on my mother's schedule. For us, being still young, it's hard (Pereira and Botelho 2011, p. 2451).

Many carers feel their homes become institutionalized (Milligan 2001). Questions of temporality feature strongly in the 'chaos' experienced by the caregivers described by Olaison and Cedersund (2006). Caregivers lose the ability to control time and are required to live in the moment, leading to a constant state of anxiety and uncertainty about the future (Pereiro and Botelho 2011; see also Nolan et al. 2003; Wallengren et al. 2008).

It is the caregiver who is betwixt and between the different temporal identities of the cared-for person (disability time) and the wider world; it is the caregiver who is at the interface between the two. In a real sense, their time is not their own as the bodies and minds of those they care for 'make time-specific demands which cannot be scheduled to some external conception of time' (Rose 1994, p. 49). Further, while objective time demands can be measured in terms of hours spent caring, the subjective demands imply giving constant attention to the needs of the cared for person (Haveman et al. 1997).

Temporal liminality involves, therefore, disruptions and loss of control over one's daily life, as well as longer term temporal questions related to disability and the loss of ability to live an autonomous, independent life. This has different implications for caregivers at different stages of the life course. Younger caregivers plan and have visions for a different future for themselves; older caregivers look forward to their own retirement, and the financial implications of this, while continuing a grueling daily caregiving schedule, are not always easy to manage as they age; and senior caregivers who are likely to be retired, have a past to consider, and less of a future, one in which they did not necessarily expect to spend time in caregiving. It is important to note that there are marked dissonances between the expectations and anticipations of caregivers and those of their peers at the same stages of the life course.

3.3.3 Liminality: Relational Dimensions

A third area in which liminality is experienced concerns social relationships. Changes in the home associated with the adoption of an informal caregiving role have an impact on social networks. Implicitly referencing the interrelationship between the spatial and the relational dimension, Csikszentmihalyi and Rochberg-Halton (1981 in Saarenheimo et al. 2004, p. 14) observe that:

> [T]he 'signs of illness', such as the presence of special hospital furniture, care equipment or particular odours and noises, get easily interpreted as obstacles for social interaction at home.

The need for informal care leads to important changes in the domestic order and in how social interaction at home is conducted. Saaranheimo et al. (2004, pp. 14–15) refer to considerable research showing the significant changes in the social networks of carers. Such research confirms there are ongoing difficulties for people to visit and go out, for socialising, or, for example, their own medical appointments. The spatial rearrangements associated with the home becoming a place of care present practical challenges which influence the ability to offer hospitality. New rules begin to regulate the visits of friends and relatives and this affects the desire, the motivation and the ability to invite people to visit.

Suitor et al. (2003) describe how networks of carers intensify and how new relationships with others in similar situations develop. Hale's observations from many years in the care sector led her to conclude that people experience a change in their social networks, one which is defined by new associations with health and allied professionals, and fewer friendship-based relationships. Her 2006 research found that carers often commented that they lost their former friends during a time of providing care for a family member, even when neighbourhood networks were strong. Some replaced their prior social networks with networks of carers in a similar position. Caregiver support groups thus become more important in these contexts (Hale 2000). But, as Saarenheimo et al. (2004) comment, there are limited opportunities for developing such carer networks, and many are unable to maintain existing friendships or develop new friendships. Changing network structures can be reflected in changing language, in particular from the 'we' of the couple to the 'I' of the carer (Hale 2000).

Relational liminality is most evident in the sense of isolation experienced when carrying the responsibility of being a primary caregiver for another human life. That isolation is both a felt and a lived reality. Informal caregivers can therefore feel very alone and abandoned with their burden of care. This is not restricted to being physically alone, without appropriate assistance. Caregivers can feel alone by missing the care receiver's old self, and the lives they shared together. There is, too, a significant feeling of aloneness with the loss of prior hopes of a shared life creating a family with a growing child (Weaver 1999).

3.4 Reconnections?

Liminality is seen in the rites of passage framework as a temporary phase in the transition process. It is followed by a phase of reconnection to the broader community with a new social standing. The Van Gennep definition of reconnection, according to Hockey and James (2003), involves movement into a new, socially recognised and valued life stage with its own set of 'rules, roles and obligations.'

Reconnections, however, are not assured, and much of the research into caregiving experiences suggests informal caregivers live in spatial, temporal and relational states of liminality. That is, many caregivers, despite aspiring to express their moral duty to help a spouse, parent, child, friend or neighbour in a way that meets their needs, have experiences of continuing liminality. The aspiration to provide help to a family member, and the actual provision of such help, is not sufficient to move the carer beyond the liminal state. Many find themselves expected to carry the responsibility for the wellbeing of the person in need of care, while having little authority to make key decisions about that care. This is particularly the case of adult children caring for once independent older people. Those who live in the same house as the person they care for are faced, often, with their home becoming a space for the delivery of care. Private spaces become public and home takes on new meanings which are defined by the disability or need for care. The need to be present as a caregiver ties them to their homes or places of care and limits their mobility. Caregivers thus find themselves losing control over the organisation of their daily lives, how they use their time being defined by the needs of the care situation.

This has a profound influence on their ability to maintain social connectedness, and social networks are thus modified, usually in the direction of becoming narrower. Many informal caregivers become disconnected as a consequence of taking on the caregiving role, and many remain in that state through their experience of caregiving.

Addressing disconnection and facilitating reconnection in a new and socially valued role is, therefore, critical. But what does it mean to say that a caregiver has become reconnected? Reconnection means the informal caregiver is not alone with the responsibility for the life and wellbeing of the person he or she cares for, but is connected through lines of support that allows the expression of the basic human inclination to care for a family member or neighbour. This means, first, being supported in the work of care, and, second, not being left to carry the weight of that work alone. Such support may come from a variety of sources, reflecting the availability of social capital, but at a basic level being connected means not being left alone in the role of caregiving. It involves being supported to develop the skills and acquire knowledge, and it means having respite opportunities and timely help. For this to occur, informal care and the work of informal caregivers needs to be recognised and valued within health and social care systems. Reconnected caregivers have their expertise, acquired through first-hand knowledge of their particular care situation, valued by the health and social care professionals with whom they interact. Support, when it is provided, will be done so in ways that are sensitive to how it may be a type of imposition on a private domain. Reconnected informal caregivers will also be able to reconcile the time demands of the care work role with other aspects of their lives. This will mean being able to maintain social connectedness and manage the temporal and spatial demands of their care situation that can undermine the ability to remain connected.

Jeggel's (2006) study of connectedness in caring emphasised the importance of formal care workers in preparing the family member for the new role of caregiving. It involves providing information and opportunities for the acquisition of specific care related skills, ensuring the availability of other appropriate help and assistive devices, and allowing the carer time to consider the implications of undertaking the care, and deciding whether or not they will undertake such care. Her study (2006) into the hospital discharges of older people suggests the notion of role fitting. By this she means giving conscious consideration to the question of whether the potential informal caregiver is suited to the role. This should be noted at the time of diagnosis and assessment of needs of the older person. If there is no one caregiver ready to take on the role, then the choice of who becomes the informal caregiver and their suitability depends on prior relationships and on convenience. In the cases where the caregiver chose to care, the role was fitted into their existing roles. Role strain and role conflict developed when those assigned the caregiving role did not choose to take it on. She notes that caregivers chosen by others often experience difficulty in fitting the role into their existing lives. Success in the caregiving role, says Jeggels (2006), depends on a positive choice by the caregiver to take on the role, and this meant giving sufficient information to make an informed choice. Heaton (1999) suggests that, in policy terms, there needs to be support for carers choosing whether or not to act as carers and with the ability to recognise situations where family members are not best placed to take up that role (p. 764).

Such connectedness has to be maintained, once someone has agreed to take on the role. Jeggels (2006) found that successful maintenance depends on the knowledge and skills of the carer, the context of care (for her study it was that of home) and access to basic resources. The problems she identified were inadequate resources for caregivers, including financial resources, lack of knowledge on how to access support, a need to leave employment to provide care, and caregiver isolation. In a nutshell, lack of income, lack of support, lack of time, lack of skills, poor public transport facilities all undermine the ability to provide suitable care. Caring is improved, says Jeggels, if there is greater support from familial, neighbourhood and professional sources.

Connectedness is taken by Jeggels (2006) to imply comfort in the role of caregiver, is associated with successful caregiving, with appropriate skills and knowledge, with good support by the broader family and social networks, including health professionals, a knowledge of entitlements, and an ability to fit the caregiving role into existing roles without excessive strain. She contrasts connected care with disconnected care as follows:

Connected care	Disconnected care
Caregiver enjoys caring	Caregiver tired, alone
Caring gives pleasure	Caregiver is frustrated
Caregiver maintains social contacts	Caregiver is isolated
Support given from family, friends, neighbours, health services	Caregiver is alone

In Van Gennep's model, reconnection was facilitated by the intervention of guides to assist completion of the passage and we too suggest that that there is potential for the formal care sector to act as guides and engage with informal caregivers for successful reconnection, in terms of acceptance of role, learning and exchange of skills, and in terms of accessing useful new supports.

Effective social ties are recognised as a key aspect of being connected. These include existing ties of kin and friends and new social linkages through formal and informal disability and caregiver networks. The potential for reconnections will be facilitated by the active construction of networks with different care providers, and the maintenance of networks with these and with other formal and informal disability and care support groups. Informal caregiving involves the constant search to find the best way to support the individual with the need for care. It involves improvisatory practices, and it leads to a well-grounded sense of what will work in a care situation and what will not. Reconnected caregivers will have this type of grounded knowledge recognised by the formal care workers with whom they engage.

3.5 Summary

In this chapter we have outlined an approach for considering key aspects of the general experience of the transition into becoming a caregiver. A secular use of the rites of passage framework which emphasises the three stages of separation, liminality and reconnections allows us to identify shared experiences of caregiving for people with long-term disabilities and chronic health conditions. The stages allow us to see commonalities in the changing personal and social dimensions of the caregiving identity.

Creating community environments where informal caregivers are socially recognised and valued could be seen to be a significant goal for many agencies interested in maintaining carer connections. Local support groups and national advocacy and support groups are important means for the achievement of this. Political recognition of informal caregiving which equates with 'work' and 'labour' rather than family responsibility, duty or affection, has potential to lead to social and financial recognition and recompense, and for support. Reconnections, then, indicate social ties at the individual, family and community level, and ties to a wider societal level.

Discussion Suggestions

Becoming a caregiver is a major life transition. What are the triggers for this change?

Discuss the word liminality and consider what a liminal experience means for informal caregivers.

Reconnection is the goal. What constitutes reconnection for caregivers? What might reconnected care practice look like? What is the value for caregivers?

From your perspective, what would you identify at each stage as the important point for intervention?

What skills do you think a caregiver could teach you and your colleagues?

Further Reading

Hockey, J., & James, A. (1993). *Growing up and growing old*. London: Sage.
Milligan, C. (2001). *Geographies of care: Space, place and the voluntary sector*. Aldershot: Ashgate.
Nolan, M., Grant, G., & Keady, J. (1996). *Understanding family care: A multi-dimensional model of caring and coping*. Buckingham: Open University Press.
Power, A. (2010). *Landscapes of care*. Farnham: Ashgate.
Twigg, J. (2000). *The body and community care*. London: Routledge.

References

Aneshenal, C., Perlin, L., Jullan, J., Zarit, S., & Whitlatch, J. (1995). *Profiles in caregiving: The unexpected career*. San Diego: Academic Press.
Barrett, P., Kletchko, S., Twitchin, S., Ryan, F., & Fowler, V. (2005). *Transitions in later life: A qualitative inquiry into the experience of resilience and frailty*. Tauranga: University of Waikato.
Bridges, W. (2001). *The way of transitions: Embracing life's most difficult moments*. Cambridge: Da Capo Press.

Bury, M. (1982). Chronic illness as biographical disruption. *Sociology of Health & Illness, 4*(2), 137–169.

Cameron, J., & Gignac, M. (2008). Timing it right: A conceptual framework for addressing the support needs of family caregivers to stroke survivors from the hospital to the home. *Patient Education and Counselling, 70*, 05–314.

Chapman, H. (1997). Self-help groups, family carers and mental health. *Australian & New Zealand Journal of Mental Health Nursing, 6*(4), 148–155.

Csikszentmihalyi, M., & Rochberg-Halton, E. (1981). *The meaning of things: Domestic symbols and the self*. Cambridge: Cambridge University Press.

Davey, J. (2006). *Research on ageing in New Zealand: Progress, gaps and the potential contribution of EWAS research* (Enhancing Wellbeing in an Ageing Society Working Paper 3). Wellington.

Ducharme, F., Levesque, L., Lachance, L., et al. (2011). Learning to become a family caregiver. Efficacy of an intervention Program for Caregivers Following Diagnosis of Dementia in a Relative. *The Gerontologist, 51*(4), 484–494.

Efraimsson, E., Hoglund, I., & Sandman, P. (2001). The everlasting trial of strength and patience: Transitions in home care nursing as narrated by patients and family members. *Journal of Clinical Nursing, 10*, 813–819.

Fine, M. (2006). *A caring society? Care and the dilemmas of human services in the 21st century*. Houndmills: Palgrave/MacMillan.

Frank, J. (2002). *The paradox of aging in place in assisted living*. Westport: Bergin and Garvey.

Hale, B. (2000). From partner to carer: A description of changes in language and networks amongst family caregivers. *Social Work Review, 12*(1), 7–10.

Hale, B. (2006). *The meaning of home as it becomes a place for care – The emergence of a new life stage for frail older people?* Ph.D. thesis for the University of Otago, Dunedin.

Hale, B., Barrett, P., & Gauld, R. (2010). *The age of supported independence*. Dordrecht: Springer.

Hallman, B. (1999). The transition into eldercare – An uncelebrated passage. In E. K. Teather (Ed.), *Embodied geographies: Space, bodies and rites of passage* (pp. 208–223). London: Routledge.

Haveman, M., Berkum, G., Reijnders, R., & Heller, T. (1997). Differences in service needs, time demands and caregiving dimensions among parents of persons with mental retardation. *Family Relations, 46*(4), 417–425.

Heaton, J. (1999). The gauze and visibility of the carer: A Foucauldian analysis of the discourse of informal care. *Sociology of Health & Illness, 21*(6), 759–777.

Hirst, M. (2005). Carer distress: A prospective, population-based study. *Social Science & Medicine, 61*(3), 697–708.

Hockey, J., & James, A. (1993). *Growing up and growing old*. London: Sage.

Hockey, J., & James, A. (2003). *Social identities across the life course* (1st ed.). Basingstoke: Palgrave Macmillan.

Hugman, R. (1999). Embodying old age. In E. K. Teather (Ed.), *Embodied geographies: Space, bodies and rites of passage* (pp. 193–207). London: Routledge.

Janlov, A., Hallberg, I., & Petersson, K. (2006). Older persons' experience of being assessed for and receiving public home help: Do they have any influence over it? *Health & Social Care in the Community, 14*(1), 26–36.

Jeggels, J. (2006). *Facilitating care: The experiences of informal carers during the transition of elderly dependents from hospital to home – A grounded theory study*. Doctoral dissertation for the School of Nursing, Faculty of Community and Health Science, University of the Western Cape, Cape Town.

Larson, J., Franzén-Dahlin, A., Billing, B., von Arbin, M., Murray, V., & Wredling, R. (2008). The impact of gender regarding psychological well-being and general life situation among spouses of stroke patients during the first year after the patients' stroke event: A longitudinal study. *International Journal of Nursing Studies, 45*(2), 257–265.

Milligan, C. (2001). *Geographies of care: Space, place and the voluntary sector*. Aldershot: Ashgate.

Montgomery, R., & Kosloski, K. (2000). Family caregiving: Change, continuity and diversity. In P. Lawton & R. Rubenstein (Eds.), *Alzheimer's disease and related dementias: Strategies in care and research*. New York: Springer Publishing Company.

Nolan, M., Keady, J., & Grant, G. (1995). Developing a typology of family care: Implications for nurses and other service providers. *Journal of Advanced Nursing, 21*(2), 256–265.

Nolan, M., Lundh, U., Keady, J., & Grant, G. (2003). *Partnerships in family care*. Maidenhead: Open University Press.

Olaison, A., & Cedersund, E. (2006). Assessment for home care: Negotiating solutions for individual needs. *Journal of Aging Studies, 20*, 367–389.

Parks, J. (2003). *No place like home*. Bloomington: Indiana University Press.

Pereira, H. R., & Botelho, R. (2011). Sudden informal caregivers: The lived experience of informal caregivers after an unexpected event. *Journal of Clinical Nursing, 20*, 2448–2457.

Power, A. (2010). *Landscapes of care*. Farnham: Ashgate.

Richards, S. (2000). Bridging the divide: Elders and the assessment process. *British Journal of Social Work, 30*(1), 37–49.

Rose, H. (1994). *Love, power, and knowledge: Towards a feminist transformation of the sciences*. Bloomington: Indiana University Press.

Saarenheimo, M., Nikula, S., & Eskola, P. (2004). *Exploring the cultural borderlines of family caregiving*. Paper presented at ISER, University of Essex. http://www.soc.surrey.ac.ukcra-gISA2004/symposia/symp_session1.htm

Suitor, K., Pillemer, J., & Wethington, E. (2003). Integrating theory, basic research, and intervention: Two case studies from caregiving research. *The Gerontologist, 43*, 19–28.

Teather, E. K. (Ed.). (1999). *Embodied geographies: Space, bodies and rites of passage*. London: Routledge.

Turner, V. (1969). *The ritual process*. Harmondsworth: Penguin.

Twigg, J. (2000). *The body and community care*. London: Routledge.

Van Gennep, A. (1909/1960). *The rites of passage* (M. B. Vizedom & G. L. Caffee, Trans.). Chicago: University of Chicago Press.

Wallengren, C., Friberg, F., & Segesten, K. (2008). Like a shadow: On becoming a stroke victim's relative. *Scandinavian Journal of Caring Sciences, 22*(1), 48–55.

Weaver, S. (1999). *Looking the other way: Raising children with special needs in Aotearoa/New Zealand*. Auckland: Harper Collins.

Wenger, C. (2002). Using network variation in practice: Identification of support network type. *Health & Social Care in the Community, 10*(1), 28–35.

Westenholz, A. (2006). Identity, times and work. *Time & Society, 15*(1), 33–55.

Wiles, J. (2003). Daily geographies of caregivers: Mobility, routine, scale. *Social Science & Medicine, 57*(7), 1307–1325.

Wilson, H. S. (1989). Family caregiving for a relative with Alzheimer's dementia: Coping with negative choices. *Nursing Research, 38*(2), 94–98.

Chapter 4
Informal Caring and Early Childhood

4.1 Introduction

This chapter examines the experience of becoming an informal caregiver when a diagnosis of an impairment which will lead to disability is given for babies and infants. We identify the experiences of parents at the different stages suggested by the rites of passage framework, and reflect on these in terms of the spatial, temporal and relational aspects of their lives. The disclosure of the diagnosis is a critical moment, but for many parent caregivers, the experience is a type of diagnostic limbo. The type of information, the manner in which information is conveyed, and the organizational context all contribute to shaping this experience. Our review suggests parents, one of whom normally goes on to become the primary informal caregiver, experience a turbulent period of transition. Becoming a caregiver in this situation presents distinctive challenges related to the family life course stage. Reconnection, in terms of the rites of passage process, we suggest, involves making sense of the disability within the family narrative, being supported to cope with the new demands of the role, and maintaining social connections.

> It is … true that the family members and carers of children with … disabilities are a high-risk group with a significant need for support, which is all too often unmet. Having a disabled child can result in parents suffering from increased stress, taking a toll on their mental and physical health, and can affect all aspects of family life, including decisions about work, education, family finances and social relations (WHO 2010, p. 21).

Informal care of children with disabilities refers to arrangements within families or wider kinship networks where the child is cared for on an ongoing basis by a parent, other family members or friends. Such arrangements typically complement formal care services to meet the needs of children with a variety of impairments, including: developmental disabilities, such as Asperger's Syndrome, autism, Down's Syndrome; mental disabilities that may include learning disabilities or phobias; physical disabilities such as visual impairment, hearing impairment, mobility impairment; head

P. Barrett et al., *Family Care and Social Capital: Transitions in Informal Care*,
DOI 10.1007/978-94-007-6872-7_4, © Springer Science+Business Media Dordrecht 2014

injury; or chronic illness. Despite the wide variety of possible complex needs in childhood requiring additional care, and the different capacities of families to cope, there are a number of shared elements in the caregiver experience.

When a child is born with a disability or suffers an injury or chronic illness requiring more specialised care, parents and families experience a period of trauma and adjustment as they make the transition into new roles as caregivers. Typically, it is women who are morally assigned to the primary caregiver role (Shearn and Todd 2000, p. 119), although many fathers and other family members contribute to this work. For parents and other family members, caring at this stage of the life course presents specific challenges distinct from those experienced by caregivers in the situations discussed in other chapters, not least because:

> It is widely recognised that becoming a parent of a child with learning disabilities implies an enduring responsibility spanning several decades … a feature that distinguishes it from other forms of family caregiving (Todd and Shearn 1996, p. 379).

We have drawn on the voices of parent caregivers of children with disabilities to convey a more detailed awareness of key moments in the caregiving experience. Through quotations from documented personal experience, and through references to relevant research, we explore family member responses to disability and the subsequent caregiving situation. As we have indicated, the material is organised around the separation, liminal and reconnection phases of the caregiving experience. This can be compared to the great turning points (and associated rites of passage) in traditional societies that move people from one stage of life to another: birth, puberty, marriage and death. May (1994, p. 17) drew a parallel between these turning points and three 'moments' for the parent of the disabled child:

- A break from the past for the whole family where loyalty to the new child requires a reorientation to the values of their culture, in particular the focus on youth and the pride in independence. Effectively, the family becomes estranged.
- A turbulent period of transition
- Entry into a new life, where the focus is on acceptance and dynamic service.

In tracing these developmental progressions, we observe the personal, emotional dimensions from the perspective of the caregiver, their development as caregivers, the links between their adjustment to this role and their social connectedness, the consequence for their own living situation and their futures, and the implication of the nature of their involvement with health and allied social care professionals. The implications of caring for a child with a disability have potential to leave an individual in an ongoing state of liminality. We consider this and reflect on what is needed to achieve a state of reconnectedness.

We begin, though, by briefly reviewing statistics indicating the prevalence and living arrangements of children with disabilities in New Zealand and the United Kingdom as examples indicating the scale and significance of this informal care situation.

4.1.1 Children with Disabilities and Household Environments in New Zealand and the U.K.

The 2006 New Zealand Household Disability Survey estimated 10 % of children between the ages of 0–14 had a disability. Of these, 63 % lived in two-parent households, 28 % lived in one-parent households, and 5 % lived in households occupied by two or more families. In New Zealand, disabled children are less likely than non-disabled children to live in two parent households (63 % compared with 72 %), and they are less likely to live in above-average income households – 27 % compared with 39 % (Office of Disability Issues and Statistics New Zealand 2009, p. 2).

Parents and caregivers of 11 % of disabled children needed help with their child's personal care or with domestic work because of the child's condition or health problem. Such home support was, however, provided to parents and caregivers of just 4 % of all disabled children. This was either direct support from a government agency or money to pay for such support. It was parents or caregivers of children with an intellectual disability who were the most likely to receive this type of support (56 %). Parents or caregivers of 3 % of all disabled children paid out of their own pocket for help with their child's disability-related personal care and for help with domestic work or shopping because of their child's condition. The cost of care meant parents of 4 % of all disabled children needed help but were unable to get this help.

Respite services and carer support services were found to have been needed by the parents or caregivers of an estimated 17 % of all disabled children in households. Of these, 40 % received some free respite care, 46 % received help from a government agency to pay for respite care, and 15 % got respite care that was paid for by their parents or caregivers. Over 40 % of the parents or caregivers of children who had such needs did not get some or all of the respite care or support they needed. This was 7 % of all disabled children. Again, the cost of such support was the primary reason, along with a lack of knowledge of entitlements to support (Office for Disability Issues and Statistics New Zealand 2009, pp. 4–6).

The situation in the U.K. is broadly similar. Blackburn et al. (2010) have carried out a secondary analysis of a national UK Family Resources Survey, which is the source of information on disability prevalence in the UK for the Department of Work and Pensions as a part of their examination of the prevalence of childhood disability for the total child population by age, sex, ethnicity and impairment type. They also examined the relationship between childhood disability and social circumstances. They estimated 7.3 % of children between the ages 0–18 had a disability. Of these, 65.9 % lived in two-parent households and 34.1 % live in one-parent households, again, this being broadly similar to the New Zealand situation. As in the New Zealand case, disabled children are significantly more likely to be living in a sole-parent household (34.1 % compared with 25.6 %). Blackburn et al. (2010) also found children with disabilities in the UK were more likely to be living in households with other siblings and adults with disability. Their housing was more likely to be rented rather than owned, and those households had lower incomes than households with non-disabled children. Their research also found that 'on almost every measure, families with disabled children were more likely than other families to report not being able to afford items and activities they wanted or needed, indicating they were experiencing greater deprivation than other families' (Blackburn et al. 2010, p. 6; Kuhlthau et al. 2005; Curran et al. 2001).

4.2 Becoming a Caregiver of a Child with a Disability

4.2.1 Separation Experiences: Diagnosis and Disclosure

The notion of a biographical disruption, in the sense of an interruption or break in one's life story, is particularly apt in defining the experience of finding out that your child has a disability which will require significant additional care. It is a defining temporal moment, but one that can extend into a state of diagnostic uncertainty. It represents a separation from an expected family future and parent identity. The experience occurs at or just after birth. Bannerman Foster (1987, p. 44) observes from her study of the politics of caring that 'all parents remembered the moment they found out that something was wrong with their child.' With reference to children born with physical disabilities or genetic disorders, parents recalled that doctors suspected a problem at the time of the birth or soon afterwards.

Awareness of developmental problems may come more gradually, beginning as a suspicion. This 'recognizing the need' (Grant et al. 2003, p. 345) follows a period of observation and anxiety when parents come to a realisation that 'something is wrong.' A key moment in this process is when a health professional formally confirms the disability. This disclosure signals the beginning of a new future, one that was not foreseen or planned. The moment of disclosure is a point in time where it is possible to identify a separation between the expectations and hopes, and the actuality of a future as a caregiver. Parents describe this as leading to a state of shock, confusion and grief as they reassess what it means to be a parent and as they begin to come to grips with facing a future of managing disability and care obligations. As Todd and Jones (2003) observed from their study:

> Parents did find coming to terms with the news that their child has a disability as a distressing and intensely emotional process (p. 232).

Huberta Hellendoorn (2009) in writing about hearing of the diagnosis of her daughter with Down Syndrome captures this trauma:

> Just before the end of the visiting hour the door of my room opened. The doctor's face said it all. How could he find the right words? And what could he say? There was no need. We knew enough about chromosomes. My face felt hot, my breath caught up in my throat, my heart was beating fast. I grabbed Dad's hand. I said 'She's not all right, is she? Our baby? What's wrong with our baby? Her eyes!' (p. 7).

Miriam Edelson (2000) described hearing the information:

> I feel like someone just kicked me in the stomach. I can barely get a breath. My mind races, scenes of the last several months flash wildly through my mind. Jake's cries, seizures, his struggle to nurse. All in all, a pretty poor quality of life lies ahead for Jake (p. 43).

Hellendoorn's descriptions of her experience and Edelson's openness about her grieving, anger, and fears provide a vivid picture of the innermost feelings of parents at this time, of the tensions between anguish, love and anger.

Hearing the news is, therefore, a significant moment. The way the news is both delivered and received does reflect broader medical, social and personal attitudes towards disability. Parental responses are shaped by the way disability, and the meanings given to having a 'disabled child,' are constructed and conveyed by medical personnel, social care workers and family and friends.

The fact is, parents experience hearing the news within the context of an attitudinal environment towards disability that tends to be negative. Their anguish and ambivalence, therefore, is also often shared by wider family members. So, while the extended family can be a source of support, it can also reinforce wider negative attitudes towards disability. Negative attitudinal environments imply less social capital, such as when disability is seen as a punishment for earlier wrongdoing (Scorgie et al. 2004, p. 95). The views of members of the wider family and social network are therefore important influences in shaping the experience of becoming a parent of a child with a disability, not only in terms of shaping the meaning of the situation, but in terms of coping, and questions about the likelihood of support from others.

4.2.2   Hearing the News

The caregiver comments referred to in the previous section also point to the importance of the way the news is communicated. In several instances, the manner in which the news was given added to the sense of shock, grief and confusion. It has become clear that historically such diagnostic communications have been grossly mishandled. An example is reported by Scorgie et al. (2004) who quote the case of a Canadian mother of a son born with Down's Syndrome:

> [The] interview began with a powerful description of Chad's diagnosis shortly following his birth. Diane was alone in her room when, she reported, the physician "… arrived, stood in the doorway and said, 'There's something wrong with your baby. He's a Mongoloid idiot. Give him up. Don't ruin your life.'" [The mother was] immediately confronted with negative images and meanings and a choice that she rejected (p. 102).

The nature of the exchange was clear – residential care was encouraged on the grounds that family care arrangements would 'ruin your life.' In this case, a social worker arrived the following day to arrange for the adoption placement of the child.

There has been an awareness of problems with processes of disclosure for some time. Cunningham (1994) claimed that the effects of disclosure were not well understood. Hasnat and Graves' (2000) investigation into parental dissatisfaction with disclosure of disability by health professionals found that clinicians were more frank with parents of children with severe disabilities than with intellectual disabilities, and such frankness was partly due to clinician assessment of the emotional stability of parents. They also observed that professionals found it difficult to communicate information about the diagnosis and additional relevant information.

The following account of another poorly handled diagnostic communication by Edelson (2000) points to the way the setting, or spatial dimension, contributes to shaping the experience.

> A doctor we have never seen before beckons for us to approach. He appears impatient. I settle Jake with the emergency ward nurse and make my way into the noisy hallway. I am somewhat alarmed to see that the doctor is flanked by five eager medical students. Their white coats belie the innocence of their fresh, young faces. The doctor practically rounds them up with his clipboard and prepares, it seems, to hold forth. My heart lurches into my throat. 'Your son has a rare brain condition called lissencephaly,' says the doctor. He is curt. It is clear that he is addressing his entourage as much as Jim and me. We still don't even know his name (pp. 41–42).

Hearing the news, delivered in such a public forum that mitigated against an empathic manner, contributed to the sense of trauma.

Huberta Hellendoorn (2009) also evocatively described hearing about the diagnosis in a clinical setting where it was the medical dimensions of the condition which dominated the exchange. She continues:

> I felt as if I was shut up in a square white tent, separating me from everyone around me, affecting everything I did or said. I listened to the other women talking about their babies, laughing together, planning visits in the future. I noticed that whenever I entered a room they fell silent. I felt their pity, but I didn't want their pity. I wanted to talk, but I didn't know what to say (p. 10).

Her feeling of being shut up in a square white tent is a reference to the significance of the hospital setting where she discovered her child had a disability, and her realisation that this had implications for her and the family's, future. The disability was defined and presented in medical terms, reflecting the orientation of the medical organisational setting. That the implications for the parent upon hearing a child has a disability are profound is not surprising. The fact that such a disclosure happens within a medical setting does mean the exchanges between the health professionals and the parents tends to be on the medical nature of the condition, and less so on the psychological and emotional consequences for the parents. Parents at this stage are faced with why? questions and anxieties about the future, and such questions tend to be ignored in these settings. As the quote by Huberta Hellendoorn (2009) suggests, she experienced the news as a type of entrapment within a sterile, medicalised situation, the consequences of which were both personally upsetting, 'my heart was beating fast,' and socially isolating. She had to deal with this alone.

Such is the meaning associated with disability that Hellendoorn felt isolated when joining other young mothers in the hospital. The other young mothers fell silent whenever she entered the room. She felt excluded from the normal camaraderie developed following the shared experience of childbirth among new mothers – the talking together, the planning of visits, the mutual support. While she recognised this was motivated by 'pity' or sympathy with her situation – the other young mothers were careful not to celebrate their own stories about their new babies – such pity only served to reinforce her exclusion and deny her the chance to talk. It was as if she had passed from what Sontag (1978) has referred to as the 'kingdom of the well' to the 'kingdom of the sick.' She commented elsewhere about how women would approach her as she wheeled her baby outside, and fall silent, or draw back, not knowing what to say. She felt unable to initiate any conversation either; she was denied the casual social contacts which women with new babies make.

4.2.3   Stranded in Diagnostic Limbo

For some parents, the news is immediate, and for others it can take a long time before a firm diagnosis is made. Bannerman Foster (1987) retells the experience of a father whose son, at 9 months, suffered brain damage after choking. His words capture the experience of waiting and the anxiety and uncertainty surrounding the diagnosis:

> [The doctor] said he was in a coma … he hoped it would be no more than a couple of days and he would come out of it. And then they would be able to take it from there to find out … if it had done any cell damage in the brain or not. And a couple of days led to a couple of weeks, and a couple of weeks led into a couple of months, and he finally woke up, but he received so much brain damage in the lapse of time … As more and more time went on, our hopes of change just went down and down. You know, most [of the doctors] said the same thing all the time … [the] chances of him coming out of it getting less and less … And then … he said that he didn't feel he was in a coma any longer, that, you know…this was it. (Bannerman Foster 1987, p. 44).

This was their son's future. We can think of this situation as one where time has gone on hold. The time between suspicion and verification, between diagnosis and confirmation, a diagnostic limbo where time has been paused.

The time it takes to fully recognise symptoms and deal with unclear diagnoses leave some families to make sense of shifts in patterns of symptoms and behavior by themselves. Further, an unwillingness by medical professionals to make any definitive pronouncements when a child is young, means that many parents continue to hope for improvement (Bannerman Foster 1987, p. 61).

Parents are likely to be the first to notice developmental problems and often report frequent requests for help based on their own observations. In some cases, there is an awareness of differences from birth. A child may be unresponsive to people or focusing intently on one item for long periods of time, or an engaging, babbling toddler may suddenly become silent, withdrawn, self-abusive, or indifferent to social overtures. Bursnall et al.'s (2009) research showed that parents are usually correct about noticing developmental problems, although they may not realize the specific nature or degree of the problem. They (p. 93) quote parents reflecting on their suspicions:

I knew something was wrong from about 18 months ... First of all I had a feeling like, 'How come I can get along with all my friends' children but like my one I couldn't?'... 'Why can't I talk to my own daughter? Why can't I play with my own daughter?' I thought, 'Is it me?'

[My child with autism] was beginning to cause me problems in playgroups ... there was just something different about the way he was relating to other babies and other children ... I ... used to go to baby groups and just sit there and sometimes cry. I think things weren't right, and I couldn't understand it. Life was very hard.

Both quotes capture the period between suspicion and verification.

4.2.4 *Separation and Grief*

References to feelings of grief, a sense of loss and mourning, feature prominently in caregiver accounts of this stage. Elva Sonntag (1994) quotes a mother in her study describing how difficult it was to accept that their 8 month old child who had undergone heart surgery had been brain-damaged through medical misadventure. The experience was one of grieving:

I think it was very hard...to accept that he had changed because he still looked the same child and he was, so the family were going through a terrible grieving stage.

The nature of the grief experience by caregivers is captured in the quote by Barbara Gill (1997, p. 16):

When our baby was born we lost something we were already in love with – our idea of what she would be. No baby could completely fulfil that idea or be that fantasy but. A most babies overlap or approach our dream baby, because our dreams come from what we know, from our idea of the norm. A child with a disability was not in our picture at all, except maybe as an occasional fear. We who have a child with a disability lost not only our fantasy but our reliance on having a 'normal' baby.

The grief was for their child, their hoped for future, their expectations of family. These accounts do convey a sense of bereavement as experienced with the death of a family member (Poehlmann et al. 2005, p. 255).

4.3 Liminal Experiences in Becoming a Caregiver

In breaking down the experience of becoming a primary caregiver for a child with disability, the notion of liminality implies parents, particularly those who become the primary caregiver, go through a period of improvisatory living, a period when the old norms and assumptions no longer apply as they search for new ways of being. It is a period when normal social codes are suspended and when future codes begin to be created. Again, we can think about these developments in terms of the themes of spatial, temporal and relational liminality. Parents such as Huberta Hellendoorn, Miriam Edelson and Elva Sonntag are among the leaders in exploring the experience of becoming a caregiver of a child with a disability. Their descriptions of experiences of discontinuity, role confusion and associated anxiety and distress are consistent with notions of liminality. Scorgie et al. (2004) capture the search for meaning by caregivers when they observe that, following diagnosis, parents ask:

> 'Who is my child? 'Who can he/she become?' They look at themselves and ask: Who am I as my child's parent? 'Who can I become? And they look at their lives and ask: What is my life going to be like, now and in the future?' (p. 94).

Parents experience a double loss, not only the loss of the child they had imagined, but also the loss of their own and the child's future life. The fit between biography (Dyck et al. 2005) and the anticipations that accompany the birth is disrupted by the disability and the need to care. This lack of *fit* implies a disordering of expectations.

The discontinuity can also be seen in the spatial dimensions of caregiving. Three researchers who focus on such discontinuity, Milligan (2000), Wiles (2003) and Power (2010), discuss the 'landscape of home' which becomes a place for specialized care and the wider community environment. In Irving's (2004, p. 317) terms, the landscape of home is made strange by the need to accommodate the needs of the disability. Bodies with 'different ways of being' require differently organized space. The presence of therapeutic aids, for example, calipers, continence bags, hearing aids, and, depending on the age of the child, a need for security to protect the safety of the child, become defining features of the home (Power 2010, p. 207). When formal paid caregivers and health professionals are involved, the private space of the home becomes a more public, therapeutic space (Hale et al. 2010; Milligan 2000; Wiles 2003). It is an area that is trespassed, changing the space from one that is 'private/domestic' to one that is 'public/domestic' (Milligan 2000, p. 55). The domestic space of the home becomes a 'site for caring', resulting in an institutionalization of carer's private space. Home takes on a different meaning, both for the family members and for visitors.

4.3.1 Spatial Liminality

New parents often comment on the loss of control over their daily life and routine a newborn brings. Such time demands are accentuated when caring for a child with a disability. The need for continuous vigilance and care is evident in the typical comment, 'I have to constantly be there.' Sonntag (1994, p. 198) refers to the time-consuming work of caring for a disabled child:

> He just screamed … he can't do anything. He can't sit, he can't feed, he can't go to the toilet. He can't have a drink, he can't play, he can't see, he can't do a thing. You have to do everything for him.

Becoming a caregiver of a child with disability and facing such demands leads to the suspension of mobility. Carers become 'tied to the home' (Power 2010, p. 205). As the house has become a site for care, being out of the house presents difficulties that relate not only to managing the care needs of the child, but also to managing or coping with interactions with others. Dealing with negative comments and reactions to disability from those outside of the home present a further ordeal (Power 2010, pp. 199–202). Shearn and Todd (2000) capture this in a quote from a mother of a child with an intellectual disability who stated, 'We're shut in, we are literally shut in. This is it. This is our world!'

Further, as parent caregivers develop expertise in managing and responding to the particular needs of their child, it becomes difficult to hand over that role to others. For many parent caregivers, this responsibility cannot be shared. Additionally, it is it is often the case that children experience separation anxiety and fear being left without a parent. This presents difficulties, with carers being unable or reluctant to leave the house for any length of time, complicating activities like shopping, socializing, professional appointments, or employment. Many outings can be made only with the cared-for person coming along (Power 2010). Taking the child out becomes even more time-consuming and presents additional challenges. Comments from caregivers refer to challenges associated with the child's feelings about unfamiliar buildings, and spaces which frighten the child or evoke memories of unpleasant interactions, such as the dentist or doctor's surgery. The following comments from (Power 2010) indicate how these are experienced:

- Years ago, taking Stacey out resulted in lots of screaming.
- 'Acting up' – he's liable to act up in the store, so you couldn't do what you wanted to do.
- I'm tied to the house; she doesn't like going away too much.
- I can't leave him with anyone else, I have to take him with me wherever I go. And he hates going away from home, so I have to go to the nearest shops. And I can't have a coffee with friends, can't take him into a cafe.
- If we go out with him, he's likely to run around, or lie on the floor yelling, hitting, biting, scratching, kicking. You can imagine what that does to an outing (pp. 205–209).

4.3.2 Temporal Liminality

The experience of being in a state of 'temporal suspension' is captured by Edelson (2000, p. 50) who describes the need to constantly revisit and re-evaluate one's expectations of the future:

> Typical milestones like college, marriage and grandchildren may not be possible. … Learning to balance conflicting feelings … is not a one-shot experience; you cannot just get over it. You have to revisit the multi-layered issues over time and grapple with them again and again.

A part of this process is caused by the development of new conditions. For some families, 'disclosure' of disability is not a singular event (Grant et al. 2003, p. 346). There is, therefore, the need to revisit expectations again and again.

For primary caregivers, time revolves around the need to provide care. The fabric of daily life is woven around care (Power 2010, p. 207). The following outline of a morning schedule from Elwy (2007) captures this:

> Each night my husband Sherin and I listen to the hum of the air compressor, to the beeps from the pulse oximeter, and for weak calls for help from our 5-year-old son Ben while we try to get enough rest to attend to him, his two sisters, and our occupations the next day. The monitor we have installed in Ben's bedroom scarcely picks up his voice over the sounds of the three machines operating in his room, and, therefore, we half-sleep, afraid of not hearing him. … At 6:30 AM, I know it will be a good day if the drink I have given Ben starts his bowels moving. Unable to hold himself on the toilet, Ben tolerates my supportive grip on his waist. Watching his 1-year-old sister Charlotte create havoc in the bathroom by dragging towels, toilet paper, makeup, and more out of cupboards helps distract Ben from his pain. … By 7 AM, Ben is ready for breakfast. Now it is time to wake 8-year-old Lucy, who would love to rise slowly with a backrub, but there isn't time because her brother's schedule is so tight. Ben still needs help eating his breakfast and taking his medicine. He must make another bathroom stop prior to the arrival of the school van. Coats must be put on, the oxygen tank and walker must be transferred to the porch for pickup, the suction machine bag must be packed with new filters, catheters, and gloves (p. 2675).

The demanding nature of these tasks does not mean that they are always experienced as stressful. Some parents are able to describe how these tasks effectively become rituals that ground the day in a sense of joy and gratitude for the life of the person with disability. The point to be emphasized here, though, is that daily life becomes organized around the demands of providing care.

4.3.3   Relational Liminality

Becoming a caregiver of a child with a disability leads, also, to experiences of social liminality, both within the family and outside of the home. As noted, the demands of caring for a child with disability can lead to being housebound. Mindfulness of the child's needs and the daily work of care inhibit social interaction outside of the household, reducing social connectedness. Shearn and Todd (2000, p. 114) sum up the consequences of this by describing how mothers of children with intellectual disabilities experience a sense of 'peripherality,' of being on the outer-edge. The trend is only accentuated where there is challenging behavior, as they described:

> I don't keep in contact with anybody now really because I can't visit. I can't take Calum anywhere. He's just too destructive. I took him over to my sister's and he smashed their brand new telly. You can't even arrange to go out in the night because not everybody can look after Calum, see (Shearn and Todd 2000, p. 114).

With the time consuming demands of caring for a disabled child, parent caregivers with other children experience feelings of anxiety about not meeting the needs of those children. When the family includes siblings, these children face similar social constraints: the space allowed for play is shaped by home being a 'landscape of care'; the space allowed for visitors is similarly constrained; even whether it is possible to have visitors in terms of the 'sleepover' variety; and the after-school exchange visits. Spicer (2007) found that parent caregivers do feel they neglect the needs of other family members and are often anxious over the implications for other children, especially their ability to spend time with all children in the family. Siblings themselves were found to feel they did not get enough attention from parents. Spicer (2007, p. 2) observed that siblings can 'harbour strong negative feelings, believing that the caring responsibility has taken their mother away from them.'

4.3.4 Liminality and the Stress of Caregiving

Becoming a parent and caregiver of a child with disability is, therefore, a significant life event with ongoing challenging consequences, what is often described as the carer 'burden'. That burden is evident in the quote from Dixon, who writes (1994):

> If being a regular parent meant doing a third of the things parents of children labelled disabled have to do, then the human race would rapidly become extinct (p. 77).

For some, the burden is ongoing, being portrayed by Kelly and Hewson (2000) as evident in the poorer emotional and physical health of parent caregivers of children with disabilities. The physical aspects of that burden are described in research that emphasizes health problems. Tong et al. (2003) who found that more than 70 % of mothers of children with physical disabilities report low back pain, particularly in cases of parents of children with cerebral palsy. Comparing the health of parents of able-bodied children with those of disabled children, Wang and Barnard (2008) found that parent carers of children with high needs and who are dependent on technology experience more anguish, anger, guilt, frustration, sorrow and social isolation, along with sleep deprivation and depression. Emerson (2003), though, has warned against over-generalising from disability parenting to distress and social disruption. This study found that:

> Only a minority of mothers reported that their child's difficulties had made them to any extent depressed or physically ill. Similarly, only a minority of mothers reported that their child's difficulties had disrupted their social and leisure activities, or had had an adverse effect on relationships within the family. Indeed, mothers were just as likely to report that their child's difficulties had strengthened their relationship with their partner as they were to report that it had weakened their relationship (p. 397).

We accept these points, but note too that other researchers draw quite different conclusions. As Leonard et al. (1993) indicated, spending more hours in caregiving tasks, expending more of the household funds on coping with the disability, and caring for children with disabilities who are older or with more complex needs increases the level of distress. For many, these are long lasting consequences.

We conclude this discussion of liminal experiences in the process of becoming a caregiver of a child with disability by quoting in full the following article by

Maryanne Twentyman, published in the New Zealand Waikato Times. The article captures many of the interconnected themes of living in this type of situation we have referred to above:

Life with an Autistic Child   **23 April 2012**

William Christie is locked in his bedroom overnight – it's the only way parents Sue and Peter can keep their son safe. "He is actually a lovely boy – he's so innocent – but he just doesn't understand," Mrs Christie said.

William, her youngest child, was born with Down syndrome and then, at age 3, was diagnosed as profoundly autistic. "I knew that was coming," she said. "He was showing traits from the age of 1, the shaking hands, the looks and the fact he simply wasn't progressing at the same rate as other children in our Down syndrome support group."

The double challenges brought many sleepless nights and almost broke the family. Mrs Christie battled depression, while her husband was forced to give up the family farm in order to concentrate on keeping his family together. For their two eldest children – Steven, 13, and Grace, 11 – helping look after William has meant growing up faster than others their age, few family outings and absorbing the barrage of attacks from their baby brother who doesn't know any different.

When Waikato Times visits the Christie family on the outskirts of Morrinsville it's lunchtime. William is being fed by his attentive father, Steven and Grace sit silently opposite, while Sue describes the battle with extreme food refusal that took "years to overcome".

On the table a plastic sheet with stick-on cards helps William to communicate – the most worn card is the one that reads: I need help.

But it's not just William that needs help. It's the whole family. Worn out, frustrated and struggling to makes ends meet with huge health-related bills for William and trying to overcome the loss of a farming position when Peter's boss was forced to sell his land. But the love and determination in the room is palpable – even if the walls around the family home show the scars of battle at the hands and feet of William.

"He just loves loud noises – the louder the better," Mrs Christie explained. "He just picks up the first thing and fires it in any direction – and he beams when it smashes and crashes." And her son feels little pain. "We found him on one occasion holding on to an electric fence which he was also holding in his mouth – plus he was wet. We were thinking thank God it's not live but then we found out it was – with 3500 volts running through it. He just doesn't understand." The latest casualty of William's destructive behaviour was his Te Aroha based carer, where William stays three nights a week. "She hadn't locked him in one night and he got out into the lounge and smashed her TV, DVD – I mean he trashed the place and we felt so bad for her," Mrs Christie said.

(continued)

(continued)

> With growth comes strength and the Christies fear William's random behaviour could worsen and that others could be injured. They want to build an extension on to the family home with a safe room for William – with reinforced walls and safety glass in the windows. "But we also want it to be an interactive room that will keep him busy. A sensory wall so he can feel and touch, music and games so he can interact and most of all a place he can be safe," Mrs Christie said.
>
> A new room would also allow Steven to move back into the family home. "We set up a room for him in garage but it's hardly ideal. The walls aren't lined and he feels disconnected but we just need more space to bring the family back together."
>
> Friends are now rallying to support the Christie family who are "so thankful" for the help and support they have received. And while their son is eligible for various government assistance, the allowances barely scratch the surface of their son's needs.
>
> "The funny thing is if the family completely fell apart, then someone would be forced to look after [William], and at what cost?" asked Mrs Christie.

4.4   Reconnections

The previous account of experiences of separation and liminality suggest parents and families who become caregivers of children with disability face significant personal and social challenges that threaten their ability to remain socially connected and cope with the demands of caring. The level of social capital clearly influences the level of available care for the child with disability as well as the level of support for caregivers. They buffer caregivers from the 'depleting effects (physically and emotionally) of normative and non-normative stress' (Shonkoff et al. 1992, p. 12). Their ability to meet the care needs of their child is shaped not only by their immediate personal and family context, but also their connectedness to social networks, and the capacity of those networks to provide necessary resources and supports.

We noted earlier the way poorly handled disclosures reinforce the trauma of separation experiences. We begin this discussion of the experience of reconnection by suggesting that an understanding of the parental experience by medical staff and assessors and an appreciation of their need for support through the disclosure process will lead to more appropriate forms of communication. Our research indicates that the journey of the family through the diagnosis, disclosure and subsequent adaptation to the demands of care is fraught with personal and social upheaval. Empathetic, sensitive and honest diagnostic communication is recommended (Sheets et al. 2011).

Caregivers who, with support, negotiate those challenges effectively, and move beyond the liminal experiences noted above, can be said to be reconnected in terms of the rites of passage framework in a new role as caregiver. This is more than simply reaching a state of acceptance of the care situation. It implies, as Pianta et al. (1996, in Grant et al. 2003) suggest, an understanding of the nature of the disability and the impact on the child, an appreciation of the impact of the disability on their own and their family's experience, making sense of and managing their feelings about the situation, and having a focus on the present and the future. Further, as Irving (2011) puts it, people learn a new 'way-of-being.' However Grant et al. (2003, p. 253) are more skeptical, commenting that reaching this state of reconciliation with their situation will take considerable cognitive skill that not every parent will possess.

Scorgie and Sobsey (2000) have identified a range of transformational outcomes associated with parenting children with disabilities. They refer to personal transformations in relation to the acquisition of roles or traits, relational transformations with regard to family relationships, advocacy relationships, friendship networks and attitudes towards people in general, and perspectival transformations, which concern changes in how people view life. Importantly, though, they insist that only over time can observers note such changes. They assert that such traumatic experiences from difficult life incidents, such as parenting a child with disabilities, can actually benefit lives. With regard to stress and coping, they observe that the implicit assumption that stress is essentially negative in its consequences is not confirmed by evidence from people's lives. They also point out that the goal of 'coping' is not necessarily to return to a former state of wellbeing.

Edelson's (2000, p. 50) comment, however, that in this care situation 'you have to revisit the multi-layered issues over time and grapple with them again and again' (p. 50) remind us there is no hard and fast boundary between stages of separation, liminality and reconnection. As parents confront and re-confront new challenges in caring for a child with disability, they face new liminal experiences. However, we suggest reconnection occurs as the parent caregiver is socially recognized, valued and supported in the new role. Pianta et al. (1996, in Grant et al. 2003) maintain that despite revisiting issues again and again, parents who are supported to develop the abilities and skills of caregiving:

> eventually focus attention on the present and future, maintain an accurate, undistorted view of the child's skills and abilities, hold a balanced view of the impact of this experience on themselves, and regulate their affective experience (p. 253).

To be reconnected does not imply the restoration of a former self; rather it is a transformation, a set of changes leading to a new and valued social identity. The transformation is evident in the common qualities that caregivers develop: a sophisticated understanding of the child's condition and needs; relevant caregiving knowledge and skills; an ability to work with care professionals; advocacy and community development skills; and not least, the ability to bring up the child, and other children. Their expertise is acquired through a combination of knowledge transfer from support services, and through the experience of daily experimentation and improvisation to find what works to improve the life of the disabled person. It is these qualities that, as Allen (2000) observes, leave many 'professional' nurses in hospital settings anxious about working alongside experienced family carers. Numerous researchers now call for recognition of parent caregiver expertise and carer partnerships with health care professionals.

The sense of expertise is evident not just in esoteric skill, but in the joy that carers can eventually find in the rituals of doing routine care tasks. When Sam Crane (2003) describes caring for his son Aidan, he controls his attention in such a way that it becomes a form of spiritual exercise.

> Every morning before taking him into the social world of school, I wash Aidan. We do this while he still in bed, lying straight on his back. Starting with his face, I slip my left hand under his head to steady it and speak to him, alerting him to the coming shock of dampness on his brow. Even with my spoken introduction, the first swipes of the warm washcloth invariably startle him. He widens his eyes in reaction to the wet assault. I carefully rub under and behind his ears, working toward his eyes to cleanse away the sleep from their inner corners. Soap comes next, soap on cheeks and forehead and chin, soap to dissolve the dirt from his smooth skin (p. 167).

4.4.1 Facilitating Reconnections Within Social Context

The social networks within which families are located are clearly important sources of support with potential to facilitate reconnection. Fathers are a critical source of support for mothers who typically continue to take on the primary caregiving role (Lee et al. 2006, p. 46; Ricci and Hodapp 2003). Families exist within broader social networks, the strength of which may be described in terms of social capital – that is, the norms of trust and reciprocity that influence the capacity for mutual support and the community resources that actually provide direct support. The level of social capital, or pre-existing social relationships, influences the potential for and realisation of support (Mirfin-Veitch et al. 2003).

The professional network of health, allied health and resource workers, including pre-school, teachers and teacher aides are critical sources of information and skills which help the parents learn about disability, and how to interact with the child and with his or her environment. Community resources such as day care, play groups (even when the parent caregiver has to be present), respite care and eventually, of course, school are social supports in place to help. Support groups for caregivers provide opportunity to share the experience, obtain knowledge and information, and strengthen endurance and resolve. Sonntag's (1994) group of participants had,

> taught themselves and sometimes forced themselves to be articulate in meetings, on committees, in public gatherings, and on school Boards of Trustees…these women worked in mothers' clubs, where they shared information and experience; in Parent-to-Parent groups; established international links with other parents (p. 198).

It is immaterial whether the support comes from parents who also have disabled children, or from those who do not. What matters is the sense of being part of a community that can talk about what is necessary:

> There are parents with disabled kids who can say "Oh, I know what you mean". And they really do. Or they laugh and tell you an even worse story about their own child. Then there's people who don't have disabled kids, and they'll say "God, I don't know how you cope… I couldn't do it." Sometimes you need to hear that too (Carpinter et al. 2000, p. 10).

4.4.2 The Importance of Respite

To have respite is to have a suspension of activity. It is needed to avoid the fatigue, physical, mental and emotional, of caregiving for a child with disability. Whether it is provided by formal services or from with the family social network, it is a means for sustaining the caregiver. Respite care can be taken to signify being connected, of not being solely responsible for maintaining the life of the child, but of being able to share the responsibility. It also signifies recognition by others of the value of the work of care.

Carpinter et al.'s (2000, p. 17) study found respite care to be the form of support most valued by parents with children with high disability support needs. It is respite which sustains their capacity to care. The demands of caring for a child with high support needs lead to a state of permanent exhaustion, a lack of time to complete other tasks (like filing and paying bills), insufficient attention to siblings, and no time for personal recovery and re-creation. Respite allows caregivers to catch up on such activities. When it is effective, it does sustain the caregiver in the role:

> We get regular respite every second weekend. That's our time. When we got that it made all the difference. Without it we wouldn't have been able to keep our daughter at home these last three years (Carpinter et al. 2000, p. 9).

It is clear that the quality of respite care matters, and being able to find alternative caregivers willing and able to meet the particular needs of individual children determines whether parents take it up. Leaving a child with specialized support needs with another caregiver is a source of anxiety for parent caregivers, and even when basic competencies are met, respite care can be a source of fear for the wellbeing of the child. Caregivers are often forced to accept something that is less than satisfactory to get a break. Further, the upheaval associated with the breaking of routines, the effort required to prepare for the break, and the aftermath in terms of separation anxiety or other child-centered problems mean parents often do not take respite. This can lead to a situation where respite seems to be under-utilized, simply because it is not safe for families to use.

4.4.3 Reconnection Through Employment

Becoming a caregiver of a child with disability is an all-consuming life transition with temporal, spatial and relational dimensions that lead to the carer becoming less mobile and more bound to the place of care, the home. The demands of caregiving have implications for those parent carers who have been in paid employment and those with future employment intentions. Many primary caregivers, therefore, do not see paid employment as compatible with their care responsibilities. A number of researchers, however, point to the potential of paid work as a means of connecting caregivers with the wider social world and the benefits from that (Todd et al. 2008;

Ramcharan 2004). It provides a different community from the world in which parent caregivers usually move. Gordon et al. (2008) have found that the same proportion of mothers of children with disabilities want to work as mothers of children without disabilities. Their conclusion is that paid work is a legitimate and powerful mechanism for addressing the striking isolation of parent caregivers.

Gaining access to paid work, however, is dependent on the ability to fit employment around the caring timetable. A willingness and ability of employers to provide flexibility, caregiver readiness to share the care, and family-friendly work environments all contribute to this. It implies working part-time or during a school term period when they child is having his or her needs met elsewhere (Baker and Drapela 2010). Paid work has much potential to sustain caregivers provided suitable employment policies are in place that provide caregivers with the means to reconcile the demands of care with the demands of employment.

As noted at the beginning of this chapter, families with children with disability are less likely to live in above average income households and parents are more likely to be required to spend their own money on meeting care related costs. Raising a child with a disability is more expensive than raising other children (Gordon et al. 2008). Disabilities are expensive to maintain, and parents who are on a one-income, low-income or benefit-income face genuine financial challenges. Making paid employment less problematic for mothers has potential to play a part in addressing such issues.

4.5   Summary

In this chapter we have explored the processes of caregiving through a transition from separation experiences associated with diagnosis and disclosure to a form of reconnection to the wider society with the identity of caregiver. We drew attention to the shock of diagnosis and disclosure, and the accompanying emotions of grief, guilt and fear. Broader social attitudes towards disability influence the way the message is both given and received. Given the fluctuating nature of many disabling conditions, parents exist in a type of diagnostic limbo. Liminality experiences, that is, the suspension of the normal', include the loss of control over daily life as it becomes focused on responding to the need for care to sustain the life of the child, and the actual physical and emotional stresses of care for a child with disability. It also is characterized by a shift towards the periphery of pre-existing social networks. Reconnection includes transformation as the primary caregiver acquires experience and develops expertise in caring, and as they become recognized and valued in this role. Opportunities for respite are critical, as is the importance of reintegration back from the periphery through, for example, employment.

These shared experiences shape who the caregivers become and leads to a shared identity. The strong ethic of care and advocacy for people with disabilities which caregivers develop is reinforced through participation in disability and caregiver networks, and contributes to wider social capital through role modeling carer commitment. We emphasize that carers become experts in caregiving, and their skills and knowledge can be useful to health and welfare professionals. Further, the comments of carers on appropriate and empathic communication reinforces the need for knowledge in how best to communicate with carers in terms of respect, empathy, timeliness of communication, and good and sufficient information.

Discussion Suggestions

Diagnosis and disclosure is a significant time for carers, propelling family members into a state of liminality. What characterises that experience?

Discuss the idea that the type of disability and degree of disability has an influence on the parents' social capital.

As a carer, what improvements would you suggest for telling new parents about a diagnosis of disabilities? What is your approach?

If you are a caregiver, what support would you like to see from your health and welfare professionals?

Further Reading

Edelson, M. (2000). *My journey with Jake: A memoir of parenting disability*. Toronto: Between the Lines.
Gill, B. (1997). *Changed by a child*. New York: Broadway Books.
Gothard, J. (2011). *Greater expectations: Living with Down syndrome in the 21st century*. Fremantle: Fremantle Press.
Power, P. W., & Dell Orto, A. E. (2003). *The resilient family: Living with your child's illness or disability*. Notre Dame: Sorin Books
Scorgie, K., Wilgosh, L., & Sobsey, D. (2004). The experience of transformation in parents of children with disabilities; theoretical considerations. *Developmental Disabilities Bulletin, 32*(1), 84–110.

References

Allen, D. (2000). Negotiating the role of expert carers on an adult hospital ward. *Sociology of Health & Illness, 22*(2), 149–171.
Baker, D., & Drapela, L. (2010). Mostly the mother: Concentration of adverse employment effects on mothers of children with autism. *The Social Science Journal, 47*(3), 578–592.
Bannerman Foster, S. (1987). *The politics of caring*. Lewes Sussex: The Falmer Press.
Blackburn, C., Spencer, N., & Read, J. (2010). Prevalence of childhood disability and the characteristics and circumstances of disabled children in the UK: Secondary analysis of the Family Resources Survey. *BMC Pediatric, 10*, 21.
Bursnall, S., Kennedy, E., Senior, R., & Violet, J. (2009). Understanding the experience of parenting a child with autism. In C. Marshall, E. Kendall, M. Banks, & R. Gover (Eds.), *Disabilities: Insights from across fields and around the world*. Westport: Praeger.

Carpinter, A., Irwin, G., & Rogers, G. (2000). *Just surviving*. Wellington: Ministry of Health.

Crane, S. (2003). *Aidan's way: The story of a boy's life and a father's journey*. Naperville: Sourcebooks.

Cunningham, C. (1994). Telling parents that their child has a disability. In P. Mittler & H. Mittler (Eds.), *Innovations in family support for people with learning disabilities*. Chorley: Lisieux Hall Publications.

Curran, A., Sharples, P., White, C., & Knapp, M. (2001). The costs of caring for children with severe disabilities compared with caring for children without disabilities. *Developmental Medicine and Child Neurology, 43*(3), 529–533.

Dixon, J. (1994). Doing ordinary things. In K. Ballard (Ed.), *Disability, family, whanau and society*. Palmerston North: Dunmore Press.

Dyck, I., Kontos, P., Angus, J., & McKeever, P. (2005). The home as a site for long-term care: Meanings and management of bodies and spaces. *Health & Place, 11*(2), 173–185.

Edelson, M. (2000). *My journey with Jake: A memoir of parenting disability*. Toronto: Between the Lines.

Elwy, R. (2007). Extended family. *Journal of the American Medical Association, 297*(24), 2675–2676.

Emerson, E. (2003). Mothers of children and adolescents with intellectual disability: Social and economic situation, mental health status and the self-assessed social and psychological impact of the child's difficulties. *Journal of Intellectual Disabilities, 47*(4/5), 385–399.

Gill, B. (1997). *Changed by a child*. New York: Broadway Books.

Gordon, M., Cuskelly, M., & Rosenman, L. (2008). Influences on mothers' employment when children have disabilities. *Journal of Policy and Practice in Intellectual Disabilities, 5*(3), 203–210.

Grant, G., Nolan, M., & Keady, J. (2003). Supporting families over the life course: Mapping temporality. *Journal of Intellectual Disability Research, 47*, 342–351.

Hale, B., Barrett, P., & Gauld, R. (2010). *The age of supported independence*. Dordrecht: Springer.

Hasnat, M., & Graves, P. (2000). Disclosure of developmental disability: A study of paediatricians' practices. *Journal of Paediatrics and Child Health, 36*(1), 27–31.

Hellendoorn, H. (2009). *The Madonna in the suitcase*. Dunedin: Hellendoorn.

Irving, A. (2004). Life made strange: An essay on the re-inhabitation of bodies and landscapes. In W. James & D. Mills (Eds.), *Qualities of time; An anthropological perspective*. Oxford: Berg.

Irving, A. (2011). Strange distance: Towards an anthropology of interior dialogue. *Medical Anthropology Quarterly, 25*(1), 22–44.

Kelly, A., & Hewson, P. (2000). Factors associated with recurrent hospitalization in chronically ill children and adolescents. *Journal of Paediatrics and Child Health, 36*(1), 13–18.

Kuhlthau, K., Smith Hill, K., Ycel, R., & Perrin, J. (2005). Financial burden for families of children with disabilities. *Maternal and Child Health Journal, 9*(2), 207–218.

Lee, T., Shandor Miles, M., & Holditch-Davis, D. (2006). Fathers' support to mothers of medically fragile infants. *Journal of Obstetric, Gynaecologic and Neonatal Nursing, 35*(1), 46–55.

Leonard, B., Johnson, A., & Brust, J. (1993). Children with disabilities: A comparison of those managing 'OK' and those needing more help. *Children's Health Care, 22*(2), 93–105.

May, W. (1994). *The patient's ordeal*. Bloomington/Indianapolis: Indiana University Press.

Milligan, C. (2000). Bearing the burden: Towards a restructured geography of caring. *Area, 32*(1), 49–58.

Mirfin-Veitch, B., Bray, A., & Ross, N. (2003). 'It was the hardest and most painful decision of my life!': Seeking permanent out-of-home placement for sons and daughters with intellectual disabilities. *Journal of Intellectual and Developmental Disability, 28*(2), 99–111.

Office for Disability Issues and Statistics New Zealand. (2009). *Disability and informal care in New Zealand in 2006: Results from the New Zealand Disability Survey*. Wellington: Statistics New Zealand.

Pianta, R., Marvin, R., Britner, P., & Borowitz, K. (1996). Mothers' resolution of their children's diagnosis: Organised patterns of caregiving representations. *Infant Mental Health Journal, 17*, 239–256.

Poehlmann, J., Clements, M., Abbeduto, L., & Farsad, V. (2005). Family experiences associated with a child's diagnosis of fragile X or down syndrome: Evidence for disruption and resilience. *Mental Retardation, 43*, 255–267.

Power, A. (2010). *Landscapes of care: Comparative perspectives on family caregiving*. Farnham: Ashgate.

Ramcharan, P. I. (2004). Getting back to work: A dead end for carers? *Journal of Intellectual Disability Research, 48*(4 & 5), 348–356.

Ricci, L. A., & Hodapp, R. (2003). Fathers of children with Down's syndrome versus other types of intellectual disability: Perceptions, stress and involvement. *Journal of Intellectual Disability Research, 47*(4–5), 273–284.

Scorgie, K., & Sobsey, D. (2000). Transformational outcomes associated with parenting children who have disabilities. *Mental Retardation, 38*(3), 195–206.

Scorgie, K., Wilgosh, L., & Sobsey, D. (2004). The experience of transformation in parents of children with disabilities; theoretical considerations. *Developmental Disabilities Bulletin, 32*(1), 84–110.

Shearn, J., & Todd, S. (2000). Maternal employment and family responsibilities: The perspectives of mothers of children with intellectual disabilities. *Journal of Applied Research in Intellectual Disabilities, 13*, 109–131.

Sheets, K., Blythe, G., Crissman, C., et al. (2011). Practice guidelines for communicating a prenatal or postnatal diagnosis of Down Syndrome: Recommendations of the National Society of Genetic Counselors. *Journal of Genetic Counselling, 20*(5), 432–441.

Shonkoff, J., Hauser-Cram, P., & Wyangaarden Krauss, M., et al. (1992). Development of infants with disabilities and their families: Implications for theory and service delivery. *Monographs of the Society for Research in Child development*, Serial No. 230, *57*(6), 1–153.

Sonntag, E. (1994). Women of action: Caring at home for a daughter or son with an intellectual disability. In K. Ballard (Ed.), *Disability, family, whanau and society*. Palmerston North: Dunmore Press.

Sontag, S. (1978). *Illness as metaphor*. New York: Vintage.

Spicer, L. (2007). Disability and family carers. *Family Matters, 76*, 30–31.

Todd, S., & Jones, S. (2003). Mum's the word: Maternal accounts of dealings with the world. *Journal of Applied Research in Intellectual Disabilities, 16*(3), 229–244.

Todd, S., & Shearn, J. (1996). Struggles with time: The careers of parents with adult sons and daughters with learning disabilities. *Disability & Society, 11*(3), 379–401.

Todd, S., Shearn, J., & Jones, S. (2008). Struggling beyond the mum-line: Employment and mothers of children with intellectual disabilities. *Journal of Intellectual Disability Research, 48*(4–5), 373–388.

Tong, H. C., Haig, A. J., Nelson, V. S., et al. (2003). Low back pain in adult female caregivers of children with physical disabilities. *JAMA Pediatrics, 157*(11), 1128–1133.

Twentyman, M. (2013, April 23). Life with an autistic child. *Waikato Times*. Hamilton. http://www.stuff.co.nz/national/health/6788756/Life-with-an-autistic-child

Wang, K., & Barnard, A. (2008). Caregivers' experiences at home with a ventilator-dependent child. *Qualitative Health Research, 18*(4), 501–508.

WHO. (2010). *Better health, better lives: Children and young people with intellectual disabilities and their families. The case for change* (EUR/51298/17/5). http://www.euro.who.int/__data/assets/pdf_file/0003/126408/e94421.pdf

Wiles, J. (2003). Daily geographies of caregivers: Mobility, routine, scale. *Social Science & Medicine, 57*, 1307–1325.

Chapter 5
Caring for a Family Member with a Lifelong Disability

5.1 Introduction

In this chapter we shift our focus from caregivers of children with disability to those who continue to care for family members with chronic disability. Care for a young and older adult with such disabilities brings up issues related to the longstanding experience of the carer. By this stage, the features of the disability are likely to be well understood and many carers will have developed a degree of expertise in their care work, along with competence in negotiating with the formal care sector and wider avenues of support. For many caregivers, their proficiency in providing care for a loved family member is a foundation upon which they become carers for other families or for caregivers facing similar situations. From our observation, many go on to support and mentor other family and informal carers, become advocates for these families, and more politically active in drawing attention to the needs of both people with disabilities and caregivers. In so doing these active carers add to the stock of social capital. The experience of caregiving can, therefore, be transformative at many levels for, the carer, the person with disability, and for the wider community. However, ongoing care responsibilities can also lead to the considerable depletion of personal and social resources with significant effects on caregiver well-being and health (Schofield et al. 1998).

In the previous chapter we reviewed key moments in the caregiving experience, from the birth of a child with a developmental or physical disability, to situations of later onset disability as a result of injury or illness. In these circumstances, we observed liminal experiences and dynamics that lead to a new role and identity as a caregiver. To reiterate: a key moment of change in the experience of the caregiver is the point of disclosure and diagnosis. At this time, caregivers are forced to revise expectations about their future as they make the transition into a new role defined by their caregiving responsibilities.

For parent caregivers, the transition to adolescence and then adulthood by the person with disability typically occurs as parents move towards their middle years. Harris et al. (1998) suggest that this transition leads to a realization by the parents that their child will experience significant life-long challenges. Parents may have considered this, discussed it, and observed others with similar disabilities making the transition, but it is not until they begin the experience themselves that it is necessarily brought home just what their child(ren) will face.

In this present chapter, we explore the mid-life course of the caregiving process, when carers have moved beyond the initial shock stage associated with diagnosis into a stage of enduring care. It takes the story forward and examines the experience of ongoing care for adolescent and adult children with chronic disabilities. Caregivers move beyond disclosure and acceptance, to finding ways of living with the demands of care. Many of the issues faced by younger caregivers are carried over into the older age group. However, a key developmental task of all adolescents is to establish a personal identity, with independence, autonomy, and emotional separation from parents. Adolescents need to take responsibility for themselves, take risks, demand rights, re-negotiate rules, develop social autonomy, and establish a sexual identity with the possibility of intimate sexual relationships (see Greydanus et al. 2002; Hellemans et al. 2007). These developmental tasks require carers to negotiate new situations in the caregiving relationship.

The dynamics of this phase revolve around the negotiation of the life course changes of the loved family member, as well as their own progression through these changes, while at the same time enduring the everyday routines of care. Older parent caregivers face continuing challenges that include feelings of loss and sadness across the lifecycle of their disabled child, and those who continue in the caring role find themselves increasingly confronted by the question of what will happen to their children when they are gone.

5.2   Lifelong Caring

Improvement in hygiene and advances in public health medicine, medical technology and improved pharmaceuticals, alongside the improved care in hospitals and care facilities, have combined to improve the lifespan of many people with disabilities. Today, these lives are lived in the community, as far as possible, rather than in institutions or care facilities, reflecting the philosophy promulgated by the disability movement during the 1980s, and mirrored in the appellation 'ageing-in-place' for older people by the OECD in 1996. The philosophy of care in the community, community living, and of rehabilitation towards independence has thus increased the number of older disabled individuals in the community, many of whom continue to live with family caregivers.

Care that continues into adult life in this way is seen as non-normative. Certainly, there is a stereotype that the parenting relationship in a nuclear family is completed when the young person reaches adulthood. This can easily be challenged in the 'normal' family which goes through many cycles of supporting adult children through the vicissitudes of adult life. In religious terms, the iconic representation of this fundamental enduring connection between a parent and the fate of the suffering individual is located in the figure of the Mater Dolorosa. In this image the suffering of Christ is imaged through the suffering of Mary. It is interesting that this iconic representation reflects the possibility of a dyadic relationship, where the care relationship imparts value both to the one cared for and to the caregiver. When we recognise this dyadic relationship, we see that the fate of the carer as being closely tied to that of the person with disability through the different stages of the lifespan. This perpetual relationship is ubiquitous in human society and is as fundamental to our humanity as any property philosophers have invoked as distinctly human. At one level, therefore, the fact that the disabled adult continues to need support should not be seen as somehow unnatural. Yet there are many subtle differences that carers must negotiate to enable them to move through adult cycles of separation and reconnection to whatever degree they are capable. A useful metaphor is to see this phase as a pathway or trajectory of care that extends throughout the period of the illness or disability.

Like the three stages of the rites of passage, multiple approaches have been developed to frame the trajectories of informal care. Most of these identify three phases, for example: entrants, new veterans and old veterans (Lawton et al. 2000); stages of encounter, enduring, and exit (Lindgren 1993); stages of transition including making the best of it, making the move, and making it better (Davies and Nolan 2006). Others identify four phases: becoming a caregiver, taking care, midwifing the death, and taking the next step (Stetz and Brown 1997; Brown and Stetz 1999); or Escandón's (2006) four phases of role acceptance: early responsibilities, role reconciliation, role imprint and providing/projecting care. What these studies have in common is that they define each phase based on the timing and type of caregiving activities provided, and how these activities change over time at key 'turning points' (Neufield et al. 2008; Wallengren et al. 2008).

These stages are useful markers and remind us there is a process of change where, at critical moments, there are specific needs for support and help. Such moments present new challenges, but these are not always easily negotiated, as Graziosi (2010, p. 24) suggests: 'Just when a parent understands one system, they are thrust into another system where the rules have changed.'

New phases in the care process require parents to manage change, both for themselves and for the person with disability. In highlighting some of these changes, we focus on the need to adjust parenting across developmental stages, managing the challenges of sandwich generation care, and adjusting to the demands of being a perpetual parent. Through these periods of change, the focus of carers is on how to endure and sustain themselves in the caring role.

Mid-life course carers are confronted daily with the fact of the ongoing dependency of the person with disability. The effort this requires is a lifelong commitment, violating what Featherstone (1980) characterises as a 'natural order.'

> When parents are young and healthy and energetic, children require vast amounts of exhausting physical care. As both grow older, this demand tapers off, and eventually the children grow independent. … .A severe disability disrupts this natural order, extending a child's dependence beyond a parent's strength, health, even lifetime (p. 19).

To focus on caring across the life course is to focus on temporal dimensions of care and, as Grant et al. (2003) observe, this has been a neglected aspect in research of family caregiving. They suggest that there has been a view of caregiving through the mid-life years as static, on the basis of broader views about stability in the mid-adult life course. The diagnosis has been made and movement into a new social role as a caregiver has occurred. However, caregiving at this stage continues to be characterised by improvisation, change and adjustment. Butler's (2007) ethnography of brain injury cases seven years after severe brain injury demonstrated that family carers were still negotiating change both in their own lives and those of their loved one with brain injury.

Lifelong caring involves many changes in response to the changing care situation over the years (Todd and Shearn 1996a, b). It is subject to re-evaluation and redefinition through the years of caring as the carer becomes further aware of the long-term implications. Some become 'perpetual parents,' a phrase borrowed from Kelly and Kropf (1995), who are constrained by the needs of the care recipients and by their own wishes to continue direct caring. Whether or not a family member moves out of home as a young adult, the responsibility and oversight for care continues.

The notion of the life course implies an understanding that at certain ages, parents will be freed from hands-on child care and be able to make arrangements for other activities, such as employment; later in the life course, children will have moved out of home and parents freed to pursue their own wishes. But caregiving parents, as Todd and Shearn (1996a) suggest, live outside such customary times:

> …parents could be characterized as living 'out of time' not only in the sense of having deviated from the normative time of family careers, but also in the sense that their non-parental lives were lived outside of the conventional times of adult society (p. 390).

This deviation of the normal time of family careers, and living 'out of time,' can lead to the isolation of lifelong carers. Home can become a lonely, isolated place, imbued with different social meanings.

5.2.1   Perpetual Parents

Kropf and Kelly (1995) emphasize the parenting side of caring and provide an example which captures well the situation of perpetual carers. They described an 81 year old mother who was continuing to care for her 61 year old daughter, Anita. Anita, who had severe mental retardation, had been cared for by her mother her entire life, and the family was described as having made tremendous sacrifices to sustain that care. Anita's impairment meant she had limited functional ability, limited vocabulary, and required assistance from her mother with all ADLs (activities of daily living). At age 61, Anita was facing new health problems. She was considerably overweight, had high blood pressure, and suffered recurrent respiratory infections. She had also begun to indicate very low energy levels and difficulty with independent walking. Anita's 81 year old mother was, at this stage, becoming more frail, and she was also reported as suffering from arthritis, high blood pressure and cardiac arrhythmia.

Anita's mother was very much a perpetual parent. Her life had revolved around caregiving responsibilities and the ongoing need to respond to the changing developmental needs of Anita. She was a veteran caregiver who had endured through the middle phase of many transition models. At 81 she was also facing the question, 'what will happen when I am gone?' Her health was frail and she was unlikely to be able to sustain the level of care.

The physical demands of caregiving are such that the capacity of perpetual parents to meet them as they age does diminish. Schofield et al. (1998, p. 27) quote a parent of a 35-year-old son with a severe physical disability. She had spent every day for years lifting him and this was undermining her own health. The mother was quoted: 'The lifting was just pulling my stomach like it was ripping the lining off my stomach, just transferring him from bed to chair or toilet.' Another quote from this research indicated similar physical strain: 'My daughter is getting a lot bigger and I have to watch my back. I go to the chiropractor every 3 months to be able to lift her because I am lifting her all the time' (p. 27).

Clearly the physical demands are taxing, but so too is the need to give constant attention. As care service co-ordinators and care researchers, we have seen many examples of caregivers who continue in a role as a perpetual parent. While all situations have distinctive features, such carers typically have a developed ability to manage the care needs of their child. They customarily know what is required for the maintenance of a stable environment, and this translates into their continual monitoring of the family member who receives care. It not only includes assistance with activities of daily living, which as indicated above becomes more demanding over time, but also observing the mental and emotional wellbeing of the cared-for person. It typically involves monitoring an individual's emotional wellbeing, supporting through depressive episodes, dealing with a constant demand for attention, or handling erratic behaviour. Such attentiveness is evident, for example, in the way carers seek to manage levels of stimulation, be that in order to prompt and encourage engagement in positive activities, or to avoid over-stimulation and the unpredictable behaviours that can result.

Family caregivers of adults with intellectual impairments often refer to the exhaustion that comes from the constant need to keep the cared-for person 'stimulated and occupied' (see also Power 2010, p. 190). Hellendoorn (2009) comments that this can range from the constant physical demands associated with care to the need to attend to the small details of checking, making sure the TV programme is right, the book is the right one, the chair is at the right angle. Many of these monitoring activities are not easily captured in the language of care tasks, but they do represent a form of constant stress.

As parents age, there is therefore a concern with questions of the sustainability of care. This is a concern for most parents of adults with chronic disability, the fact that there is likely to be a period, sometimes up to 30 years, when they are not present to oversee the care. Jennings (1993) has, observed that such older parents have a heightened sense of fear over their own death, and are often less prepared for dying, because of concerns associated with leaving a disabled child.

One of the key issues during this phase of care is beginning to establish systems to address the long-term sustainability of care. From our observation, many carers address issues of mortality by working to establish sustainable situations for their children. The best case scenario may be creating a situation where the person with disability will be able to maintain his or her activities after the parent leaves or dies. To this effect some parents will begin to put pressure on siblings to support and care, advocate for good group homes, develop micro-businesses, and focus increasingly on whatever independence is possible for the person with disability.

5.2.2 Sandwich Generation Caregivers

Mid-life adult carers are also recognised as 'sandwich generation' carers given the increased likelihood that at the same time as caring for children and/or children with disabilities, carers in mid-life may be caring for elderly parents, or at least, ensuring care is delivered to them. Chisholm (1999) presented the following definition, which is broader in scope:

> The sandwich generation refers to individuals who, by dint of circumstances, find themselves in the position of being caregivers for their young children and/or adult children as well as one or both of aging parents. The individuals of the sandwich generation tend to be in the 40 to 65 years of age group (p. 178).

As people live longer, delay marriage and birth of the first child, and with the trend towards community care for people with disabilities and ageing frailties, more people find themselves in this situation. Although the term 'sandwich generation' refers to caregiving for the older generation while looking after and bringing up dependent children, we draw attention to the way these challenges are greater when caring for two generations of people with disabilities. As a result of these trends, greater numbers of middle-aged adults are faced with the challenge of balancing the needs of their own disabled children with the demands and needs of ageing parents. Typically, the individuals or couples involved are between the ages of 45 and 65 (Lindgren and Decker 1996).

Such caregivers face many challenges. The most salient issues confronting them include finding time, energy, and resources to balance the competing demands of the needs of ageing parents, the needs of dependent children, and responsibilities associated with work and careers. At the same time that the population is ageing, families are smaller, more women are single parents, and more are impoverished as a result of divorce. This scenario of increased demand in an era of decreased capacity threatens to reduce the quality of life for many women. The resulting intensification of caregiving demands has potential to leave many women carrying responsibilities for care and other domestic roles and, thus, further reinforce the exclusion of women from the formal economy (Aronson and Neysmith 1997).

5.3 Developing Expertise as a Family Care Practitioner

Caring across the life course, as a perpetual parent or sandwich generation carer, leads to the accumulation of care-related knowledge and expertise. Caregivers develop as 'practitioners' in their capacity to oversee the wellbeing of the individual with disability. Ruddick's (1989) anthropological and philosophical work on maternal practice gives one of the most thorough descriptions of what is involved in care. While heralded as the pioneer of the subject of care ethics, her work has been questioned because it seems to describe only the practice of mothers. However, in the introduction she very clearly outlines how what she describes is relevant to the practice of all carers.

Practices, according to Ruddick (1989), are collective human activities distinguished by the aims that identify them and by the consequent demands made on practitioners committed to those aims. The aims or goals that define a practice are so central that in the absence of the goal you would not have that practice. In caregiving practice, the goal is the preservation, growth, and social integration of the person being cared for. To be engaged in the practice of care means that the carer is committed to meet these goals. Carers more or less consciously create a practice as they simultaneously pursue these goals and make sense of their pursuit. Understanding shapes the end, even as the practical pursuit of the end shapes the understanding. By the time they are caring for an adult, the carer has gone a long way towards being able to understand and articulate this practice. Kittay (1999), noted above as the mother of an adult daughter with severe disability, describes from her perspective the parallels between caring for a normal child and one like Sesha.

> What I have learned from the experience of mothering Sesha, and what the many accounts of parenting such a child reveal, is that the differences we encounter redefine the sameness. Raising a child with a severe disability is not just like parenting a normal child – but more so. It is often very different. Yet in that difference, we come to see features of raising any child that otherwise escape attention or that assume a new valence (p. 163).

Through the process of providing hands-on care and oversight for the wellbeing of the loved one, caregivers acquire specialized knowledge of the disability or disease, knowledge of possible treatment options, medications and assistive technologies, and experience in managing the demands of the care situation, including behavior management. They have typically reached a point where they will no longer passively wait for others to provide solutions. An indication of the types of skills they acquire through hands-on experience in the nine dimensions of informal care identified by Schumacher et al. (2000; in Nolan et al. 2003). They are:

- Monitoring – keeping an eye on things in order to know how well the care recipient is doing;
- Interpreting – making sense of what is observed;
- Making decisions – choosing a course of action;
- Taking action – carrying out caring decisions and instructions;

- Providing 'hands-on' care – giving care safely and with comfort;
- Making adjustments and progressively refining care until it is 'fine-tuned' to the care-receiver's needs;
- Accessing resources such as information, equipment and help;
- Working together with the care receiver and providing care appropriate to the needs of both parties; and
- Negotiating healthcare systems – working with the system and getting the most out of it (p. 288).

It is through the daily work of care, the search for what works best to enhance the life of the person with disability, through trial and error, that mid-life caregivers become experienced in these areas. Expertise develops over time and evolves out of an active process of searching to find ways of supporting a sustainable and good life for the person with disability.

This process of learning to care is characterized by a continual search for better ways to manage conditions and a willingness to try new strategies when old approaches are no longer effective. Lessons are learned through the hard knocks that come with trial and error, and when a strategy is not working, it is described as being like 'hitting a brick wall.' For example, one of the carers in Butler's (2007) study described how they tried to leave their son with a transitional rehabilitation unit. The hope was that a team of professionals might be able to help him to make the transition away from home and into a flat of his own. The experiment was unsuccessful because he refused to take direction from staff. However, it was helpful to family because they realized yet again that they had to draw on whatever resources were available to them in order to find a way forward. In this case the exercise of looking for new solutions to meet his developmental needs opened up new pathways and options they had not thought of before. The carer found out they would be able to use a small amount of compensation as a down payment on a house. This was a gamble, but it paid off and it was the first step towards a new life for this young man with brain injury. This moment was described by the primary caregiver as an epiphany which led to new knowledge about how best to care for her son. It was one of the many leaning moments in her journey of development as a carer.

5.3.1   Working with Professionals

Many parents of children with special needs assert that the majority of decisions regarding their adult children are still being made by professionals, leaving them marginalized, and even alienated, by the 'system' (Scorgie et al. 1999; Soodak and Erwin 1995; Valle and Aponte 2002). For a time parents can feel forced to assume 'passive' roles, becoming 'the recipients of information rather than the providers' (Garriott et al. 2000, p. 42). Some have described encounters with professionals who treat them with condescension, even suggesting that their goals for their adult children are 'unrealistic, unreasonable, and/or incompetent' (Soodak and Erwin 1995, p. 271).

Non-supportive interactions with care professionals are categorised by Neufield and Harrison (2008) as interactions which question and, therefore, undermine the credibility of the caregiver; interactions where the caregiver's concerns are minimised or disbelieved; interactions which lead to inappropriate advice or offers of aid; interactions where the expected care was inappropriate or not forthcoming; and interactions where the professional either failed to recognise the needs of the carer, or refused to address such needs even if they were recognised. Such interactions inevitably weaken the capacity of informal caregivers to meet the needs of their loved one.

We suggest reconnected carers are those who are able to negotiate formal care systems, and work with care professionals as they monitor the wellbeing of the person in need through this process. It is clear that achieving good support from care professionals is necessary at key times in the life of the person with disability. Negotiating the relationship with such professionals, however, is not always straightforward. Primary caregivers face the need to develop the judgment to discern which individuals are most likely able to facilitate the development of their loved one. Liaising with professionals is not always straightforward given the many claims to professional competence within the formal, professional care sector. It is through processes of working with professionals that informal caregivers develop competence in advocacy and other aspects of the care work role.

These are many difficult questions to negotiate with professionals, one of which is balancing the competing goals in the care of the person with disability. We observe that many care professionals continue to be fixated on independence as the sole goal of any worth for the individual, even those with severe disability, and even when it can seem relatively meaningless. Independence has been a touchstone among the disability movement, but it is not necessarily the most important goal in terms of supporting wellbeing and enabling growth.

Having first-hand, grounded knowledge of what works for the person with disability means family care practitioners are often better positioned to negotiate the balance between supporting independence without leaving the cared-for individual to bear the full brunt of poor decisions. The following example by Butler (2007) outlines the situation where the family caregiver recognizes the loved one simply needs to try things out until he is able to find what works for him. This carer talks about letting her son (who has a brain injury) learn from his mistakes, but also keep a watchful eye on the situation, in case it got out of hand:

> [He] learns best by experience, so we let him experience the good and the bad. If he does something then he has got to experience the bad and it is a bit like the flatting situation. I mean, that's been a great learning curve, that managing people coming in and out has really been a good learning curve for him. I cringe at some of the problems and that, but I keep my mouth shut. Like Jack and I will talk about things, but I don't say half of what I think to [him]. God forbid! (p. 194).

Supporting the development of children and adults with severe disability is never as straightforward as that of non-disabled children and adults. Attaining developmental milestones is only possible where carers are able to attune precisely to the needs of the person with disability. Whereas it might be possible for a single family care practitioner to ensure the survival of an individual with severe disability through the intensity of their preservative love, it is virtually impossible for a single individual to tend to all the developmental needs of any person. Working with professionals is therefore necessary. Attaining a level of confidence to articulate what is required for the person with disability when working with professionals is an indicator of development as a family care practitioner.

The world-wide movement towards variations of individualised funding is leading to change in the relationships that families and people with disability have with care professionals. Their spending power has potential to create a market for services that are more specifically tailored to their needs. As Powers et al. (2006) note:

> Models are being developed that avoid the oversimplified notion that service users are either autonomous or non-autonomous, permitting both collaborative direction of services by individuals and trusted others, and delegated autonomy to surrogates (p. 67).

With individualized funding models, there is potential for greater flexibility and therefore responsiveness to meet the needs of both the person with disability and family caregivers.

5.4 From Family Care Practitioner to Community Advocate

Non-supportive interactions with health professionals often precipitate the first actions towards a broader advocacy role by family caregivers. Having concerns about the person with disability minimized or disbelieved, or having inappropriate services offered does lead to a clear realization by family caregivers that they carry the primary responsibility to the person with disability. While this can lead to feelings of isolation in the care role, it can also be a spur to advocacy. When this leads to participation in community groups which reach out to other caregivers, or others in similar situations, family caregivers can be seen to be making a contribution to the wider community. Such activities often extend to adopting activist or political lobbying roles. From our observations, many parents become more self-assertive, and more prepared to stand up for their child and for others in similar situations.

Generally, when reference is made to the transformative impact of caring on the caregiver, the focus is on the transformations that come about within the individual care dyad. However, carers tend to talk more about the ways that care transforms them as they develop strategies that empower both themselves and their families. Empowerment is a personal process that develops in response to frustrations within the caregiving situation, with the health care system, and with themselves. It is typically involves a process of critical reflection, a determination to take charge of the situation, and a will to persevere that results in the development of these qualities. It can lead, according to Gibson (1995), to the development of 'participatory competence,' an ability to advocate for their child and for others. The efforts of these caregivers do lead to societal transformations as they create social spaces for their loved one. They play an essential role in creating new supports and systems for families of people with disability, but they are also important in providing an education for the next generation of health practitioners.

Transformation through care is most possible for those with the greatest degree of social capital available to them. In Neufield and Harrison's (2008) study of the responses of carers to adversity, they acknowledged that the women in their study were all educated and had the initial perspective that encouraged empowerment. Those with wealth, access to information, and skill in dealing with professionals are likely to be advantaged when drawing on social bonds and bridging social networks, and so are likely to secure better outcomes than those who are 'resource poor' (Arksey and Glendinning 2007, p. 168). Family caregivers with less education and other social and economic resources, it would follow, are less able to access the transformative stage of caring.

Carr's (2003) feminist perspective describes empowerment practice as a process in which a critical consciousness develops over time and yields a new understanding that becomes the basis for action. Interaction with others in a similar situation facilitates this new understanding and generation of possibilities for action as political aspects of their personal situation are identified. The context of women's life experience is influential as they experience repeated exposure to difficult situations, such as non-supportive interactions with professionals, and positive or negative feedback in response to their efforts. A key contribution of Carr's perspective is acknowledgment of the importance of exposure to an originating position that mobilizes a process of empowerment. A distinct feature of her perspective is her view that the basis of powerlessness includes the absence of external supports, as well as social or political forms of oppression.

5.4.1   Care and Social Capital

We know, therefore, that caregiving can confer benefits on the carer (Hastings and Taunt 2002, in Siegel et al. 2009), but whether such benefits are realized is determined by whether there are supportive conditions in the broader environment (Arksey and Glendinning 2007). Caregiving is more likely to be burdensome in environments where there is limited social capital (Singer et al. 2009) and where society does not allocate adequate resources to the care of people with severe disability. In such environments, personal and social resources are likely to be depleted.

Obviously the lack of income associated with reduced capacity to engage in paid employment is one significant factor that gradually erodes the capital (both social and economic) available to family. The advantage of paying family carers is that it creates a sustainable situation, which also tends to create a degree of flexibility and choice in the life of the individual with disability. The other clear advantage is the removal of stress and burden from the family, such that it becomes possible to achieve positive transformations and turning points (Butler 2007).

The recognition of informal caregivers as expert carers is more obviously seen in the mentoring roles many end up playing in community support groups. Generally, health professionals have very little hesitation in referring new caregivers to such groups. In the best cases 'new' carers find friendship and someone to mentor them as they traverse the steep learning curve associated with their new role. Gubrium (1986, in Bytheway and Johnson 1998) observed this dynamic in his observation that, 'Those closest to the victim, who are the 'real experts' in the care and management of the disease – the caregivers – are taught or teach each other that they all share the same travail' (p. 209). From our observation and participation in such groups, skills are usually passed on orally and with a great deal of generosity. Through the expression of such outreach in community organisations which reach out to give care, social capital is evinced and enhanced (see also Bellah 1994).

Informal caregiving is the 'giving' of care, and of commitment, skills and knowledge. When informal caregivers extend these activities beyond their responsibilities as primary caregivers within, say, the private family relationship, they become part of a systematic response to societal needs. The carer donates knowledge, empathy and expertise and thus grows the overall social capital available to new generations of carers. We can think of social capital, therefore as not only influencing the capacity of informal caregivers to care, but also as something they build up, contribute to and expand.

5.5   Meeting the Needs of Those Who Care Across the Life Course

We end this chapter with an interesting comment by philosopher Eva Kittay, whose observations on community responsibility relate to our belief in the value of effective social networks leading towards a fund of social capital. She offers an approach to conceptualizing the support necessary for carers that is centred around the idea of 'doulia.' This notion was adapted by Kittay from the Greek concept of 'doula,' where women were cared for during the vulnerable stage following giving birth. Kittay, as a philosopher, proposed that 'doulia' might be a way of sustaining equality. She based this notion of equality on the idea that carers should be entitled to support when their vulnerability is increased through the *unpaid* caring relationship, giving rise to a constructed dependency. Public support would ensure some reciprocity, knowing that the dependents themselves cannot reciprocate. The concept of 'doulia' is a way of understanding the responsibilities of the wider community to caregivers. This idea recognizes the inevitability of mutual dependence within families and communities. Kittay (1999) developed the notion as a part of her critique of the way we understand dependency, and drew on her experience as a philosopher and mother of a child with a severe disability. The common conception of society as a community of equals, she suggests, ignores how dependencies of childhood, old age and disability fall most heavily on those who care for them. Caregiving responsibilities mean carers must put aside the pursuit of their own interests to care for those completely dependent on their actions. Any form of equality, she says, requires the wider community to recognize this putting aside of self-interest by carers and it obliges society to support them while they do. This she described as a type of 'generalised reciprocity,' or in colloquial terms an explicit social recognition that 'what comes around, goes around,' or 'doulia.'

Typically, however, carers do not have any certainty that what they give will ever come back to them, but they are still taken aback to find that this labour is invisible to others. Kittay's assertion that 'we are all-equally-some mother's daughter,' is a way of indicating that this work would never be invisible to those who care for the carer in environments where there is generalised reciprocity. A mother would not abandon a daughter to her fate. In the same way, a society of equals would not stand by and render invisible the labour of an army of carers. Doulia is a call for society to recognise the work done by carers and, alongside this, the worth of the individuals they care for. It is a call,

> … to provide caregivers with conditions that allow them to do their work well and receive just compensation. They need appropriate training, the opportunity to grow in their work, a voice in the care of their charges, compensation that matches the intensity of their labor and encouragement in their sympathetic and empathic response to their charges (Kittay 2002, p. 270).

'Doulia' is therefore one way of describing what 'should' happen if the relationship between society and the carer is not to become exploitative. The need for some degree of equality within society becomes particularly pressing for carers as they move into the middle phase of care. It is during this period that the personal resources of the carer are most likely to be overreached. Without support, the 'turning points' will become a series of crises for which they are not prepared.

5.6 Summary

The present chapter has taken the story of informal caregiving across the life course forward and examined the experience of ongoing care for adolescent and adult children with chronic disabilities. These phases of care are a reminder that informal carers manage complex processes of change, both for themselves and also for the person with disability. In this chapter we highlight some of the phases of change, including turning points and transformations. The focus of the carer is on enduring across these phases, while still shouldering the essential care practice necessary to care for the person with disability. In the final section of this chapter we examined mechanisms through which society's stock of social capital is enhanced by the work of carers who have become expert through experience. The most basic resource that such carers bring is their competence, which when developed is, typically, given freely. This competence is extended politically through dynamics of advocacy which ensure that the expertise held by carers is made more widely available. The role of carers in educating health professionals is rarely reflected upon, and the importance of their role in educating the next generation of carers is generally brushed over. Out of all the many ways carers contribute to social capital, perhaps the greatest is the way that care practice challenges neoliberal notions of equality. Both care and disability together insist that it is not possible to overlook dependency. They are a constant reminder that dependency must be taken into account, hence making the world more human for all.

Discussion Questions

Discuss the various meanings of the term 'perpetual parents'.

Discuss the fears of a parent who is dying and leaving child with disabilities. What would it take to reassure such parents? Is it possible to do so?

What do you consider to be significant features of mid-life course caregiving? Can you add to those offered in the chapter?

Further Reading

Biegel, D., Sales, E., & Schulz, R. (1991). *Family caregiving in chronic illness: Alzheimer's disease, cancer, heart disease, mental illness and stroke*. Thousand Oaks: Sage Publications.
Grant, G., & Whittell, B. (2000). Families with children or adults with intellectual disabilities: The relevance of gender, family composition and the life span. *Journal of Applied Research in Intellectual Disabilities, 13*, 265–275.
Held, V. (2006). *The ethics of care: Personal, political, and global*. Oxford: Oxford University Press.
Wallengren, C., Friberg, F., & Segesten, K. (2008). Like a shadow – On becoming a stroke victim's relative (a view from inside the family – Long term care giving). *Scandinavian Journal of Caring Science, 22*, 48–55.
Woog, P. (1992). *The chronic illness trajectory framework: The Corbin and Strauss nursing model*. New York: Springer.

References

Arksey, H., & Glendinning, C. (2007). Choice in the context of informal care-giving. *Health & Social Care in the Community, 15*(2), 165–175.
Aronson, J., & Neysmith, S. (1997, Summer). The retreat of the state and long-term care provision: Implications for frail elderly people, unpaid family carers and paid home care workers. *Studies in Political Economy, 53*, 37–66.
Bellah, R. (1994). The crisis of care: Affirming and restoring caring practices in the helping professions. In S. Phillips & P. Benner (Eds.), *Understanding caring in contemporary America* (pp. 21–35). Washington, DC: Georgetown University Press.
Brown, M., & Stetz, K. (1999). The labor of caregiving; A theoretical model of caregiving during potentially fatal illness. *Qualitative Health Research, 9*(2), 182–197.
Butler, M. (2007). *Care ethics and brain injury*. Ph.D. (unpublished thesis), Otago University, Dunedin.
Bytheway, B., & Johnson, J. (1998). The social construction of 'carers'. In A. Symonds & A. Kelly (Eds.), *The social construction of care in the community* (pp. 241–253). Basingstoke: Macmillan [0 333 66298 9]. Reprinted in Johnson, J., & de Souza, C. (Eds), *Understanding health and social care, an introductory reader*. London: Sage.

Carr, E. S. (2003). Rethinking empowerment theory using a feminist lens: The importance of process. *Affilia, 18*(1), 8–20.

Chisholm, J. F. (1999). The sandwich generation. *Journal of Social Distress and the Homeless, 8*(3), 177–180.

Davies, S., & Nolan, M. (2006). 'Making it better': Self-perceived roles of family caregivers of older people living in care homes: A qualitative study. *International Journal of Nursing Studies, 43*(3), 281–291.

Escandón, S. (2006). Mexican American intergenerational caregiving model. *Western Journal of Nursing Research, 28*(5), 564–585.

Featherstone, H. (1980). *A difference in the family.* New York: Basic Books.

Garriott, P., Wandry, D., & Snyder, L. (2000). Teachers are parents, parents as children: What's wrong with this picture? *Preventing School Failure, 45*(1), 37–43.

Gibson, C. (1995). The process of empowerment in mothers of chronically ill children. *Journal of Advanced Nursing, 21*, 1201–1210.

Grant, G., Nolan, M., & Keady, J. (2003). Supporting families over the life course: Mapping temporality. *Journal of Intellectual Disability Research, 47*(4/5), 342–351.

Graziosi, E. (2010). Valuing support groups. *Exceptional Parent, 40*(4), 24–25.

Greydanus, D., Rimsza, M., & Newhouse, P. (2002). Adolescent sexuality and disability. *Adolescent Medicine, 13*(2), 223–224.

Harris, S., Glasberg, B., & Delmolino, L. (1998). Families and the developmentally disabled adolescent. In V. VanHasselt & M. Hersen (Eds.), *Handbook of psychological treatment protocols for children and adolescents* (pp. 519–548). Mahwah: Lawrence Erlbaum Associates.

Hastings, R., & Taunt, H. (2002). Positive perceptions in families of children with developmental disabilities. *American Journal on Mental Retardation, 107*, 116–127.

Hellemans, H., Colson, K., Verbraeken, C., et al. (2007). Sexual behavior in high-function male adolescents and young adults with autism spectrum disorder. *Journal of Autism and Developmental Disorders, 37*(2), 260–269.

Hellendoorn, H. (2009). *The Madonna in the suitcase.* Dunedin: Hellendoorn.

Jennings, J. (1993). Elderly parents as caregivers for their adult dependent children. *Social Work, 87*(5), 430–433.

Kelly, T. B., & Kropf, N. P. (1995). Stigmatized and perpetual parents: Older parents caring for adult children with life-long disabilities. *Journal of Gerontological Social Work, 24*(1/2), 3–16.

Kittay, E. F. (1999). *Love's labor: Essays on women, equality and dependency.* New York: Routledge.

Kittay, E. (2002). When caring is just and justice is caring: Justice and mental retardation. In E. F. Kittay & E. K. Feder (Eds.), *The subject of care: Feminist perspectives on dependency.* Oxford: Rowman & Littlefield.

Kropf, N. P., & Kelly, T. B. (1995). Stigmatized and perpetual parents: Older parents caring for adult children with life-long disabilities. *Journal of Gerontological Social Work, 24*(1/2), 3–16.

Lawton, M., Moss, M., Hoffman, C., & Perkinson, M. (2000). Transitions in daughters' caregiving careers. *The Gerontologist, 40*(4), 437–448.

Lindgren, C. (1993). The care giver career. *Journal of Nursing Scholarship, 25*(3), 214–219.

Lindgren, H. G., & Decker, H. (1996). *The sandwich generation: A cluttered nest.* http://digitalcommons.unl.edu/cgi/viewcontent.cgi?article=1560&context=extensionhist

Neufield, A., & Harrison, M. (2008). Advocacy of women family caregivers: Response to nonsupportive interactions with professionals. *Qualitative Health Research, 18*, 301–310.

Neufield, A., Harrison, M., Stewart, M., & Hughes, K. (2008). Advocacy of women caregivers: Response to nonsupportive interactions with professionals. *Qualitative Health Research, 18*(3), 301–310.

Nolan, M., Lundh, U., Grant, G., & Keady, J. (Eds.). (2003). *Partnerships in family care.* Maidenhead: Open University Press.

Power, A. (2010). *Landscapes of care.* Farnham: Ashgate Publishers Ltd.

Powers, L. E., Sowers, J., & Singer, G. H. S. (2006). A cross-disability analysis of person-directed, long-term services. *Journal of Disability Policy Studies, 17*, 66–76.

Ruddick, S. (1989). *Maternal thinking: Towards a politics of peace.* Boston: Beacon Press.

Schofield, H., Bloch, S., & Herrman, H. (1998). *Family caregivers: Disability, illness and ageing.* Sydney: Allen & Unwin.

Schumacher, K. L., Stewart, B. J., Archbold, P. G., Dodd, M. J., & Dibble, S. L. (2000). Family caregiving skill: Development of a concept. *Research in Nursing and Health, 23,* 191–203.

Scorgie, K., Wilgosh, L., & McDonald, L. (1999). Transforming partnerships: Parent life management issues when a child has mental retardation. *Education and Training in Mental Retardation and Developmental Disabilities, 34,* 396–405.

Siegel, B., Bear, D., Andres, E., & Mead, H. (2009). Measuring equity: An index of health care disparities. *Quality Management in Healthcare, 18*(2), 84–90.

Singer, G., Biegel, D., & Ethridge, B. (2009). Toward a cross disability view of family support for caregiving families. *Journal of Family Social Work, 12*(2), 97–118.

Soodak, L., & Erwin, E. (1995). Parents, professionals, and inclusive education: A call for collaboration. *Journal of Educational and Psychological Consultation, 6*(3), 257–276.

Stetz, K. M., & Brown, M. A. (1997). Taking care: Caregiving to persons with cancer and AIDS. *Cancer Nursing, 20*(1), 12–22.

Todd, S., & Shearn, J. (1996a). Struggles with time: The careers of parents with adult sons and daughters with intellectual disabilities. *Disability Society, 11*(3), 379–401.

Todd, S., & Shearn, J. (1996b). Time and the person: The impact of support services on the lives of parents of adults with intellectual disabilities. *Journal of Applied Research in Intellectual Disabilities, 9,* 40–60.

Valle, J., & Aponte, E. (2002). IDEA and collaboration: A Bakhtinian perspective on parent and professional discourse. *Journal of Learning Disabilities, 35*(5), 469–479.

Wallengren, C., Friberg, F., & Segesten, K. (2008). Like a shadow – On becoming a stroke victim's relative (a view from inside the family – Long term care giving). *Scandinavian Journal of Caring Science, 22,* 48–55.

Chapter 6
Caring for Adults with Acquired Disabilities

6.1 Introduction

When working age adults experience physical or sensory impairment or the onset of disabling illness which causes multiple concurrent losses, they can be said to have an acquired disability. It involves the loss of functionality and in many instances requires additional care. Caring for an adult with an acquired disability presents particular challenges, many of these related to the meanings of independence that are associated with adulthood. Discourses about care related to adult disability have been made problematic by the definition of adulthood as a quintessentially independent phase of life (Shakespeare 2006). It is precisely around concepts of adulthood that much of the tension between the care movement and the disability movement has revolved. Disabled people have criticized the concept of care, and the research stemming from it, because it tends to position disabled people within society as dependent and non-autonomous. Caregivers, on the other hand, tend to be perplexed by concepts of disability that deny the complex interplay between 'disability' and 'need for care' in order politically to position the person with disability as having power in the care relationship.

Tension over the meaning of care has led to a rejection of the concept of care by many of the most articulate spokespeople of the disability movement. In their attempts to avoid the negative positioning of 'disabled' and claim political power in discourses about disability, they have proposed an alternative language, preferring words such as 'support' or 'help' (Shakespeare 2000). This endeavour to redefine the care relationship through changing how we represent it is important in terms of the shift to individualized funding for people with disability, supporting the independence of adults with disabilities, since this funding provides the means to employ formal caregivers to do the work which many informal carers have carried out in the past.

It is hardly surprising that both the disability and care movements have been caught in the cleft created by the view that adulthood means individual independence and autonomy. This notion, that adulthood can be constituted as complete independence, powerfully shapes expectations about how the relationship between people with disability and caregivers should be structured, but thinking of independence in this way is inherently problematic. As Oliver (1989; see also Oliver 1990 and Oliver 1996) has stated:

> In reality, of course, no one in a modern industrial society is completely independent: we live in a state of mutual interdependence. The dependence of disabled people, therefore, is not a feature which marks them out as different in kind from the rest of the population but different in degree (pp. 83–84).

While people who are dependent as a consequence of acquired disability are at the centre of concern in this chapter, our focus is on informal caregivers who support them. Potential caregivers, be they spouses or other family members, before they ever engage in the caregiving role, face the loss of an adult companion at the very same time that they must take on both caregiving responsibilities and, often, other responsibilities previously held by that person. The impact on family caregivers is very much shaped by their location in broader social networks, the availability of resources within those networks, and their ability to obtain assistance from those networks. More broadly, the level of support through formal care arrangements very much influences the extent to which family caregivers are able to negotiate the transitions into their new role and remain connected.

6.2 Onset: Adult Disability and Caregiving

The majority of individuals who have a disability actually develop the disability as adults. Burchardt (2003, p. 1) reports that:

> 11 per cent of disabled adults of working age were born with a health problem or impairment, 12 per cent become disabled during childhood, and the remaining three-quarters become disabled during working life.

By working life she means between the ages of 16 and 65. The onset of disability through illness or injury may be sudden or gradual. The severity of the impairment and related experience of disability is likely to be highly variable.

Survival rates have steadily improved for disability acquired in adulthood, particularly where there have been improvements in surgical methods, for example in brain injury (Brown et al. 2004) and spinal cord injury (Frankel et al. 1998). Whatever the age of the onset of disability, increasing numbers of people with disabilities that once resulted in premature death now live as long as the average person (Panko Reis et al. 2004).

With disability being such a dynamic phenomenon, the experiences of limitation may be transitory or permanent, with the impact on the caregiver also likely to vary enormously, depending on the nature of the impairment or illness and the degree of support. The contribution of the wider family in the process of caregiving is critical. Foster et al. (2012, p. 1856) emphasize active family involvement is one of the most significant factors in rehabilitation and degree of recovery.

The onset of disability in adulthood represents a profound biographical disruption for the person with the disability and for his or her family. Primary family relationships come under particular stress. Initially, there tends to be an exclusive focus on the needs of the person who has been injured or sick (Crimmins 2000, p. 275). Stressors for family caregivers are not only the obvious ones of the need to give up time in response to the demands of this new situation, along with the associated anxieties and grief of seeing a loved one suffer. Families face both practical and emotional upheavals, the need to reorganize their ways of working, responsibilities need to be reallocated and multiple roles balanced. Cameron et al. (2002), therefore, conclude that family caregivers tend to have elevated levels of emotional distress at this time, particularly as their new responsibilities affect participation in other activities.

The practical implications of adult onset disability for employment and income contribute to these difficulties. Those who became disabled in adulthood were found by Burchardt (2003) to experience decline in household income, with those making a sudden transition experiencing a more rapid decline. Her study argues that it is clear that becoming disabled in adulthood is associated with a transition into household poverty, and a raised likelihood it will be sustained poverty. Moreover, if the non-disabled caregiving partner leaves employment to provide 'unpaid care for the newly disabled partner, the fall in income and consequent shock in living standards can be substantial' (Burchardt 2003, p. 63). She also observes that partnership dissolution is greater when there are such changes in a couple's income status. These wider work and income related stresses have a bearing on the primary relationship of the household when one partner becomes disabled.

When the person who acquires a disability is a spouse, the possibility of maintaining the marital relationship is increased if the injury is less severe, if the couple is older and if they have been married for longer (Arango-Lasprilla et al. 2008). And when caregivers find they cannot tolerate the strain, some do abandon the role. Statistics indicating relationship breakdown for people with acquired brain injury, for example, suggest that for many caregivers the situation does become unbearable (Webster et al. 1999). Numerous studies point to marital breakdown following a brain injury, in many cases this occurring within the context of what were stable relationships at the time of injury. Measurements of the actual proportion of marital breakdowns vary widely, from between 25 % and 78 %, and are generally depressing, especially for those with severe traumatic brain injury (Arango-Lasprilla et al. 2008).

People who become primary caregivers, therefore, come to a point when they need to revisit their own expectations for their lives – for companionship, in terms of work or career interests and responsibilities, and in terms of leisure. New tensions emerge between the demands of paid employment, domestic management and childcare (Elbaum and Benson 2007; Dell Orto and Power 2000). Being placed in a situation of needing to care for a disabled adult family member, therefore, leads to significant changes involving the redistribution of competencies and responsibilities, as well as a rethinking of present and anticipated lives.

Such is the impact on families, that they have been found to experience at least as much distress as the person experiencing the disability (Crimmins 2000). Caregivers have similar emotional responses to those of care-recipients (Pinto 2008, p. 14). In these situations, the vulnerability of the person with the disability is shared with family members, particularly primary informal caregivers.

Arthur Frank (2002), an anthropologist who wrote a memoir on his personal transformation as he suffered disabling illness, observed a parallel transformation in his wife who was acting as his caregiver.

> Caregivers are confronted not with an ordered sequence of illness experiences, but with a stew of panic, uncertainty, fear, denial, and disorientation … Terms like pain or loss have no reality until they are filled in with an ill person's own experience. Witnessing the particulars of that experience and recognising all its differences, is care (p. 49).

What is clear is that, yet again, disability does not just happen to one person, it affects the whole family and it has implications for how the family is integrated within its own wider social network. From our observations, formal care services are ill-prepared to support families, particularly primary caregivers who are family members, through these processes (see also Elbaum and Benson 2007). Family members often need to learn new skills, become familiar with new technology, and create and draw upon new networks.

These first observations relate to separation and liminal experiences. Our main focus in this chapter, however, is the relationships between the caregiver and the adult with the disability. This is a fluid and dynamic process which shows a variety of different caregiving responses to the needs of chronic disease and disability.

6.3   Experiences of Caregiving in the Mid-life Course

In this section we draw on several works on mid-life course caregiving which cover a range of issues. The first develops the notion that when a family member acquires disability, it represents a significant disruption in the life of the family. Johansen (2002) in her book 'Listening in Silence, Seeing in the Dark' reflects the way families with members who become brain damaged respond to the new situation. Johansen, a literature and narrative theory teacher, is the mother of a young man, Erik, who has suffered a traumatic brain injury in a motor vehicle accident. She writes about how the family worked with Erik and the associated medical professionals to help bring him through the trauma and to a new selfhood. She comments, too, on the impact of the trauma on the rest of the family:

> Erik's loss of self through injury, unconsciousness, and confusion contributed to Robert's, Sonia's and my loss of soul. Our sense of being integrated body-mind-spirits participating in a benign and generative universe was split asunder with Erik's accident. Sometimes in shock we felt like bodies whose minds had walked away: at other times our bodies ached without consolation from the spirit; occasionally, in fatigue and sympathetic identification with Erik, we experienced the diminishment of our cognitive functions (Johansen 2002, p. 179).

Her view of the world was 'split asunder' and she intimates she and other family members also felt Erik's own losses in a kind of 'sympathetic identification.'

The accident and subsequent disability led to a re-evaluation and redistribution of roles within the family in response to the new need. Johansen (2002) quotes her adult daughter's explanation of the way the family was in a state of constant adjustment and readjustment as it sought to respond to the crisis being experienced by one of its members.

> The family unit itself—whatever form it takes—can be understood as an organism, each member influencing the others. Perhaps we balance each other's energies in harmony. As an organism the family might be analogous to the human brain. If injury to the brain produces loss or impairment of function in one area, other pathways may be created, or one can compensate through new strategies or by strengthening other senses. It is helpful for me to imagine the family as one body with multiple capacities, perspectives and responses. With injury and loss or new life to a family come new responses, reassigned capabilities, and revised roles for each member of the unit. To have undying faith in some frozen view of 'normalcy' is to live in constant fear of transformation (Johansen 2002, p. 204).

The onset of disability was experienced as a family – there was a group dimension to the experience, and it led to compensatory adjustments within the group, the taking on of new roles by some members to accommodate change in others, to sustain this core unit of mutual social support.

The ways that caregivers and adult disabled persons relate after an injury tends to reflect long-standing patterns of expectations and strategies that have developed through pre-existing relationships. These established patterns of relationship impact on how family members respond to the sudden onset of disability, dependency and the need for care, and can be both constructive and destructive. Some families are able to re-distribute roles in the ways described by Johansen: other pathways may be created or losses can be compensated for through new strategies, or by the strengthening of other sources. There are new responses, reassigned capabilities and revised roles for each member. This can include those who seem to be best positioned to help the person with the disability not choosing to take on the task of care.

Following a serious injury or disabling illness, the spouse or parents of the patient are typically cited as the primary source of support. Research into caregiver experiences indicate this is a period of significant psychological distress, such that it might be said to match that of the person with the injury (Stiell et al. 2007), Johansen's (2002) 'sympathetic identification.' Partners of stroke survivors, for example, have been found to have high rates of depression, and are more likely to experience depression than the actual stroke victim, with 30 % in one study and 41 % in a second study (Sit et al. 2004; Suh et al. 2005). When the disability is associated with cognitive and emotional difficulties, with symptoms of mood swings, confusion, restlessness or agitation, family caregivers have not only to deal with the physical demands of caring, but with coping with or 'managing' the behavior of another adult. Caregivers with inadequate support find themselves in a constant state of liminality, operating at the maximum level of coping.

This liminal phase of anxiety and bewilderment, of a focus on the moment, is a time of need for families to talk about the trauma and their own feelings and needs. This is an ongoing requirement as Foster et al. (2012) say. They comment on the needs that families have for clear and consistent information about their loved one's needs, and to be regularly updated on treatment and care. At the same time, say these authors, research has shown that families need to have the opportunity to discuss their own feelings and develop realistic expectations for their loved one's recovery. Over time the needs of the family will change as they adapt to the ongoing difficulties and make plans for the future, suggesting that families need to be engaged throughout the entire rehabilitation journey.

6.3.1 Relationships in Ongoing Caregiving

Without diminishing the trauma of the person who experiences the onset of disability, these examples also capture the real stress families, and primary caregivers in particular, experience. This has significant implications for spousal relationships and informal care. The impact of the injury or illness, and resulting disability, presents a threat to the attachment with a loved one, an 'irreplaceable other.' The adult attachment literature identifies four basic styles of attachment: secure, preoccupied, dismissive, and fearful avoidant (Bartholomew and Horowitz 1991; Stiell et al. 2007). It is accepted that secure attachments are profoundly shaken with the sudden onset of adult disability.

The disability can give rise to rage and frustration on one side, fear and avoidance on the other. The unpredictability and disorder that occurs leads, for example, to strategies of avoidance as a way of coping. Stiell et al.'s (2007) account of the experience of stroke on a couple's relationship illustrates this. She describes the experience of a couple where one partner was affected by severe aphasia following a stroke. The frustration associated with the disability led to avoidance of contact as a way of coping – something that might be classified as 'fearful avoidance.' Aphasia, the loss of the ability to process language due to damage to the speech center located in the left side of the brain, is an example of a condition which suddenly breaks down a couple's ability to communicate. It is associated with difficulties in one or more of the acts of talking, understanding speech, reading, writing, or working with numbers. Unlike dementia, individuals living with aphasia are aware of their loss of language and indeed their thoughts are unaffected. Awareness of their loss contributes to frustration. The husband in this story repeated over and over again: 'I know, I know, I know, but, but, words … ugh!' In this story the wife, Judy, was very anxious about husband Rick coming home from the hospital. He had only mild physical deficits, but global aphasia left him with both expressive and receptive language difficulties. Much of his frustration he took out on Judy, who was with him during the day. He knew what he wanted to say but the only words that seemed to come out were *'Tee, tee, tee ...'* Rick would try to say something and give up in frustration as Judy did not understand. There would be angry outbursts after several such attempts and gradually Judy withdrew from him. She commented:

> I just give up. I am exhausted. It's easier than the frustration of not getting it or the risk of angry outbursts. And I don't want to make him feel stupid when I can't get it (in Stiell et al. 2007, p. 71).

The demands of providing care in this situation included the emotionally draining experience of trying to understand, failing, knowing that failure contributed to the frustration of her spouse, and being unable to cope with the consequences of that in a way that did not reinforce his frustration with his impairment. Her response was to avoid confronting situations and that led to her revaluation of her bond or attachment to Rick. Such frustration and challenge is common.

When couples respond to such difficulties in an adaptive way, it can lead to the reestablishment of secure attachments. Such threats or challenges have been shown to bring about a predictable series of responses in order to re-instill the bond and to develop adaptive responses to the threat (Bowlby 1988; in Stiell et al. 2007). Stiell et al. (2007) describes how this couple found a way of re-engaging. Over time, and with the support of a therapist to address their relationship stress, they learned ways around their withdrawal from each other. Not getting the message in or out no longer created a crisis and they learned to laugh or cry at failed efforts and take time out when frustration levels went too high. They eventually began to reestablish their relationship to one which could, again, be described as secure.

6.3.2 Communication Issues and Violence

The relationship between the caregiver and the cared-for person, then, faces particular challenge as a consequence of difficulties in communication. The challenges are all the greater where relationships were already strained (Finkelstein and French 1993, in Mazur 2006). Communication between those who do not have a strong relationship before the onset of disability is likely to lead to continued dismissiveness or fearful avoidance. The inability to find a way through these dynamics can lead to more permanent withdrawal and a breakdown in situations where constructive communication is necessary. In some cases, the relationships with the significant other are anything but caring, this being evident in the way adults with disabilities are more likely to be victims of personal violence, including rape, and less likely to lay complaints with the police and receive legal protection. In a recent review of the incidence of violence against people with disability, Hughes et al. (2012) found disabled adults were 1.5 times more likely to suffer violence than the general population.

Violence, too, can be a part of the experience of caring for an adult with disability. For example, a harrowing account by caregivers of young adults with disability is provided by Carpinter and Irwin (2000), who describes situations where the care is characterized by an ongoing risk of violence, and captures the impact on the caregivers:

> I find that I am operating at my very maximum level of coping all the time with my daughter. When she was at home unwell, I had to lock all the doors of the house as she wanted to run away. She was screaming and hitting. She grabbed me, hitting and scratching. I hardly had the energy to get out of the situation.
>
> Sometimes when he's hitting me I think 'I love you, I look after you, I fight for you – how can you do this to me? That's what really hurts... If I was a battered wife they'd be falling over themselves to help me and the kids – somewhere to stay, counseling, the works. Because it's my son and he's got a disability suddenly it seems to be ok. Take it from me, it's not ok (Carpinter and Irwin 2000, p. 8).

Caring for a family member who is abusive or combative is like being in a constant battle. When intimate family members who receive care become violent, caregivers are not only at risk of physical harm, but are left bereft and emotionally depleted.

Neurophilosopher, Grant Gillett (2002), discussed this phenomenon where the identity of an individual becomes distorted by a neurological event. In a paper entitled, 'You Always Were a Bastard' (2002), he outlines how the impact of an illness such as Alzheimer's Disease or a stroke, or an accident such as a brain injury, can lead to a change in personality which will see someone who has always been a gentle person suddenly become paranoid, contrary, belligerent or difficult. Gillett comments that remarks such as that in the title of the paper reflect the inability of the person with the disability to organize and edit thoughts, or as he says, 'weft and weave the tapestry that is my mind' (Gillett 2002, p. 28).

When such neurologically disabled individuals lose control over the process of editing their thoughts and constructing their own life story, when they have lost control of the process of weaving their autobiography, the carer can be one who maintains something of a narrative thread that holds together the identity of the disabled adult. This might be thought of as a part of the reconnective care process, and is commented on further later in this chapter.

6.4 Reconnective Caregiving

Reconnective caregiving includes responding to situations beyond the family and assisting the adult with disability negotiate relationship challenges and maintain social connections outside of the home. It includes being able to support the person with disability to become more widely connected. The extent to which the family has access to networks of support, therefore, is critical. It is through the family's ability to access such networks that people with acquired disability become reconnected. In this regards, support groups and family to family link programmes which promote mutual support between families are valuable (Butera-Prinzi et al. 2010).

An important form of this support revolves around the area of reintegration through work and employment. The construction of adulthood as a uniquely *work-able* period of life is central in the literature of both the disability and the care movements. It explains, also, why disability becomes such a feared concept in an environment where the function of all adults is signified by their capacity to be associated with productive activity within the economy. Being excluded from opportunities for participation in such activity characterises the experience of adults who develop disability through accident or illness. A high proportion of adults in this situation state they would like to work but, also, that they are unable to find a job, and such adults have no or very limited cognitive impairment.

In many cases where an adult acquires a disability, much of the initial care work is oriented towards sustaining life, but it soon becomes oriented towards assisting and adjusting to the new way of being. This often involves assisting adults with disability into independent housing, into employment, or with acceptable leisure activities. The task is very much one of supporting the social reintegration of the person with the acquired disability and the associated benefits of emotional support, self-esteem, and recognition. The effectiveness with which family caregivers are able to achieve such tasks is linked closely to their ability to access and exploit existing social networks or develop new ones. Success, in the form of successful reconnection and acceptance of the person with the disability in a new role is very much linked to the ability to draw upon social capital resources.

Assisting a disabled adult to become engaged in a productive work life, however, is rarely considered as part what carers do, unlike some other carers of people with developmental disabilities who negotiate to support their disabled child to find and keep a job. Yet for those individuals who have the potential to work, it is a way of returning to or achieving some semblance of what it means to be an independent adult, and to the associated benefits of social integration. As Berry (2009, p. 57) observes, being in a workplace can provide some income, but as important is the way it is a strong source of social interaction and social support, not only for the disabled adult, but for caregivers. It, thus, leads to improvements in psychological well-being, it reduces social isolation, and it can relieve caregiver stress. It is a way of achieving reconnection with wider social networks for both the disabled adult and the informal caregiver.

Reconnective caregiving here involves becoming an advocate for the wellbeing of the person with disability and the need to live a life that is socially valued and that has meaning. The stronger the pre-existing social networks, the greater the capacity to achieve these goals for the disabled adult. Generally, the facilitation of productive work for the person with severe disability requires complex negotiation on the part of the carer and the capacity to maintain the invisibility of the process. The following example outlines the role of family caregivers in arranging sustainable employment for an individual with a brain injury.

Barry had a severe head injury at age 18 and for the following six years he was either in rehabilitation or in the process of being assessed while his family tried to get the funding which would allow him to move away from home safely. There were several attempts to help him move into a place of his own, but each time he came home more miserable and unwell. His neuropsychologist said that he would never work and could 'only ever do attractive leisure pursuits'. His physiotherapist said that it was 'not so much a question of having a faulty starting motor, it was more one of not having a starting motor at all.

In looking for an employment opportunity for Barry we initially researched the possibility of attending the one sheltered employment opportunity in town. Barry was vehemently opposed to it. His feelings did not change over time. We then approached the all the employment agencies in town, but none could help. We asked around, like at local dairies, but they refused as soon as they heard of the brain injury. We then used personal contacts to get him a job at a printers. People were friendly, and he was careful and precise in doing the work. After a few months we asked whether he could be paid and they said that he would have to go. Eventually we found him a job at the Student Association, helping to put notices on boards. They paid him a little and we topped up the wage out of his care package, so that it was the minimum wage. This solution worked effectively for over ten years and gave him regular part time work with all the benefits that came with that in terms of self-esteem and friends (Butler 2010).

In another case described by Butler (2010), a family was able to also provide employment for their brain-damaged son using individualised funding. With the individualized funding the family was able to put into place a number of creative solutions that matched the fluctuating ability of their son. For instance they made an arrangement whereby a builder was paid to supervise their son while he worked on a building site. This gave the son great satisfaction, even though he was working as a volunteer and even though he was not able to sustain regular work attendance. The family also used the funding to employ a handyman to work alongside their son and together they began to renovate houses. This gave the son some income, because he was eventually able to rent out rooms to tenants in these houses. The family set up a trust so that he would be able to benefit from this income and this proved to be a sustainable work solution over time.

Both cases illustrate the often unseen work of caregivers in supporting the person with disability to become reconnected with the wider community through employment. Interestingly, the sheltered workshop movement in New Zealand was driven by families who believed that it was important their family members be given a way of benefiting through engagement in productive work. This was particularly for those with intellectual disability, but such workshops were also used by a wide range of people with acquired severe disability, particularly those with brain injury. The disability movement has subsequently, and quite legitimately, labelled sheltered employment as an example of a paternalistic charity model which exempted people with disabilities from the normal employment conditions and protections afforded all other workers. Exemptions have now been removed from minimum wage laws and this has effectively forced the closure of these parent driven initiatives. This has, however, in the New Zealand context, had a significant impact on those who are not able to get paid work in the employment market.

6.4.1 Facilitating Connectedness and Ensuring Formal Care Sector Responsiveness

As noted earlier, an intrinsic but unrealized part of the work of family carers to facilitate reconnection is the way that they embed the person with disability within their community and family narrative. During the time of treatment and rehabilitation this community typically includes medical personnel. The narrative work, as we have suggested, involves re-making connections and helping others to see the person with disability as someone worthwhile in spite of the impairment. Johansen (2002) realized in the early days following her son's injury the extent to which she was trying to create a narrative. She described, here, how she felt as she left the first hospital that had cared for him and transitioned to the next stage in his rehabilitation.

> What I longed for at the time of this transition was some kind of marking to place on our path or some ritual that would help us convey the significance of all that had transpired in our lives... we appeared to walk out of the medical narrative as impersonally as we had come into it... Only retrospectively have I realised the extent to which I was conceiving Erik's journey through brain injury as a narrative. As I reached into the profound silence of coma with words and images, I was attempting to weave a story from the chaos that might help Erik and us eventually hobble toward meaning (Johansen 2002, p. 75).

We outlined in Chap. 4 difficulties when informing the parents of the diagnosis, focusing on the medical information and failing to integrate it into a personal narrative. Here, Johansen (2002) is describing creating a new narrative around her son, Erik, following his brain injury. This narrative became a way of bridging gaps through the different worlds that she had to help him traverse.

> I discovered how sharply our lived personal stories –which were sustained by multiple subplots, extended across generations, laced with symbols and filtered through our values – were shattered and ignored by the medical world. Despite their vocation as healers, the medical personnel held a far narrower and more mechanistic view of reality than ours. Faced with this alarming realization, I learned quickly that for Erik's survival we would find a way to bridge the gaps in language between the two styles of discourse and their purposes (Johansen 2002, p. 75).

When she began to realize her experience as a caregiver was poorly understood by the medical professionals, she began to assume responsibility to ensure her story, and that of Erik's, was better appreciated. She assumed responsibility to ensure that those working with her son saw him within the context of his whole life, and not merely in narrow medical terms. She connected the narrower medical focus to the wider holistic reality of Erik's life. Only a close family member with an intimate knowledge of his life would be able to provide such a perspective. Amongst other things, this part of her role emphasizes what in other contexts is referred to as the 'expertise' of informal caregivers in terms of the knowledge they bring to the care situation. This, too, is very much a work of reconnection, and attempt to reconnect the threads of Erik's life with the family and with the new social world he would inhabit.

Through this narrative work, she was able to draw other people into Erik's story. She came to the realization that she depended on everyone who came into contact with him to be answerable to his situation. In this way her informal care was the bridge to other forms of care, far beyond the immediate family. Answerability in this sense refers to the way that the sense of responsibility is extended beyond the immediate informal caregiver to everyone who comes in contact with the disabled person. It involves communicating that formal carers can make a difference beyond their assigned care work roles by responding to the whole person. They greet Erik on entering the house, his room, they tell him what they're doing for him, with him, they take an interest in his activities, or interests. Their response is to Erik, rather than a task-focused set of actions for him. It involves communicating that formal carers can make a difference beyond their assigned care work roles by responding to the whole person. Johansen was aware that she was trying to influence others to respond with care to her son from the moment that he had his brain injury.

> While he was comatose Erik was not only apparently far beyond our discernible reach but also totally dependent on the expertise of people whom we didn't know and who didn't know us. With the exception of two hours each twenty-four hour period for the first three weeks, we had to relinquish our vulnerable son to the care of those unknown. This absence of control to protect, to care for, or even to try to rescue endured. Sometimes our powerlessness battled brutally with our determination to influence, what others might have regarded as control, the quality of care Erik received and to affect its outcome (Johansen 2002, p. 186).

The sense of answerability points to the wider social network context and to the permeability between the boundaries of formal and informal care.

> From our personal decision to stay aggressively engaged with Erik through every stage, and from the generous attention Erik received from a host of people, the ground of our ethical thinking radically shifted from justice to care to answerability (Johansen 2002, p. 195).

Johansen had to very palpably learn of her own helplessness in the face of the full range of needs that Erik had. Yet she was able to trust that those who came in touch with him would be accountable for good care, to Erik himself and to her. Through the responsibility and focus on empowerment of everyone who came into contact with him he eventually made his way into a life where he gained qualifications and a job. What Johansen does not make explicit in this account is the extent to which she facilitated the capacity of others to remain responsive to the whole person needs of her son.

6.4.2 Advocating to Ensuring Formal Care Sector Accountability

The section above shows the way caregivers develop skills as advocates in support of the person with the acquired disability. There is, however, another form of advocacy that is important and it relates to the way family caregivers hold others who work with the care-recipient responsible and answerable for their actions.

We currently know very little about the extent of abuse and what form it takes among those who are being cared for in the community by low paid workers with little training or supervision. Occasionally there are headlines which bring extreme cases to public attention.[1] Family caregiver oversight is critical in terms of monitoring the potential for abuse in cases of severe disability as even the most articulate and experienced adults can experience abuse. Family caregivers often become aware that abuse has happened by subtle signs of disturbance in a family member who cannot articulate their experience. This is one of the worst nightmares for a family carer who may only use paid care as a respite when they are already at the end of their tether.

In cases of severe disability there is often a requirement for high levels of both formal and informal care. Ensuring formal care workers remain answerable for and to the person with disability extends beyond the general advocacy for the relationship-based care referred to above, to a concern with protecting the care-recipient from neglect. This is particularly the case in situations where poorly paid and untrained formal care workers provide care that is inadequate. The quality of formal care, be it provided regularly or as respite, very much reflects the conditions under which it is given. All too often, care providers face a shortage of trained staff, and a lack of financial and other resources. Family carers in need of respite often face further anxieties, therefore, around the level of training of formal caregivers and the ability of these caregivers to meet the needs of their loved one.

The role of informal family carers in ensuring continuing responsibility is further highlighted in the following case:

> John was employed at the docks and running his own small farm when he was involved in an accident involving an exploding tyre. This left him so severely brain injured that it was impossible to assess the full extent of his cognitive damage. He was cortically blind, partially deaf, incontinent and unable to communicate except through random sentences. He lacked the capacity to regulate temperature and was very sensitive to noise and confusion. At the time this story was written his wife had become overwhelmed by the task of supervising the numerous paid carers who came into the house. His daughter arrived and she realized quickly that he was being neglected to the point where it was life threatening.
>
> 'When I came back I would spend hours and hours reading up in the diary about him because I was concerned when I saw the fact that he had two drinks in sixteen hours, two drinks of coffee. He actually asked me for a glass of water, he actually said 'water,' so I gave him water and I got very spun out when I saw this and thought 'my god what has been going on?' Dad was in bed; the house was freezing cold up in dad's end where the bedroom was. He was lying with a sheet over him and he was wet with urine' (Butler 2010, p. 7).

The oversight of paid carers is often part of the work of ensuring that others remain answerable to the person with disability. Kittay (1999) was in the enviable position

---

[1]For example, a situation such as that of a 56 year old man with tetraplegia killed by his paid worker (van Beynen 2010, Thursday, 17th June).

of being able to employ a carer to work with her daughter Sesha. This person (Peggy) stayed with her for over 20 years, which permitted Kittay to develop her career while still having her daughter live with her at home. She called the model she moved to as one of 'distributed mothering': 'I am Sesha's one mother. In truth however, her mothering has been distributed across a number of individuals: her father, various caregivers and Peggy.'

Kittay's situation is relatively unusual. More often when support is offered to family carers it is frequently offered in the form poorly paid and untrained carers. This effectively acts as a form of rationing (Duffy and Waters 2008) since family carers can feel forced to make a judgement that the disabled person would not be safe.

Recognising caregivers and people with disability as experts within their own lives can present a profound challenge to the professional. This is highlighted particularly clearly when arguments are developed against the payment of family carers, as is evident in the example of the group of New Zealand families taking a case against the Ministry of Health to the Human Rights Review Tribunal in 2010. The position of the Ministry reflects first, concerns over cost containment and secondly, a reluctance to recognise significant caregiving work of family members. If attention is paid to what families actually do as caregivers, such arguments against the payment to carers cannot be sustained (Butler 2010). Our argument throughout the book is that caregiving is a significant extension of what families normally do, and when it constrains the caregiving family member from leading a normal life, then that caregiving should be considered as work.

6.5 Summary

When an adult acquires disabilities, the experience of individuals and their families is traumatic. A key part of the trauma relates to the challenges to meanings of independence and autonomy associated with adulthood, and the transition for the person with disability towards dependence on care. The disability movement has rightly drawn attention to the way meanings of dependence and care can have significant negative implications for people with disability. Becoming a caregiver of an adult who through injury or illness develops disability brings these issues to the fore. It leads to fundamental existential questions for the person with the disability and for family members. It leads to the redistribution of roles within the family in response to the new need and to stresses on family relationships and spousal relationships in particular.

However, caregiving is experienced in many different says. It should not be automatically supposed that carers will frame their experience in terms of burden, especially in the early days of caring. Coping mechanisms tend to be initiated at various levels: intrapersonal, interpersonal and through practical strategies (McKenna et al. 2012). Some carers in McKenna et al.'s (2012) study identify areas of post-traumatic growth, indicating, in our view, a sense of reconnection.

In this chapter we have focused on the potential for the family to develop and construct its own narrative as a way of making sense of the new adult identities, as a way of making sense of the disability and of retaining the connectedness with the person with disability. Reconnections in this situation also include attempts to reestablish links outside of the family, these efforts being usually focused on the labour market and meaningful work. While the focus is on the adult with disability in efforts to reestablish those links, doing so has significant implications for the informal caregiver. Informal caregivers therefore become involved in working to maintain connectedness of the person with disability as a way of supporting their own connectedness.

Discussion Questions

What unique challenges does adult onset disability present for both the person with the disability and the person who takes on the role of primary caregiver? What are the implications for spousal or other close family relationships?

What is meant by reestablishing connection through narrative?

Give examples of the contribution of caregivers (such as their knowledge, skills, creating networks, and advocacy).

Discuss the idea that family caregivers should be paid for their work. How could this be done? What would be the basis for this? How would the work then be monitored?

Further Reading

Berry, J. (2009). *Lifespan perspectives on the family and disability*. Austin: Pro-Ed.
Dell Orto, A., & Power, P. (2000). *Brain injury and the family* (2nd ed.). Boca Raton: CRC Press.
Johansen, R. (2002). *Listening in the silence, seeing in the dark: Reconstructing life after brain injury*. Berkeley: University of California Press.
Nelson, H. L. (2001). *Damaged identities: Narrative repair*. Ithaca/London: Cornell University Press.
Priestley, M. (2003). *Disability: A life course approach*. Oxford: Polity Press/Blackwell Publishing Ltd.

References

Arango-Lasprilla, K., Dezfulian, T., Kreutzer, J. S., et al. (2008). Predictors of marital stability 2 years following traumatic brain injury. *Brain Injury, 22*(7–8), 565–574.
Bartholomew, K., & Horowitz, L. M. (1991). Attachment styles among young adults: A test of a four-category model. *Journal of Personality and Social Psychology, 61*(2), 226–244.
Bowlby, J. (1988). *A secure base: Parent-child attachment and healthy human development*. London: Routledge.
Brown, A., Leibson, C., & Malec, J. (2004). Long-term survival after traumatic brain injury: A population-based analysis. *NeuroRehabilitation, 19*, 37–43.

Burchardt, T. (2003). *Being and becoming: Social exclusion and the onset of disability* (CASE Report 21). Report prepared for the Joseph Rowntree Foundation, ESRC Centre for Analysis of Social Exclusion, London School of Economics, London.

Butera-Prinzi, F., Charles, N., Heine, K., et al. (2010). Family-to-family link up program: A community-based initiative supporting families caring for someone with an acquired brain injury. *NeuroRehabilitation, 27*(1), 31–47.

Butler, M. (2010). *How should we care for the carers?: A care ethic for informal carers*. Wellington: Ministry of Health.

Cameron, J., Franche, R., Cheung, A., & Stewart, D. (2002). Lifestyle interference and emotional distress in family caregivers of advanced cancer patients. *Cancer, 94*, 521–527.

Carpinter, A., & Irwin, C. (2000). *Just surviving: Talking with parents of children with very high disability support needs about how they get by*. Wellington: New Zealand Ministry of Health.

Crimmins, C. (2000). *Where is the mango princess?* New York: Alfred E. Knopf.

Dell Orto, A., & Power, P. (2000). *Brain injury and the family: A life and living perspective*. New York: Springer Publishing Company.

Duffy, S., & Waters, M. (Eds.). (2008). *The economics of self-directed care*. London: Control Publications.

Elbaum, J., & Benson, D. (2007). *Acquired brain injury: An integrative neuro-rehabilitation approach*. New York: Springer-Science Media.

Finkelstein, V., & French, S. (1993). Towards a psychology of disability. In J. Swain, V. Finkelstein, S. French, & M. Oliver (Eds.), *Disabling barriers – Enabling environments* (pp. 26–33). London: Sage.

Foster, A., Armstrong, J., Buckley, A., et al. (2012). Encouraging family engagement in the rehabilitation process: A rehabilitation provider's development of support strategies for family members of people with trauma. *Disability and Rehabilitation, 34*(22), 1855–1862.

Frank, A. (2002). *At the will of the body: Reflections on illness*. Boston/New York: Houghton Mifflin.

Frankel, H., Coll, J., & Charlifue, S. (1998). Long term survival in spinal cord injury: A fifty year investigation. *Spinal Cord, 36*, 266–274.

Gillett, G. (2002). You always were a bastard. *The Hastings Center Report, 32*(6), 23–28.

Hughes, K., Bellis, M. A., Jones, L., Wood, S., Bates, G., Eckley, L., McCoy, E., Mikton, C., Shakespeare, T., & Officer, A. (2012). Prevalence and risk of violence against adults with disabilities: A systematic review and meta-analysis of observational studies. *The Lancet, 379*(9826), 1621–1629.

Johansen, R. (2002). *Listening in the silence, seeing in the dark: Reconstructing life after brain injury*. Berkeley: University of California Press.

Kittay, E. F. (1999). *Love's labor: Essays on women, equality and dependency*. New York/London: Routledge.

Mazur, E. (2006). Positive and negative events experienced by parents with acquired physical disabilities and their adolescent children. *Families, Systems & Health, 24*(2), 160–178.

McKenna, A., Wilson, F. C., & Caldwell, S., et al. (2012). Decompressive hemicraniectomy following malignant middle cerebral artery infarctions: A mixed methods exploration of carer experience and level of burden. *Disability and Rehabilitation, 34*(1), 1–11.

Oliver, M. (1989). Disability and dependency: A creation of industrialized societies. In L. Barton (Ed.), *Disability and dependency* (pp. 6–22). London: Falmer Press.

Oliver, M. (1990). *The politics of disablement*. Basingstoke: MacMillan.

Oliver, M. (1996). *Understanding disability: From theory to practice*. London: Macmillan.

Panko Reis, J., Breslin, M., Leszzoni, L., & Kirschner, K. (2004). *It takes more than ramps to solve the crisis of healthcare for people with disabilities*. Chicago: Rehabilitation Institute of Chicago.

Pinto, P. E. (2008). *Impact of brain injury on caregiver outcomes and on family quality of life*. Ph.D. Dissertation, State University of New York, Buffalo.

Shakespeare, T. (2000). *Help*. Birmingham: Venture Press.

Shakespeare, T. (2006). *Disability rights and wrongs*. London: Routledge.

Sit, J., Wong, T., Clinton, M., Li, L., & Fong, Y. (2004). Stroke care in the home: The impact of social support on the general health of family caregivers. *Journal of Clinical Nursing, 13*(7), 816–824.

Stiell, K., Naaman, S., & Lee, A. (2007). Couples and chronic illness: An attachment perspective and emotionally focused therapy interventions. *Journal of Systemic Therapies, 26*(4), 59–74.

Suh, M., Kim, K., Kim, I., Cho, N., Choi, H., & Noh, S. (2005). Caregiver's burden, depression and support as predictors of post-stroke depression: A cross-sectional survey. *International Journal of Nursing Studies, 2*(6), 611–618.

Van Beynen, M. (2010). *Killer thought victim better off dead*. Christchurch: The Press. 17 June 2013.

Webster, G., Daisley, A., & King, N. (1999). Relationship and family breakdown following acquired brain injury: The role of the rehabilitation team. *Brain Injury, 13*(8), 593–603.

Chapter 7
Caring for Older People

7.1 Introduction

As the population ages, a growing amount of the additional care needed will come from informal caregivers. This chapter reviews the experiences of becoming a carer and caring for an elderly spouse, partner, parent or neighbour. The rites of passage framework is employed here to identify the transition processes of separation, liminality and reconnection. The impact of the disability and the extent of the caring relationship are seen in spatial and temporal reconsiderations of daily life, in the changing relationships between spouses and kin, and in the introduction of health service personnel. Reconnection is considered as finding meaning and making sense of one's life story in the new care role. Further, at a practical level, reconnection implies connectedness with others, both kin and care professionals, and a shared responsibility in the caregiving role.

This chapter examines the implications of ageing-in-place for older people who become frail and/or disabled and their caregivers. Our focus here is on the experience of informal caregivers. How do family members and friends who take on the role of caring experience that change in their lives? Community dwelling older people who become frail or disabled receive most of their care from family and friends (Jette et al. 1992, pp. 193–194; Noonan et al. 1996, p. 314). Barrett et al. (2005) found that frail older people who continued to live in their own homes were sustained by the help and care of spouses, adult children and grandchildren. Adult children provided a raft of tangible and intangible supports that made possible their remaining at home, and if not mitigating the need for externally provided services then they were able to complement formal services. The support ranged from assisting with personal care, providing transport, social contact and outings, preparing meals, shopping, paying bills, gardening, lawn mowing, home maintenance, spring cleaning and more. In a similar way, being in a couple household provided for the practical support of frail partners. In couple-households there was often a cooperative exchange of abilities where the losses of one partner were compensated for by the abilities of the other, and vice versa – something that might

P. Barrett et al., *Family Care and Social Capital: Transitions in Informal Care*, 109
DOI 10.1007/978-94-007-6872-7_7, © Springer Science+Business Media Dordrecht 2014

be described as 'cooperative compensatory living' (Barrett et al. 2005). Having a spouse as a caregiver did protect against the need to move into more supported housing arrangements.

7.1.1   Defining Informal Care in This Situation

Caregiving in this context needs to be distinguished from intergenerational and spousal assistance or help. Caregiving for an ageing family member who ages-in-place involves giving assistance 'beyond that which is required as a part of normal everyday life' (Walker et al. 1995, p. 402). Such care may be provided for an ageing family member as a consequence of debilitating conditions such as arthritis, sensory loss, Parkinson's Disease, or following the onset of frailty. Helping and giving assistance are a part of the normal exchanges within family relationships. It is well known that gender is an important factor in explaining caregiving in family contexts, with women carrying out many tasks that might be considered as a part of everyday household work, such as meal preparation, cleaning and laundry. Many women may not, therefore, distinguish such tasks as divergent from the norm, when such care extends to that which is required as a part of normal everyday life. Walker et al. (1995) point out that this subjective dimension to the definition of informal caregiving means there is a need to look more carefully at care in this context. What distinguishes informal care from normal intergenerational or spousal care is 'dependence on another person for any activity essential for daily living' (Walker et al. 1995, p. 403), both instrumental activities of daily living (such as cleaning, laundry and meal preparation) and activities of daily living (such as bathing or walking). So shopping for a spouse or parent is not considered informal care unless the spouse or parent is unable to do that alone. It is the level of frailty or disability of the care-recipient rather than the actions of the caregiver that is important. Care and support can be given to both non-dependent and dependent spouses and parents. When the care-recipient is dependent, however, there are important differences in the frequency and amount of care given, and, significantly, the meaning of that help from the perspective of the caregiver.

Social and emotional support is also a part of caregiving in this situation. Exchanges involving the provision and receipt of social and emotional support are very much two way, and are well known to affect the quality of the care relationship. The social and emotional dimension is central to caregiving and is closely tied up with the actual instrumental assistance that is provided. The social and emotional aspect of care is also closely linked with the consequences of caregiving and care receiving. Walker et al. (1995, p. 404) emphasise, too, that care-recipients continue to play an important role in such affective exchanges, particularly in care situations involving ageing family members, by providing social and emotional support themselves.

The experience of caregiving for an ageing parent will be influenced by the gender and generational dimensions of the care exchange, by the relationship between the caregiver and the care-recipient, and by their personal history (Fine 2007; Finch and Mason 1993). As Walker et al. (1995) suggest, the meaning associated with becoming a caregiver will therefore vary according to these dimensions:

> An older man may believe he is not dependent for assistance in household tasks, even if he is clearly unable to do them because his wife has always done these tasks. Her perception of his dependence may be quite different from his. Further, caregiving tasks may be less stressful if caregivers perceive them to be an extension of intergenerational or spousal assistance they have provided for years. In fact for women who provide IADL assistance, it may not be the tasks that are stressful, but the meaning assigned to those tasks when a loved one is *dependent* on their care. … In contrast, men (and women) who lack experience in IADL and ADL task provision may [find it more of an adjustment] to cook, clean, bathe, and provide other care efficiently and effectively (p. 404).

Individuals will experience becoming a caregiver quite differently. Jeggels (2006) describes this as 'role fitting,' as individual family members adjust their family role to the new needs caused by the disability. Taking on the caregiver role is normally an expression of duty, affection or reciprocity within the context of families or among neighbours, an expression of Putnam's (2000) bonding social capital. With care among spouses, it is an indication of an ongoing commitment to a partner. While care flows in both directions throughout the family life course, at earlier life stages care and practical help tend to flow from parents to children. When parents age and become frail or disabled, the dynamic tends to be reversed, although practical financial help may continue from parents to children and grandchildren.

The motivations for spouses and adult children to care does derive from a sense of family with handed-down expectations of behaviour. Motivations to care are often based on the nature of the care expressed in earlier life stages (Fine 2007). This sense in which belonging within a kin group adds a 'moral dimension … is closely related to identity' (Finch and Mason 1993, p. 170). Identities such as a reliable son, a generous mother, a caring sister are constructed and then confirmed through the caring process. This is evident when caregivers say they are merely acting 'like my mother did'; 'I saw my mother care for my grandparents.' The significance of a family's oral history of caregiving cannot be underestimated: 'Mother cared for her parents, because her mother, my grandmother, cared for her parents,' and so a moral family identity has been constructed.

Becoming an informal caregiver to an ageing spouse, parent or neighbour beyond that which is a part of everyday life is, we suggest, an important transition point in a person's life. It is a point where some 'sort of enduring psychological shift' takes place (Rutter 1996, in Nolan et al. 2003, p. 92). Although not ritualized in the accepted sense of ritual, the processes are sufficiently routinized with identifiable marking points to merit designating them as 'stages' and we relate these stages to the rites of passage concept which enables us to gain new insight. One of those flashes of insight identifies an initial stage of separation, which we suggest comes at the time of assessment, diagnosis, and disclosure. Another insight relates to the recognition of experiences of caregiver liminality, of being on a threshold with its concomitant anxieties and fears. Reconnection in the Van Gennep (1909) description implies reintegration into the community and societal acceptance of the new identity. We might think of this in terms of social recognition and valuing of informal caregivers and acceptance of informal caregiver claims in government policy.

7.1.2   The Increasing Importance of Informal Care in This Situation

What follows is our review of the experience of passage through these stages when becoming an informal caregiver for an older person. An increase in the number of older people in industrialised countries ageing-in-place does mean there is a concomitant increase in the need for aged care and support, and this is most often provided by family members. For couples, caregiving usually means staying together and continuing to share a household and home, and adapting their lifestyle to cope with disabilities. Adult children who are the other main caregivers for older people, can house their elderly relative, but more usually live separately and provide care through regular visits (Grundy et al. 1999), with most older people preferring to live independently, i.e., in their own homes (Peace and Holland 2001; Grundy 2006).

In many countries these trends of living 'independently' at home have been reinforced over the past 20 years by greater emphasis being placed on provision of home-based services and growth in the number of retirement villages which provide for various levels of supported housing. The trend is clearly evident in a comparison of the proportion of older people in long-term care in Auckland, New Zealand in 1988 and 2008. Broad et al.'s (2011) research shows that while the size of Auckland's population over the age of 65 increased by 43 % over the 20 year period between 1988 and 2008, the actual numbers in residential homes fell. Proportionally, it fell from 1 in 13 to 1 in 18, or in age-standardised rates, from 65 to 33 per thousand. Broad et al. (2011) found that if the same proportion were in long-term rest-home care in 2008 as were in such care in 1988, the number of people in rest-homes in 2008 would have been 74 % higher than it was. The age-standardised rate of older people in residential aged care has therefore been halved over the 20 year period from 1988 to 2008, this being powerful evidence of the ageing-in-place philosophy being implemented in practice. The researchers speculated that the tighter implementation of standardised needs assessments before entry, growth in the availability of home-based services, and growth in the number of retirement villages had led to the lower rates of residential care use. It is in this context that there is an increasing demand for care from family members and friends. The trends in New Zealand are evident in many countries. Further indication of the growing demand for informal caregivers can be found in Pickard et al.'s (2000) analysis informal care in the U.K. She projects an 81 % growth in the U.K. informal care workforce over the next two decades. As it is, the 2001 U.K. Census found that around six million people provide care on an unpaid basis for a relative, friend or neighbour in need of support due to old age, disability, frailty or illness.

7.2 Separation Experiences

Becoming a caregiver of an aged spouse or parent involves taking on a role which goes beyond the usual norms of kinship (Biegel et al. 1991; Finch and Mason 1993; Cook 2007). There is a point where there is a realisation of the significance of the new role, this being reinforced by the recognition by friends and other family members of that role, and wider recognition by health professionals. It is a point, as Janlov et al. (2006) observe, where there is a commitment and realization that there is 'no turning back' (p. 30). The separation experience can be sudden – as when a family member suffers a traumatic health event, but often the separation experience is one that occurs slowly – the slow accompaniment to an increasing level of frailty or disability. Self-awareness of this is often retrospective: 'It can sneak up on you' and 'by the time you recognize what you are doing, you're into it,' as one of Hale's (2006, pp. 144–145) respondents said.

Wilson (1989) and Willoughby and Keating (1991) refer to the 'noticing' stage in the care transition, the noticing of unusual behaviours and of taking on of new roles: 'I never used to have to do this' or 'it's different from when he was well.' It is the noticing of a gradual change of gait or pattern of speech, with, perhaps, an increasing slurring of words. Initially, such changes are explained as tiredness, over-busyness, stress, but these 'rationalisations' tend to be replaced by suspicion of something more serious. Noticing and searching for explanations tend to be followed by visits to health professionals and diagnoses. With diagnoses, caregivers begin to reflect on how the role of spouse or child has changed and are likely to change.

Awareness of the significance of the role occurs in large part through the acknowledgement of others such as health professionals who carry out assessments and develop care plans. It is these exchanges that lead to caregiver support and respite opportunities to enable the care to continue as a substitute for residential care. A significant indicator is being included in information distribution and in care decision making. Finding out information, meeting with professionals supporting at the bedside, being involved in discharge plans, grows into a role of managing the care of the parent or spouse. It ultimately can include persuading a parent or spouse to move into residential care or take advantage of formal care or respite care opportunities, or working with health professionals to achieve this goal.

7.2.1 Realising Responsibility: Temporal and Spatial Dimensions

The temporal dimensions to separation experiences associated with becoming a caregiver at this life stage include either gradual or sudden role adoption. The nature of disability or illness determines whether there is a single decision or action, embodied in an 'impulse to care' or whether there is a series of actions moving the family member deeper into the caregiving role (McGrew 1991, in Atchley and Barusch 2003). Gradual role adoption, where the 'caring sneaks up on you' often involves a family member beginning by taking over different domestic duties, or taking responsibility for driving, for organising home matters, or for bill payments. Sudden role adoption sees the spouse or adult child catapulted into responsibilities for domestic and personal care work, decision-making and oversight of the wellbeing of the cared-for person. Diagnosis and disclosure, usually by a doctor, is one significant point in time when suspicions and the slow onset and noticing are crystallised into a certainty of a continuing role change for both the person in need of care and the caregiver.

The formal needs assessment which follows a diagnosis, where the older person in need of care is appraised within his or her living environment is a critical event. Assessment of the 'environment' includes taking into account possible forms of informal support. The assessment therefore also takes account of the potential caregiver and his or her ability to give care. Such recognition of a spouse or adult child as being the responsible provider of help and care at home is a type of official social recognition of the role of caregiver. It is a confirmation of the adoption of the caregiving role, a clear marker of the new identity of caregiver, and is often associated with entitlement to formal home care, respite care, and other caregiver support and information.

Becoming an informal caregiver leads to changing daily rhythms, these shaped by the care needs of the older person. It implies adjusting to the slower disability time of the cared-for person, and to the temporal schedules of formal care services that become involved. The public world of the formal care system intrudes into the private world of home. The formal care worker arrives at times which suit her and her agency, and other services such respite care and caregiver supports create a new household rhythm to fit in with officially defined entitlements. The former temporal rhythms of the home are broken.

Temporal dimensions of change are closely linked with spatial dimensions. The time taken to help the care-recipient to go out, the time taken for personal care, for domestic cleaning exemplify this. When a spouse or adult child becomes a caregiver for a frail or disabled older person, they often face change in their physical living environments in spatial terms. It may involve relocating 'home' to co-reside with or be near to the person in need of care, it may involve bringing the person in need of care into the home, or it may involve a reorganisation of space within the home. The ability of adult children to provide care is affected by their proximity to their disabled parent. One response of families which are geographically dispersed is for the parent to move in with the adult child and his or her family. Caring at home within the context of ageing-in-pace introduces tensions between the home being a space for family and wider social interaction, and with the home becoming a space for the delivery of care. These might be thought of as changes that challenge the meaning of home.

One of the most common changes for older people who remain in their own home is the reorganisation of space to accommodate the disability and need for care: the changing use of rooms for example, where a caregiver might create a 'hospital-at-home' room for his/her spouse, with a hospital bed, a commode, space for walker, wheelchair, and other paraphernalia of disability. The toilet might have a raised seat and grab rails, the shower a special shower chair, or a bath-board across the bath. This assists not only the family caregiver but also the formal caregiver to provide the care, but in spatial terms it signifies the changing meaning of the home. So, for the caregiver, the meaning of home is changed – it becomes a site for the delivery of care. When formal care is provided, Hale (2006 p. 157) observed a considerable emotional impact in watching someone else do what the family carer normally did: 'she takes my space.' The formal care worker worked with the familiar body, the familiar home space, but did things differently from what the wife or adult child was accustomed to do.

7.2.2 Negotiating New Relationship Dynamics

Becoming an informal caregiver for a parent or spouse also involves important changes in the social world of the caregiver. These include relationships with the cared-for person, with other family members, with the wider social environment, including relationships with the workplace, and with medical and allied health and social care professionals. One interesting socio-linguistic marker of change in relationship dynamics between the caregiver and cared-for person was identified by members of a caregiver group initiated by Hale (2000), where the caregivers who were spouses began to stop using the pronoun 'we' of couples, and began to use the 'I' of an individual indicating, amongst other things, a change in relationship, in authority and in responsibility for making decisions. One of Hale's (2006) participants commented: 'Holding my husband's penis for the district nurse to insert a catheter was the turning point for me' (p. 145).

This signifies an important change to, and even the loss of, a significant relationship with a frail or disabled loved one. Accepting responsibility for the spouse or parent and taking actions mark the move to a caregiver role; initiating contact with health professionals or a care agency, ensuring discharge plans for care are in place, and keeping an eye on the care worker. Accepting responsibility and taking action in terms of hands-on body work is an important indicator of change in the relationship – a separation from what had been before. When formal care is a part of the support provided to the older person, it is the acknowledgement by health professionals which leads to caregiver support and respite opportunities.

7.3 Liminality or 'Living on the Brink'

Liminality indicates discontinuity, a threshold between what has been and the future, a state of betwixt and between and, as such metaphors suggest, the emotions here are of anxiety, bewilderment, confusion and fear. Stoltz et al. (2006) observe that family caregivers do 'worry a great deal about the future' and there is 'much despair.' There is a continuing anxiety about the future, both that of the care-recipient and their own. Wilson (1989) referred to the type of experience we describe as 'living on the brink,' a comment fitting well with the notion of liminality or of being on a threshold. Liminars, in Van Gennep's (1909) writing, were usually spatially separate from the rest of the tribe, until their knowledge of the new stage was complete, when they would be allowed to return to the tribe and be recognised in their new identity. The separation we are considering does not see informal caregivers removed from the situation of care. The liminal experience takes place in the familiar environments of home and the less familiar environment of a hospital ward or doctor's surgery.

For an individual who is becoming a caregiver, a lack of familiarity with assessment processes and eligibility criteria leaves them in a state of confusion and dependence of the health and care professionals involved. Their ambivalent status in medical environments is linked with the little recognition they receive from health professionals for their interest in and knowledge of what is needed. The experience of liminality, as Olaison and Cedersund (2006) suggest, is not only one of confusion, anxiety, and of searching for a way through bewildering new systems, but also of learning to negotiate within these systems. There is an important stage, therefore, of learning the game. This is, however, a game where the assessors are in charge, controlling the dialogue with the recipient and, when included, the caregiver. The subsequent allocation of care responsibilities affects caregiver capacity to control the organisation of their daily lives, influence choices about housing and household organisation, and constrains the capacity for social participation as an individual, couple or family. Again, we examine this experience of being betwixt and between in temporal terms of daily rhythms and future care, in spatial terms as decisions are being made about care needs, and in relational terms.

7.3.1 Temporal and Spatial Liminal Experiences

Becoming an informal caregiver of a parent or spouse introduces new demands on one's time, simply to meet the practical and emotional aspects of care. Caregivers continue to experience a loss of control over the organisation of their daily routine, they feel bound to the house, unable to travel too far away for too long, and find it essential to limit their own personal activities. As we saw in reviewing experiences of separation, new time schedules are introduced within the care household. The schedules of formal care workers and of health practitioners begin to shape the organisation of household routines. These often conflict with the private time and expectations of care households. There are considerable tensions between the different time frames of care recipients, family carers and formal care workers (Twigg 2000). While older people structure their lives through domestic and social routines, and the slow time of disability, they perceive time and priorities differently from public health service agencies (Biggs 1993; in Richards 2000, p. 37). These care service agencies need to manage the competing claims of numerous clients and the need to coordinate care worker times, both of which have an impact on the long-experienced home routine.

Spatial liminality involves a loss of the order which previously existed and the trial and error of changing spaces, of improvisatory practices as caregivers learn how to give the care required. For some families, the space of home changes its meaning as it becomes dominated by aids. The reorganisation of rooms and the presence of aids leaves a sense that home just does not seem the same anymore. Moving bedrooms to accommodate a cared-for person, reorganising a front room, a public room, to accommodate the personal care and functional needs of a care-recipient change the landscape of the home and, in a way, publicise the care needs.

As we have seen in other chapters, the spatial and behavioural impact of care at home will have an impact on the caregiver's other relationships, both close and those in more distant social networks. Households with aged members have built up long established modes of social participation within the home and outside of it. Such modes of participation tend to be associated with family and wider social conventions, something Saarenheimo et al. (2004, p. 13) refer to as specific 'rules regulating the visits of friends and relatives.' When there are difficulties in offering hospitality and in actively maintaining pre-existing networks, these factors lead to changes in the social networks for both husband and wife. Close family networks may become more closed, or new networks of professionals and caregiver supports may develop around the care situation. Temporal, spatial and relational dimension of caregiving in this situation are therefore closely connected.

7.3.2 Relational Liminality

The experience of liminality includes feelings of uncertainty that accompany the introduction of formal home help. This can be a relief that help is available, according to some caregivers. Such formal help can be seen both as a 'wonderful support,' 'I don't know what I'd do without her,' or it can accentuate negative feelings such as a threat to independence; a sense of failure in fulfilling promises for better or worse; feelings of intrusion of a non-family member into the intimate spaces of the home; and, an extension of that feeling, a realisation of the gatekeeping power of health professionals in care situations. This points to experiences of relational liminality (Milligan et al. 2005; Aronson 1999).

Relational liminality can be seen in the ambivalent status informal caregivers have in relation to health and formal care professionals. Many are excluded from full participation in decisions made for the older person, but which have life changing implications for the caregiver. Concerns by health and care professionals to protect the privacy of the cared-for person can reinforce this. Informal, family caregivers often, therefore, can be left with the responsibility of meeting care needs but not be recognised or given due consideration in decisions about the cared-for person.

In becoming informal caregivers, individuals build up detailed knowledge about the cared-for person. Caregivers learn the skills of caring by doing – by the hands-on care, emotional and behavioural care, and coping with, for example, the difficulties of dementia. Some health professionals are meticulous in asking for caregiver input, acknowledging their expertise and knowledge. Others are less able to recognise this knowledge, and, in fact, may give very little time to become involved with the family care situation. Family caregivers at this stage in the process are, however:

> at a loss of what to do … family carers might feel confused about which services are available and from which institutions or agencies. … Not knowing what to do and feeling abandoned or alone with caregiving could be labelled as feeling unsupported, for although the family carers are in need of support, they are also expected, sometimes by others but also by themselves, to support the person they care for (Stoltz et al. 2006, p. 603).

The sense of responsibility to meet the needs of the cared-for person and a feeling that it is to be faced alone can be overpowering. Within this context, the experience of engaging with health and care professionals is critical. The quality of service at this stage of the care process determines the extent to which carers feel supported or alone. Where there are too few resources allocated, and where limited time for both face to face and other forms of support is constrained, caregivers are left with a sense of isolation in the new role.

Family caregivers also face wider social isolation as the demands of the new role weaken their ability to maintain social connectedness. The constraints of the caregiving situation on spontaneity and mobility outside of the home, a reluctance to leave the care-recipient alone, and difficulties in entertaining friends and family all come together to reduce opportunities for wider social engagement. Difficulties in sustaining leisure activities and related social networks can lead to increasing isolation. Twigg (2000) and Janlov et al. (2006) emphasise that there is limited understanding of these issues, and it is our observation that such social isolation reinforces feelings of anxiety typical of the liminar.

At the same time, the relationship between the caregiver and cared-for person also changes. Becoming a caregiver involves carrying out personal care tasks that challenge earlier bases of a spousal or parent-child relationship, such as showering or toileting. The structure of the relationship in terms of traditional roles changes when one partner becomes dependent on the other for care. Spouses often experience a tussle for authority (Hale 2006, p. 149). These relate to the management of medication, the performance of domestic work, the preparation of meals, personal care, and house maintenance. Each of these can be a point of some resistance and opposition from the cared-for person. The comment from one carer, 'I've stopped being a wife' captures this role change.

Taking responsibility for physical safety and hygiene is another part of the role change in the transition from an adult child to a filial caregiver; for the dirty intimate work of toileting, showering, 'cleaning up' a parent's body. Adult sons and daughters who care face similar liminal experiences. In one sense, the relationship is a continuation of family care norms, yet in another, it exceeds these norms, by redefining the boundaries and content of the son or daughter-parent relationship.

Personal care is difficult for an adult child to manage, especially when different genders are involved. Such work is often seen as a taboo area for adult children. Daughters showering fathers, sons helping mothers on the toilet, find the intimacy intrusive and embarrassing, as indeed do many of the care-recipients (Jeggels 2006; Hale 2006).

Many adult children who care for a parent, particularly daughters, are also recognised as facing 'sandwich generation' issues – caring for individuals at both older and younger life stages. Changing work practices mean more women in their middle years are in employment and, as we have seen in other chapters, balancing care work and employment is increasingly a challenge. Employment consequences for adult children caregivers include loss of income and difficulties in returning to the workforce if time is taken out for caring (Bourke 2009; Stoller 1983; Raschick and Ingersoll-Dayton 2004; Cook 2007).

Caring for an older parent or spouse is also linked with health problems, physical and mental. Caregivers in this situation often face pressure to leave the workforce to meet caregiving expectations or to take lower paying jobs (Bourke 2009, p. 10). Davey and Keeling's (2004) research showed that for the New Zealand women with caregiving responsibilities, their care work was 'invisible,' not appreciated and not taken into consideration in their place of work (in Bourke 2009, p. 10). Further, many older women involved in caring for a spouse of parent are often reluctant to let their employer know about the extent of their care work as it is expected to lead to forms of discrimination in their workplace. A large number used work time for caring, as well as annual leave. Many took advantage of flexible working hours (Bourke 2009, p. 11). Decreasing work hours is common, and the pressure to do so is greater if the condition of the older person deteriorates. The lack of understanding from workplaces and assumptions that there are networks of support for family caregivers, leaves many daughters who become caregivers of parents stressed, concerned that they may need to take more time off as the need increases, and isolated. These demands and stresses do tend to lead to a higher degree of negative feelings about the care situation.

7.4 Reconnections

Becoming a caregiver of a dependent, aged parent or spouse challenges the meanings attached to earlier roles and relationships. Searching for meaning is a part of the liminal experience. Finding meaning and making sense of the care situation in terms of one's life story implies reconnection. While becoming an informal caregiver presents many difficulties and stresses, the capacity to make a 'larger sense' of the situation, as Pearlin et al. (1990, in Noonan et al. 1996, p. 314) observe, has been found to be an important factor in coping. The way caregivers see their situation and ascribe meaning to it is linked with their ability to cope. Meaning in this sense, as Rubinstein (1989) defines it, is 'the often affectively laden array of significations and associations individuals attribute to the events they experience' (p. 119).

Giuliano et al. (1990, p. 2) define meaning in this context as 'positive beliefs one holds about one's self and one's caregiving experience such that some benefits or gainful outcomes are construed from it.'

Positive outcomes do tend to be disregarded in the caregiving literature (Jorgensen et al. 2010), although there are studies that report both stress and satisfaction. There is an association between high levels of caregiving and both high stress and high satisfaction (Walker et al. 1995, p. 404). Both can co-exist. As we have noted, caregiving can lead to lives that are rigidly scheduled, with less flexibility and a loss of privacy, but it also leads to emotional satisfaction (Scorgie and Sobsey 2000). Studies that identify positive outcomes for caregivers suggest it can be an enjoyable and a positive transformational experience. It can improve the quality of the relationship and, within the context of that relationship, can be an important form of social and emotional support to both the care-recipient and the caregiver. With this in mind, we turn now to consider issues of reconnection.

Reconnection implies a social context – connection with others – and in caring we believe Stoltz et al. (2006) have captured this sense of connection when they describe the experience of 'togetherness with others' and 'togetherness with oneself.' Stoltz et al. (2006) have studied the experience of caregivers of older people at home with a view to understanding the meaning of support. Their findings are most helpful in making sense of the meaning of reconnection at this stage of life. Their analyses pointed to the importance of a sense of togetherness with others in the care tasks as a key to managing and coping. While they acknowledged that there was a large amount of evidence indicating that the 'effectiveness of interventions for family carers is not convincingly strong' (Stoltz et al. 2006, p. 595), with much research focussing on the negative outcomes of caregiver burden and stress, they were concerned with understanding better what characterised positive outcomes. They examined what support for family caregivers, in the form of day care services, respite care, telephone support, online support and group sessions, meant to those receiving that support.

In the context of our concern with reconnection, the idea of being connected can be taken to imply not being alone in the caregiver role and being able to share the responsibility for decision-making or the practical tasks of caring. It is this sharing of the role that provides caregivers an assurance in, as Stoltz et al. (2006, p. 595) state, the 'resourcefulness of others.' Being connected to support provides caregivers an assurance that others, be they health professionals, care workers, or wider family and friends will ensure things work out well, and that they will be 'helped to help their loved one' (p. 595). It his having their needs recognised that provides reassurance, and this can be contrasted with the feelings of abandonment, of having care situations dismissed or unacknowledged which occurs when support is not forthcoming.

Alongside a strong sense of assurance in the resourcefulness of others, Stoltz et al. (2006, p. 595), along with Scorgie and Sobsey (2000), identified confidence in the 'resourcefulness within oneself,' a sense of calm and confidence in knowing how to respond in caregiving situations and in where to turn for rightful help. Caregivers who felt this assurance of their own resourcefulness were said to be connected with themselves, their own strength or ability to cope, and their capacity to ensure their own needs were met within the caregiving situation.

Connectedness in caregiving, therefore, was understood as meaning 'togetherness with others' and a sense of 'togetherness with oneself.' When caregivers felt a sense of togetherness with others, they described 'feeling encircled by action potential ... [a] sensing of a network that would step in, should they need it, ... [this being] a great asset to them in the reassurance of honouring the promise that many had made to care for their relative at home' (Stoltz et al. 2006, p. 600). A strong sense of trust that someone else 'could step in and take over caring, should the need arise' provided reassurance that family caregivers would be assisted in coping with the practical and felt demands of caregiving. It was a sense of shared responsibility and knowledge that someone else could step in if required that provided this assurance, and of not being 'the sole accountable bearer of the wellbeing of their relative or for making decisions pertaining to the health of the person cared for' (Stoltz et al. 2006, p. 601).

While these experiences imply reconnection, a lack of connection implied ongoing liminality – being alone with the responsibility, feeling overwhelmed by that responsibility and as a consequence, feeling unsure and apprehensive. The feeling of having nowhere to turn, no one to turn to is captured in the comments of one of their respondents:

> Because this was unbelievably tough, this was probably the toughest time when nobody listens, they listen to you and say certainly, right, sure we will do that, and then nothing happens. I think that is really bad because you should keep your promises ... You called: "No it's not our pigeon"; "No, it's not us"; "No, we have to have a referral from the physician" ... so that it was, mmm, yeah five, six places before we got hold of someone who could help (Stoltz et al. 2006, p. 601).

Our suggestion is that to assist such reconnection there needs to be an acknowledgement and use of both bonding and bridging social capital. Where natural bonding resources, such as the family and wider networks within a local community do not exist, it is formal health and welfare agencies which have the potential to create and maintain informal networks of care. Supporting a strong volunteer network is one means of ensuring this; another is constructing and maintaining community resources so individual situations are recognised and isolation is diminished.

7.4.1 The Meaning of Care in This Situation

While there are many difficulties and costs for caregivers, the capacity of caregivers to deal with those consequences is influenced by the meanings they give to caring. Noonan et al.'s (1996) study of informal caregivers of older people found themes of 'gratification and satisfaction, friendship and company, improved relationships and personal growth' (p. 324) typified the positive meanings given to the role. They outlined the case of Ms A., a 54-year-old widow who took care of her co-resident 80 year old mother.

Ms. A.'s mother was bedridden and required substantial care given a progressive muscular disorder. Her mother had difficulty speaking and Ms A. bathed her, prepared her meals, did her laundry, and provided company. She was assisted by a neighbour and her older sister who checked in on her mother while she was at work, and she received some assistance from her son and daughter on weekends. Apart from this, Ms A. received no further assistance. As well as being the primary caregiver for her mother, she kept the house and worked full-time as a nurse. Ms A. was found clearly to enjoy caring for her mother and she intended to continue doing so, believing she provided better care than that which would be given in a nursing home. She took pride in the care she provided and saw her role as maintaining her mother's dignity. Ms A. saw her care as an expression of family responsibility and a form of reciprocity.

> Well, I suppose it is a burden in the respect that … you don't have as much freedom and leisure time as a lot of your peers, or … other family members. … But I figure … I'm doing the best I can, and if I can give her the care that she needs, as long as I can, I'll be glad to do it. … It's a labor of love. …
>
> I'm very proud … Everybody tells me I should be proud that she has no broken sores. Her skin is very soft, you can take her hand and feel it. Her skin, everybody remarks, "God, her skin is like a baby." I say, "Well, she's being reborn." … I mean, you bathe them in just the way you bathe yourself, But, don't take their privacy away from them, either. … She's fully covered at all times. I mean, don't expose them. I think that humiliates and degrades the people who are bedridden, or that need to have care. … I know, it would degrade me, especially, if you're a proud person. … It helps them to maintain their dignity. … I don't mind it. You only get one mother. … She did a lot for nine children that she raised. And, I mean, one way of paying back. I think that … the world needs … a lot more people to take care of their parents. They took care of them all their lives. And, we have to pay them back, one way or another.

Noonan et al. (1996) also told the story of Mr B. a 49 year-old man who cared for his 81-year-old mother. His mother had moved to be closer to Mr B. and she lived 5 minutes away. She had a number of medical problems and was also being treated for depression. Like Mrs A., Mr B. provided a great deal of care – he prepared meals, oversaw her medication and diet, provided transport for medical appointments, managed her finances, and performed various other day-to-day chores. Mr B. was assisted in the care of his mother by a home health worker who prepared meals and provided assistance with bathing some afternoons. Mr B. also saw his care work as an expression of family responsibility and reciprocity:

> It has to be done. Somebody has to do it. It's my mother. So, I don't mind doing it. Because it's my mother. But I wouldn't want to make it a lifelong profession. . I've just resigned to the fact that I'm gonna do it. I have to do it… Nobody else is gonna do it, so I just do it it's automatic. Yeah, I'd like to have my own life. But I know I can't. … I still got a long life ahead of me. She's not gonna live a million years. … She gave me the best years of her life.
>
> She's not gonna get the care at a nursing home that she would get here. … Some people just put 'em away. You don't have to deal with them. … Let someone else deal with them. And all you got to do is pay 'em. Some people think like that. I can't think like that. I couldn't do it. … I could make life easier for me just putting her somewhere. … But . I haven't got it in me to do that to her. … And, I feel that if I'd a put her in the nursing home that she wouldn't be here today.

The positive interpretations of the care work role implied a sense of reconnection. Both Ms A. and Mr B. had taken responsibility, but they were supported in the role, and while they were the primary caregivers, they were not alone. A combination of wider family and neighbourly support, and formal care services were combined to sustain the caregiving in these situations.

7.4.2 Policies to Support Reconnection

Formal care services, therefore, have potential to play a critical role in supporting connected caregiving. They can complement the day-to-day, round-the-clock care of family caregivers by providing episodic support and more specialised care to the older person when required. Day care services, respite care, education, telephone support, online support and group sessions for caregivers have potential to supplement and enhance informal care. Seen as something that complements rather than supplants informal care challenges views which suggest formal care services somehow weaken the incentives for family members to care for their own. Such views are influential among policy makers who look for arguments to cut the costs of formal care, but they are not empirically supported and serve only to weaken the capacity and sustainability of family and informal caregiving. The resources of the formal care sector, in terms of information, expertise and funding need to be seen as complementary to the resources of informal caregivers.

Within the context of the aging-in-place philosophy and the expansion of services oriented towards keeping people in the community and in their own homes, policies are being developed to encourage informal caregivers to care for as long as possible. In the UK, the Carers (Recognition and Services) Act 1995, and subsequent Acts, recognised 'those who were providing substantial levels of informal care and support … [as having] the right to an assessment of their own needs over and above the person the cared for' (Milligan 2009, p. 65). The 2008 UK 'Carers at the Heart of the 21st Century' report has recognised the dichotomous social trends of ageing-in-place and its associated dependence on informal care, and trends in labour force participation and family structure. This policy has stated the need to place informal, family care at the centre of family policy, acknowledge informal caregivers as 'expert partners in care,' provide access to support to reduce caregiver vulnerability to caregiving related hardship and begin to recognise and value informal care. Similarly, in New Zealand, the 2008 Carers Strategy and Five Year Action Plan has been developed to value and support New Zealand family caregivers. The strategy aims to:

> improve the choices of … informal carers so they can better balance their paid work, their caring responsibilities and other aspects of their lives, [and ensure caregivers are] properly recognised and supported in their caring role so every New Zealander can have choice and opportunities, in a society that respects and values them (Carers NZ 2008, p. 5).

Whether these policy goals are continuing to be pursued by the allocation of government resources in the current financially constrained environments remains to be seen. Nevertheless, these initiatives do point to the need for good information and the need to support informal caregivers to make connections with other caregivers.

Informal caregivers of an ageing spouse, parent or neighbour face the real threat of social isolation and the breakdown of prior social connections as a consequence of the responsibilities and demands of caregiving. Meeting with other informal caregivers through caregiver support groups is an important way of promoting the development of new connections and friendships. Such groups often develop a momentum of their own and informal caregivers can move from being a recipient of support in such environments to being providers of support and knowledge to other informal caregivers. Support groups of this type do address the feelings of being alone in the caregiving role; they do facilitate new friendships; they are a valuable repository of information and knowledge and a grounded vehicle for sharing that knowledge. As Milligan (2009, p. 131) says, they are a way of sharing the experiences and challenges of caregiving – the 'frustration, anger, guilt, betrayal and grief.' They facilitate reconnection in a practical way and offer a new and valued social identity. The interaction provides an opportunity for decisions about caregiving to be shared, and can help deal with the negative feelings associated with informal caregiving. Sharing decisions with group members or with members of the wider family does help the caregiver cope. Specialised caregiver support groups, such as those for Parkinson's Disease, stroke victims and Alzheimer's Disease, are also important for the specialist knowledge they impart. They are disability specific, which has the advantage of informing caregivers about the progress of the disability, as well as providing for the exchange of practical tips for caring. In the absence of specialized groups, neighbourhood-based supports have potential. Helping out through visiting, sitting with the cared-for person while the caregiver has a break, washing, shopping, and rubbish disposal might be seen as the spontaneous expression of neighbourliness. Such neighbourliness is often available but not encouraged and little notice tends to be taken of community willingness to help.

When caregiving is socially valued and informal caregivers recognised for what they do, they are more likely to feel connected with others and confident in the identity as a caregiver. There is a movement to raise the profile and recognition of informal caregivers. The same concern to increase choice and control for health and social care services is beginning to be extended to caregivers. Following their comprehensive review of databases on choice and decision-making in social care services, Arksey and Glendinning (2007) found limited attention given to the issue of choice for caregivers. An earlier literature search by Arksey et al. (2005) found data from a number of studies showed there were a variety of constraints that impacted on caregiver choice. These included limited budgets for statutory services, tight eligibility criteria, a restricted range of service options, and the limited availability of agencies and paid care staff to provide the care required. Those with responsibility for allocating services were also found to constrain choices by not explaining available help, by describing limited choices or by operating unofficial rationing procedures (Arksey et al. 2005). The new concern to observe and address issues of caregiver choice is an outcome of the struggle for improved recognition and support for the informal caring role. Choice, however, is only possible if there are options which people value and would choose. Choice requires a variety of service options to different situations and requirements. In pursuing this, the UK Caregivers strategy proposes policy makers pursue 'active partnership with caregivers and their organisations to help ensure that services are responsive to the needs of caregivers' (Arksey and Glendinning 2007, p. 168).

7.5 Summary

As the population ages, much of the care and support for older people will be provided by informal caregivers, primarily spouses and/or adult children. Becoming a caregiver in this situation involves taking on a role that goes beyond the normal bounds of familial care and support. Spousal relationships change as one partner becomes dependent on the other and new relationship dynamics occur. We reviewed spatial and temporal liminal experiences for the caregiver. They also share the vulnerability to social isolation that the cared-for person faces. Reconnections in this context, therefore, involves not being alone with the responsibility for the life of another, but having support and respite. Reconnected care is that which is socially valued and which has positive meaning for the caregiver.

In our discussion of reconnections we have described different social assets available to carers. We have concluded by focusing on the availability of choices as a means of sustaining care. Choices relate to reconnecting to the wider society, whereby carers can either be employed, with flexible working hours to fit with caregiving, or can at least have the time and spatial freedom given by, for example, respite care, a daycare or day-sitting service. These choices, both informal and formally created, relate to the social capital which can sustain the carer. Being connected in the role, therefore, includes having the situation recognised as a priority to others, be they professionals, adult children or friends. It means that the caregiving is not unacknowledged or invisible, but that the role is known, understood for what it is and socially valued. Being connected implies having the struggles associated with caregiving in this situation acknowledged and being listened to.

Discussion Suggestions

In what ways does informal care for an ageing parent or spouse differ from the normal patterns of kinship support within families?

What is the impact on the relationship between the caregiver and the care-recipient?

What does reconnection mean in this situation?

How might support from the formal care sector facilitate reconnection in this new role?

Further Reading

Finch, J., & Mason, J. (1993). *Negotiating family responsibilities*. London: Routledge.
Janlov, A., Hallberg, I., & Petersson, K. (2006). Older persons' experience of being assessed for and receiving public home help: Do they have any influence over it? *Health & Social Care in the Community, 14*(1), 26–36.
Pickard, L., Wittenberg, R., Comas-Herrera, A., Davies, B., & Darton, R. (2000). Relying on informal care in the new century? Informal care for elderly people in England to 2031. *Ageing and Society, 20*, 745–772.
Twigg, J., & Atkin, K. (1994). *Carers perceived: Policy and practice of informal care*. Buckingham: Open University Press.

References

Arksey, H., & Glendinning, C. (2007). Choice in the context of informal caregiving. *Health & Social Care in the Community, 15*(2), 165–175.
Arksey, H., Kemp, P., Glendinning, C., Kotchetkova, I., & Tozer, R. (2005). *Carers' aspirations and decisions around work and retirement* (Research Report No. 290). London: Department for Work and Pensions.
Aronson, J. (1999). Conflicting images of older people receiving care: Challenges for reflexive practice and research. In S. M. Neysmith (Ed.), *Critical issues for future social work practice with aging persons* (pp. 47–70). New York: Columbia University Press.
Atchley, R., & Barusch, A. (2003). *Social forces in aging*. Belmont: Wadsworth.
Barrett, P., Kletchko, S., Twitchin, S., Ryan, F., & Fowler, V. (2005). *Transitions in later life: A qualitative inquiry into the experience of resilience and frailty*. Tauranga: University of Waikato.
Biegel, D., Sales, E., & Schulz, R. (1991). *Family caregiving in chronic illness: Alzheimer's disease, cancer, heart disease, mental illness and stroke* (Family caregiver applications series). Thousand Oaks: Sage Publications.
Biggs, S. (1993). *Understanding ageing: Images, attitudes and professional practice*. Buckingham: Open University Press.
Bourke, J. (2009). *Elder care, self-employed women and work-family balance*. Palmerston North: Massey University.
Broad, J., Boyd, M., Kerse, N., et al. (2011). Residential aged care in Auckland, New Zealand 1988–2008: Do real trends over time match predictions? *Auckland: Age and Ageing, 40*(4), 487–495.
Carers NZ. (2008). *Carers strategy and Five Year Action Plan – Ministry of Social Development*, Wellington. http://www.carers.net.nz
Cook, T. (2007). *The history of the carers' movement*. London: Carers U.K.
Davey, J., & Keeling, S. (2004). *Combining work and eldercare: A case study of employees in two city councils who provide informal care for older people*. Wellington: Department of Labour.
Finch, J., & Mason, J. (1993). *Negotiating family responsibilities*. London: Routledge.
Fine, M. (2007). *A caring society? Care and the dilemmas of human service in the twenty-first*. Basingstoke: Palgrave Macmillan.
Grundy, E. (2006). Ageing and vulnerable elderly people: European perspectives. *Ageing & Society, 26*(1), 105–134.
Grundy, E., Murphy, M., & Shelton, N. (1999). Looking beyond the household: Intergenerational perspectives on living kin and contacts with kin in Great Britain. *Population Trends, 97*, 19–27.
Giuliano, A., Mitchell, R., Clark, P., Harlow, L., & Rosenbloom, D. (1990, June). *The meaning in caregiving scale: Factorial and conceptual dimensions*. Second Annual Convention of the American Psychological Society, Dallas.

Hale, B. (2000). From partner to carer: A description of changes in language and networks amongst family caregivers. *Social Work Review, New Zealand, 12*(1), 7–10.

Hale, B. (2006). *The meaning of home as it becomes a place for care – The emergence of a new life stage for frail older people?* Ph.D. Thesis, University of Otago, Dunedin.

Janlov, A., Hallberg, I., & Petersson, K. (2006). Older persons' experience of being assessed for and receiving public home help: Do they have any influence over it? *Health & Social Care in the Community, 14*(1), 26–36.

Jeggels, J. D. (2006). *Facilitating care: The experiences of informal carers during the transition of elderly dependents from hospital to home – A grounded theory study.* Ph.D. Thesis, University of the Western Cape, Cape Town.

Jette, A., Tennstedt, S., & Branch, L. (1992). Stability of informal long-term care. *Journal of Aging and Health, 4*, 193–211.

Jorgensen, D., Parsons, M., Jacobs, S., & Arksey, H. (2010). The New Zealand informal caregivers and their unmet needs. *The New Zealand Medical Journal, 123*(1317), 9–16.

McGrew, K. (1991). *Daughter's decision making about the nature and level of their participation in the long-term care of their dependent elderly mothers: A qualitative study.* Oxford: Scripps Gerontology Center.

Milligan, C. (2009). *There's no place like home: Place and care in an ageing society.* Aldershot: Ashgate Publishing Ltd.

Milligan, C., Bingley, A., & Garell, A. (2005). 'Healing and feeling': The place of emotions in later life. In J. Davidson, L. Bondi, & M. Smith (Eds.), *Emotional geographies* (pp. 49–62). Aldershot: Ashgate Publishing Ltd.

Nolan, M., Lundh, U., Grant, G., & Keady, J. (2003). *Partnerships in family care; Understanding the caregiving career.* Maidenhead: Open University Press.

Noonan, A., Tennestedt, S., & Rebelsky, F. (1996). Making the best of it: Themes of meaning among informal caregivers to the elderly. *Journal of Aging Studies, 10*, 313–327.

Olaison, A., & Cedersund, E. (2006). Assessment for home care: Negotiating solutions for individual needs. *Journal of Aging Studies, 20*, 367–380.

Peace, S., & Holland, C. (2001). *Inclusive housing in an ageing society: Innovative approaches.* Bristol: Policy Press.

Pearlin, L., Mullan, J., Semple, S., & Skaff, M. (1990). Caregiving and the stress process: An overview of concepts and their measures. *The Gerontologist, 30*, 583–594.

Pickard, L., Wittenberg, R., Comas-Herrera, A., Davies, B., & Darton, R. (2000). Relying on informal care in the new century? Informal care for elderly people in England to 2031. *Ageing and Society, 20*, 745–772.

Putnam, R. (2000). *Bowling alone.* New York: Simon & Schuster.

Raschick, M., & Ingersoll-Dayton, B. (2004). The costs and rewards of caregiving among aging spouses and adult children. *Family Relations, 53*(3), 317–325.

Richards, S. (2000). Bridging the divide: Elders and the assessment process. *British Journal of Social Work, 30*(1), 37–49.

Rubinstein, R. L. (1989). Themes in the meaning of caregiving. *Journal of Aging Studies, 3*(2), 119–138.

Rutter, M. (1996). Transitions and turning points in developmental psychopathology: As applied to the age span between childhood and mid-adulthood. *International Journal of Behavioural Development, 19*(3), 603–626.

Saarenheimo, M., Nikula, S., & Eskola, P. (2004). *Exploring the cultural borderlines of family caregiving.* Paper presented at ISER, University of Essex. www.soc.surrey.ac.ukcragISA2004/symposia/symp_session1.hm

Scorgie, K., & Sobsey, D. (2000). Transformational outcomes associated with parenting children who have disabilities. *Mental Retardation, 38*, 195–206.

Stoller, E. P. (1983). Parental caregiving by adult children. *Journal of Marriage and the Family, 45*(4), 851–858.

Stoltz, P., Lindholm, M., Uden, G., & Willman, A. (2006). The meaning of being supportive for family as narrated by registered nurses working in palliative homecare. *Nursing Science Quarterly, 19*(2), 163–173.

Twigg, J. (2000). *The body and community care*. London: Routledge.

Van Gennep, A. (1909/1960). *The rites of passage* (M. B. Vizedom & G. L. Caffee, Trans.). Chicago: University of Chicago Press.

Walker, A., Pratt, C., & Eddy, L. (1995). Informal caregiving to aging family members: A critical review. *Family Relations, 44*, 402–411.

Willoughby, J., & Keating, N. (1991). Being in control: The process of caring for a relative with Alzheimer's disease. *Qualitative Health Research, 1*(1), 27–50.

Wilson, H. (1989). Family caregiving for a relative with Alzheimer's dementia: Coping with negative choices. *Nursing Research, 38*(2), 94–98.

Chapter 8
Caregiving Across the Generations

8.1 Introduction

Children and teenagers often play a central role in providing care to another family member, and increasingly grandparents are being recognised for their role as caregivers of their grandchildren. Caregiving at these ages is recognised as constituting a unique experience requiring responses appropriate to the specific needs of either early or latter stages of the life course. In this chapter we highlight these informal caregivers and the particular needs they face. Perhaps more than other caregivers, children and grandparent caregivers share the vulnerability of those they care for. These caregiving situations involve particular experiences, each with its own challenges and need for age appropriate forms of support.

Younger and older caregivers have their own distinctive vulnerabilities, unique to their different ages. Older people who care in this situation are often facing their own age-related frailties or disabilities, and children and teenagers are seen as needing care and support themselves. Our aim in this chapter is, first, to recognise and draw attention to these groups and, second, to identify how their experience of caregiving is both similar to and different from other care situations. What follows is a review the issues faced by each group – the practical, personal, social, and financial implications of providing care in these contexts. We conclude by considering the types of supports necessary to support caregivers of these ages and facilitate effective caring in these contexts.

8.2 Young Carers

Child labour in the formal economy continues to be a problematic issue in some 'developing' countries, but in 'developed' economies, children are largely protected from expectations that they participate in paid employment, except in ways that supports their development or within family enterprises as a part of the family

P. Barrett et al., *Family Care and Social Capital: Transitions in Informal Care*,
DOI 10.1007/978-94-007-6872-7_8, © Springer Science+Business Media Dordrecht 2014

endeavour. Child labour as we understand it today is, historically, a relatively new concept. Depictions of children in pre-seventeenth century European paintings capture the predominant views at the time. Children were seen as 'mini-adults' who worked to contribute to the family income during the Industrial Revolution, working in the streets, in mines, factories, as chimney sweeps, and as agricultural workers (Aries 1962). Internationally, the trend has been to develop policies which outlaw child labour.

Childhood is now widely accepted as a life stage where the focus should be on nurturing growth and development towards adulthood. In theory it is viewed as a 'special' or 'protected' phase, with adults, state agencies and social welfare professionals charged with safeguarding and protecting children and young people until they make the transition into adulthood (Dearden and Becker 2000; Frank et al. 1999). Social expectations and cultural norms today see children as dependents. It is a time of age-related play and socializing, these being recognised as important in supporting their informal and formal learning. In western constructions of childhood, it is an age without the responsibilities of adulthood, where children are seen as being dependent on care and are not expected (or encouraged) to take on significant or regular caregiving responsibilities (Becker 2007, p. 1). It is against this backdrop of norms and social expectations which translate into policies to support childhood as a time of learning, growth and development, that we can consider the experiences of children who become informal caregivers.

Estimates of the numbers of young carers are difficult to obtain, although a 2010 BBC survey in the United Kingdom found there was an 'invisible army' of children carers that was considerably greater than the 2 % estimated from the UK 2001 census. But there are difficulties in counting such numbers in different countries. Fares and Raju (2007) comment on difficulties in estimating rates of child labour in the developing world, particularly when it comes to counting work performed by girls given the greater likelihood of that work being focussed on the family household. They observe that domestic work performed by girls is not classified in many countries as child labour and it is therefore not counted (see also the International Labour Organisation, Conventions and Recommendations on Child Labour, 1999, on caring labour).

In developed countries, however, caregiving is generally assumed to be an adult responsibility, with children not usually expected to provide care beyond that which is considered 'normal' within the context of mutual exchanges within family interactions. To describe such activities as 'normal' is to recognise they involve age-appropriate care tasks well within the child's capabilities. But over the past two decades there has been a growing level of attention to the characteristics and experience of younger people who take on informal caregiving roles.

Identifying younger caregivers as a group does bring greater visibility to the role and distinguishes the defining activity of caregiving from what children 'normally' do. The term 'young carer', then, embodies major contradictions. The term 'young caregiver' does juxtapose 'child' against 'caregiver' and, according to Stables and Smith (1999), creates a contradiction which challenges our notion of both terms:

The idea of a young (child) carer sets up a series of contradictions – an adult is dependent on a child/children are dependent on adults – that combine to threaten ideological constructions of both childhood and parenting (p. 259).

Such contradictions are as significant for the adult as for the child. For example, by highlighting the dependency of the adult are we confronting the success or otherwise of the parenting? How far can different societies support these adults or parents in terms of their disability, to empower them to continue parenting? By highlighting the independence of the child, we are confronting our cultural notions of childhood and beliefs that it is a time to be without responsibilities. How can we support both partners in this care relationship?

Being open about the role played by younger caregivers is not something families are always prepared to do. Gays (2000; see also Aldridge and Becker 1994; Becker 2007) suggests that families can become anxious about health and welfare officials intervening in their care arrangements, fearing their child may be taken into care. As a consequence, when describing the way care is provided within families, parents tend to downplay the actual role of younger caregivers. Younger caregivers themselves do this too, motivated by the same fears and from family loyalty, affection and love.

Our awareness of this group and its particular characteristics has developed somewhat more slowly than the awareness of adult informal caregivers. One reason for this is that children caregivers have been a hidden population. There are several reasons for this; the first is that care and help is expected as part of family duty, just as it is for adult caregivers, and such caring tends to be taken for granted. A further reason is that families dependent on child caregivers are often hidden given the stigma attached to the conditions requiring the care, and the fear the child will be removed by welfare authorities if the extent of their care work is known, with the consequence that the family unit be broken up (Becker et al. 1998). There is growing recognition of the need for support for child carers by organisations such as the UK National Young Carers Coalition and like organisations in developed countries.

8.2.1 Who Are Young Carers?

We define young carers as children or young people up to the age of 18 whose life is affected by looking after a family member with a chronic illness or disability, or who is coping with an injury or mental illness (Lunn 1990; Franklin 2002; McDonald et al. 2009). There is a sizeable but somewhat hidden group of younger caregivers. Reports of the number and situations of young caregivers are beginning to become available, although, as we have noted, there are challenges in surveying this hidden population (see also Cass et al. 2009). These challenges are illustrated in the re-analyses of UK census data which attempted to measure the size of this group in 2001. The 2001 census estimated 1.4 % of all children between 5 and 15 were providing informal care to a family member. Re-analyses of these results, however, by the Loughborough-based Young Carers Research Group concluded this was a significant undercounting. Dearden and Becker (2004) estimated the rate to be at least twice that reported. They noted that the census did not define the amount and nature of the care provided, and they suspect that under-reporting was a consequence of the reluctance of young people to disclose their situation to officials or even to other young people.

In the US, Hunt et al. (2005, p. 6) found there were approximately 1.3–1.4 million child caregivers between the ages of 8 and 18, with 3.2 % of households with a child of this age having a role of informal caregiver. With a total of 28.4 million households, this meant 906,000 households had a child caregiver. These households tended to be those of minority groups with lower incomes and they were more likely to be single parent households. The most common conditions leading to the need for care were Alzheimer's disease or dementia, and diseases of the heart, lung, or kidneys, arthritis, and diabetes. Over half of these child caregivers helped with at least one activity of daily living and nearly all with instrumental activities. School performance and achievement were found to be affected and these caregivers were found to be more likely to show symptoms of anxiety and depression.

McDonald et al. (2009) have studied the experiences of young carers in New Zealand and they estimate that, in 2006, between 4 and 5 % of those aged between 15 and18 years cared for a member of their own household who was ill or had a disability. Additionally, 3.5 % reported having looked after someone outside their own household. This initial piece of research on the experiences of young carers in the New Zealand context arrived at similar findings to those reported elsewhere.

8.3 Becoming a Child Caregiver: Growing into the Role

Children take on caring roles for a number of reasons, primarily related to their family circumstances (Charles et al. 2008). It may be a sudden response to accident-related needs or a slower transition in a more taken-for-granted force of circumstances when, for example, a parent develops a disabling illness (Lunn 1990; Robson 2003, 2004). This is particularly the case where young caregivers become a primary carer for a parent or grandparent due to parental disability or illness. The intensity of caregiving is related to the need for care, and children often take on the role as members of a wider family caregiving team. Family caregiving norms are powerful drivers in these contexts. Those who become caregivers do so by simply growing up in a family where there is a member in need of care.[1] They grow into the role by virtue of membership of the family with caring a part of day-to-day family life. In many situations there is no one else to take on the role.

---

[1] A comment made to Beatrice Hale in 2012 by a group of young Australian caregivers emphasised that caregiving was part of family life and their role within the family.

Given that children carry out caregiving tasks because of the family relationships and the cultural expectations, we need to ask, what differentiates 'young caregivers' from other children? Morrow (2005) suggests that we make the distinction by focusing on the performance of tasks associated with supporting another person in the activities of daily living. Such activities include providing help with dressing, toileting, showering or bathing, and getting into and out of bed. They also include assisting with medication and having involvement with health professionals on behalf of another family member. In some situations it can include assisting in managing the behaviour of a family member. So young carers do whatever adult carers do (Dearden et al. 1994).

Supporting an individual in these activities of daily living can be distinguished from the instrumental activities of daily living, such as taking out rubbish and cleaning. These latter are qualitatively different and imply much less personal involvement and responsibility for the wellbeing of the cared-for person. Assisting with bodily care, toileting and mobility are deemed as adult responsibilities, yet are typically performed by children and adolescents in caregiving situations (Gays 2000).

Children who carry out personal care and support with activities of daily living are also more likely to be given responsibility for housework from a younger age, and they are more likely to perform a wider range of jobs around the house, more frequently and regularly, than children and young people who are not carers. Moore et al.'s (2005) study of 50 Australian young carers found that their caring responsibilities are more intense than their non-caring peers and were most often provided without supervision or support.

8.3.1 Positive Consequences

By successfully undertaking complex caring tasks, younger caregivers do acquire feelings of self-efficacy and satisfaction, and the greater responsibility can lead to feelings of maturity beyond their years (Banks et al. 2002). Such maturity is linked with a sense of self-worth which is derived from being needed as a caregiver and good relationships with peers and with older people (Charles et al. 2009). Some young carers, when compared to their non-caregiving peers, have a heightened understanding of the needs of other people (Grossman 1972). Young people also report that they have a positive reaction to being needed and that this contributes to a developing sense of themselves as being worthwhile, contributing individuals (Aldridge and Becker 1993; Charles et al. 2009, p. 39). There are, therefore, positive outcomes for young carers.

A further example of this is the closer attachment caregiving brings:

> [It's] good to spend time with my Mum, family stuff – it's good. I think it's good having someone care from your family because it's close family. It's not supposed to be, 'I don't do this for you, the caregiver does that.' We're family, [we] do this for each other (McDonald et al. 2009, p. 119).

Obviously, too, the skills learnt are different from those of their peer groups. They become a very skilled workforce indeed. The extent to which young caregivers develop a specialised knowledge and understanding of the care situation is evident in the following comment by Anne, a young woman who posted a brief description of her experience on the Young Carers NSW website. Her situation is a prime example of a young carer in a complex situation:

> My mother has BPD (Borderline Personality Disorder) She has had several suicide attempts and is an emotional alcoholic. She has been going on a downward spiral for about six years now and I'm almost 17. She relies on me to be her sole carer as she has on, off relationships with those around her. If someone is having a problem, she believes it is a direct cause of her or she is hurting more than they are. She then distances herself from them and continues her depressive cycle. My mother also has several incurable health conditions such as IST (Inappropriate Sinus Tachycardia) and severely low blood pressure, lung conditions, bleeding conditions, blood sugar conditions and so on. … She doesn't seem to grasp the concept of other people and their feelings towards situations and it's very frustrating. … We all love her dearly and are at a loss as to what to do. I wish I could make her okay.[2]

Not only does this statement indicate her maturity, her sense of responsibility and a quite sophisticated understanding of the care situation, it also conveys a strong sense of family.

8.3.2 Developmental Issues and Relationships

A common observation of the implications of caregiving at this age is that younger caregivers are forced to grow up too quickly and in so doing lose their childhood and their innocence. Family relationships change and roles are redefined as children shift from being dependents to responsible individuals and care providers. Being forced to deal with the world of sickness and disability and the responsibilities of caring, especially in situations of primary caregiving, leads to significant changes in the nature of the relationship with the person in need of the care, especially if he or she is a parent or grandparent.

The implications for the young person in taking on caregiving responsibilities are often reduced time for school-related activities and for initial forays into the world of paid employment. This threatens access to work and related economic opportunities in both the short and long term. They have less time for leisure, friendships and other social activities, and this contributes to social isolation. At a life stage when the younger person typically widens his or her social networks beyond the family into the world of paid employment, younger caregivers face shrinking networks, increasing their vulnerability (Hill et al. 2011, p. 194).

Young caregivers are also known to be vulnerable to physical health problems, abuse, neglect, and developmental delay, especially in the area of caring for parents with severe and enduring mental illness. Morrow (2005), in an Australian study, suggests that young carers report more injuries than other children. Muscle strain, fatigue and exhaustion are a direct result of the caring role, with the care given

---

[2] http://www.youngcarersnsw.asn.au/StoryView.aspx?PageID=1370

placing 'heavy physical and mental demands on young carers' (Gays 2000, p. 2; Aldridge and Becker 1993; Liddiard et al. 1997). They also face the stresses of the care situation. They have the emotional pressures of caregiving but often lack the support shown to adult caregivers. For young caregivers in this type of situation, according to Butler and Parr (1999, p. 60), the idea of home as a safe and secure place is contradicted by their expressions of anxiety, confinement and responsibility. This is reinforced by Fallon's (1990) comments:

> For a young carer it is not uncommon for the day to start at 5.30 a.m. with preparation of breakfast and attendance to the personal needs of the parent. The child may call home at midday to toilet the parent and prepare lunch. In the evening, shopping, cooking, cleaning may take priority over school homework. Often a child puts the parent to bed and sleeps in the same room in order to attend to him or her during the night.

As in other caregiving situations, many young carers feel tied to the home, with limited ability to do anything else, such as games, sports, leisure activities. Butler and Parr (1999) have commented that such spatial and temporal restrictions depend on the social environment of the care recipient and caregiver. In the case of sibling care, parents can make sure the non-disabled child has the ability to go out and do things. Nevertheless, Charles et al. (2009) have reviewed a number of different studies which identify the isolating nature of caregiving, not just because the young carers feel different from their peers, but also because they are unable to spend time with friends because of their home responsibilities, either in the community, at school, or back home. Frank's (2002, p. 23) comments point to some of these:

> It can be very difficult to invite friends back to our homes. This can lead to us feeling isolated and it can be very depressing and lonely. Having a boyfriend/girlfriend (inviting them home, having time to go out, and spending time together,) can be very difficult.

However, much depends on the needs of the care recipient and on the caring environment. Butler and Parr (1999) emphasise that not all young caregivers are completely tied to the home and not all parents or grandparents who become care recipients are helpless, even though they may require major assistance for activities of daily living.

8.4 Education and Employment Issues for Young Carers

A key issue for young caregivers is the impact of caring on education. Dearden and Becker (2002) examined this and observe that some educational impacts are easy to observe, such as missing school as a result of caring roles, or persistently being late from waiting for home care services to arrive, or failing to complete homework because of caregiving duties. Absenteeism, poor homework, tiredness and poor attention are all recognised as typical characteristics of young people with responsibilities as caregivers. Dearden and Becker (1995, p. 6) point to the following example where caring has had an impact on the young person's ability to focus at school:

> I just worry when I've got to go to school … I ring him [father] up at break and dinner to see how he is … I can't concentrate at school, even when I am there, there's no point in going really. When I was at school I would worry about him, whether he was OK, whether

he'd fallen, because if he fell he couldn't get up, so I did used to worry about that … I often used to phone him from school to make sure he was OK, but I'd make an excuse, 'I'm just phoning to see if the catalogue stuff has come', or something.

In more extreme situations, persistent absences from school are a result of caring responsibilities. When caring in situations where the need is related to mental health problems, for example, children may be afraid to leave family members, especially when they have a history of self-harm or suicide (Aldridge and Becker 2003). Some physical illnesses are marked by periods of exacerbation and remission and during acute phases children may also end up staying at home to *be there* in case they are needed. All of these influence educational attainment, especially when absences are regular or persistent:

> I'm not really sure [how often I miss school] it just depends how bad my dad is. If he's too bad I won't go and he says 'Go' but I won't, I say 'I'm staying here' (Dearden and Becker 1995, p. 6).

Unlike adult and older caregivers, younger caregivers are in the early stages of their lives and the responsibilities of caring have an impact on their futures, especially in they are unable to participate fully in education or successfully make the transition into paid employment. Hill et al. (2011, p. 188) show lower rates of participation in both education and employment by young caregivers compared with their non-caregiving peers. The impact on young people's futures may be most profound if they are unable to participate in either education or employment at the crucial stage of transition from high school to adulthood. The need to continue to provide care, a lack of qualifications, and a lack of money have all been identified as barriers to participation (Warren 2007, p. 143).

There is a general agreement, therefore, that younger caregivers face particular challenges. These range from personal challenges, the emotional upheaval of watching a family suffer, the difficulties of managing a complex care relationships where they have the responsibility for the wellbeing of the cared-for person, the need to develop personal skills and knowledge outside of the caregiving context, and financial and housekeeping management. There are also the challenges in maintaining social networks outside of the caregiving environment, and in managing health and injury problems (Ahmad 2000).

8.5   Reconnections? Support for Young Caregivers

As awareness of the issues facing young caregivers is growing, so too is an awareness of the types of supports with potential to enable them to remain connected. It involves, first, recognizing them and valuing their work. It implies raising awareness of young caregivers and the specific issues they face, and supporting them to become connected with formal care agencies and organisations. Young caregivers should, therefore, be included in caregiver assessments and services should be made available to support them. This will require an explicit acknowledgement of their caregiving skills and abilities, rather than patronising or excluding them from decision making about formal care that might be provided in their home. Younger caregivers acquire knowledge and skills in the same way as parent caregivers. This needs to be recognised and recognised for its contribution to social capital. At the very least, this will change the way we value their activities and contribute to ensuring young caregivers receive the similar supports made available to adult caregivers in related situations.

The following guidelines from Carers Australia (2009) outline a series of rights of young caregivers that if recognised will contribute to supporting their social wellbeing and connectedness. These include the right to be:

- Able to choose to be a carer.
- Treated separately from the person needing care.
- Heard, listened to, and believed.
- Respected.
- Able to receive respite and other health, social and practical support that are specific to your needs.
- Protected from physical and psychological harm.
- Offered access to trained individuals and agencies who can provide information, advice and support.
- Able to access independent and confidential representation in terms of needs, strengths, weaknesses and racial, cultural, and religious preferences.
- Able to appeal and complain.
- Able to choose to stop caring

(Carers Australia 2009, p. 39).

Reconnecting young carers who are susceptible to missed schooling opportunities and related educational difficulties includes, also, providing opportunities for educational support. In addition to providing help with schooling, assistance with careers advice aids the transition into the paid workforce and, more broadly, the transition into adult life. A range of support services have been developed in the UK, such as peer support networks, respite care opportunities, advocacy services, and counselling when required. These are community based services which acknowledge the uniqueness of the circumstances (Charles et al. 2008, 2009). The result has been the development of a range of support services for these young people (Bibby and Becker 2000; Thomas et al. 2003).

8.6 Grandparent Caregivers or 'Skip-Generation' Caregiving

We move now to the opposite end of the life course, the situation where older people, specifically grandparents, become carers for grandchildren. Our focus is on those who become caregivers of children with disabilities, situations where children with special needs caused by intellectual, physical or mental health disabilities are cared for by their grandparents, either as secondary or primary caregivers. The immediately recognisable similarity between grandparent caregivers and young caregivers is that caregiving at these lifecourse stages is considered as non-normative.

Numerical population ageing implies the number of older people is increasing and structural ageing implies that the proportion of older people within the population is growing in relation to other age groups. Older adults today are, however, likely to be healthier, more affluent and more active than in earlier generations. As a consequence, they are likely to experience grandparenthood and great grandparenthood for longer periods of their lives. Other social and economic changes are resulting in more older people continuing to work outside of the home, this being a change from the typical retirement scenarios of leisure, volunteering, socialising and, for some, travel. For many older people, caregiving is becoming a part of this stage of life either through caring for an ageing spouse, sibling or adult child with needs, including disability. Over the past two decades, there has been growing recognition of the role grandparents are playing in caring for grandchildren.

Much of the emerging research on grandparent-grandchildren care focuses on custodial and guardianship issues relating to caring for children without disabilities. Cass (2007), for example, links young carers with grandparents as carers for children without disabilities, reasoning that this 'second parenting' or fostering role is also a role outside the norm for this life stage. We distinguish the group of grandparents, more often grandmothers, who become caregivers for children with disabilities. This group comprises those who are fully substituting for parents, taking on fulltime the care of the children, and those who look after the children while the parents work.

8.6.1   Becoming a Grandparent Caregiver

Grandparents take on primary caregiver roles for a variety of reasons. Grandparents have tended to be a back-up to parents who were unable or unwilling to care for their child. Throughout history, and within the context of multi-generational households, this has been a common form of support for mothers. However, through the mid-twentieth century, with the decline in the size of families and the delaying of childbirth, the need for grandparent assistance has been reduced. But Janicki et al. (2000) state that recently there has been a marked increase in the number of grandparents who are becoming caregivers of grandchildren for reasons other than employment, and 'universally grandparents are becoming the exclusive caregivers for many of these children' (Janicki et al. 2000, p. 38).

The idea of family is a key motivation for grandparents who become caregivers. It is this active decision to put their family's needs first, to seek to maintain family relationships, and thus act in a way that will sustain or promote the quality of life for the family in the future that drives them (Miller et al. 2012). Grandparents become caregivers because they value keeping the family together and the importance of family ties. When they become informal caregivers, it is to support their own children who are struggling and/or who are unable to fulfil their own parenting role (Janicki et al. 2000).

While people can become grandparents at younger ages, typically the grandparenting stage of the life course is associated with people who are nearing a traditional retirement age. As such, they are more likely to face health or physical difficulties resulting from the ageing process, and they are likely to be preparing financially for retirement or be retired from full engagement in paid employment. Becoming a grandparent does not typically involve becoming a primary caregiver. It is a clearly recognised social role transition with the specific title and social obligation to support new parents. However, becoming a primary caregiver has more extensive role implications – the active, hands-on looking after, tending, monitoring, supervising and teaching tasks associated with caring for a child. Typically grandparent caregivers are women and for them caregiving becomes an all-consuming activity.

Grandparents are typically drawn into the role of primary caregiver after a precipitating family trauma. It is often sudden and unexpected, and unwelcomed (Hayslip and Patrick 2006; Minkler and Roe 1993a, b). Grandparents in this situation thus become caregivers at a time of family crisis, and this itself makes the transition more difficult (Burton 1992; Minkler et al. 1992; Shore and Hayslip 1994). The consequences for grandparents are not always positive (Burton and Bengtson 1985).

As with parents, at the time of diagnosis and disclosure, grandparents struggle with conflicting emotions – fear, anger, disbelief, but also, often, a determination to stay strong, to 'hold their emotions', for their own children as the parents of the disabled child. Grandparents have similar emotional reactions on learning of an infant's or child's disability (see Chap. 4). Katz and Kessel (2002) found that:

> Frequently grandparents find themselves in a situation where they lack the knowledge and skills to provide adequate care for the disabled child. This tends to increase feelings of despair and helplessness... However, studies have indicated that with time, grandparents adjust more positively to the child's disability than the parents, especially if they are involved in the care of the child (p. 115).

Miller et al. (2012, p. 105) refer to grandparents, too, as developing 'an emotional toughness and resilience to work positively to influence family dynamics.'

Becoming a primary caregiver as a grandparent has significant consequences, many of which are not positive. It has negative economic consequences and adverse impacts on the personal and interpersonal lives of the caregivers. These include:

> poorer physical and mental health, role overload and role confusion, and more isolation from age peers and other grandchildren. ... the incidence of such illnesses as depression, diabetes, hypertension, and insomnia is greater among grandparent caregivers, who often report more difficulty than their age peers in performing activities of daily living (Hayslip and Kaminski 2005, p. 262).

This stage of life and the ageing process brings particular needs, and Dunne and Kettler (2008) summarise these as:

limited finances resulting in having to draw on savings or retirement funds, conflict with
children's birth parents and other family members, strain on the grandparents' relationship,
lack of understanding of legal issues, restricted access to family benefits, demands of repar-
enting, difficulties dealing with schools, lifestyle changes, loss of peer friendship groups
and a return to work instead of retirement (p. 333).

In couple grandparent households, it has consequences for both partners.
Fulltime grandparent caregiving changes anticipated life course issues for older
people who are beginning to face the physical changes that ageing implies. For
example, the common plans of many retirees to migrate to a retirement zone had to
be abandoned by one couple who had assumed the role of caregiver in Miller
et al.'s (2012) findings:

[M]y husband's been talking about moving away and particularly since we've found out
about [our grandchild with disability]. I've just felt that now is not the time, so I'm not
thinking about us as far as moving away. My husband wants to retire. … he wants to go
away from the coast, I just said to him [our daughter's] situation is so difficult, she needs
the back-up and I'm not prepared to go just yet. I do see myself as a hands-on grandparent
to help her wherever I can (p. 106).

8.6.2   Family and Wider Social Relationships

Miller et al. (2012) found a significant impact on quality of life and family relationships
following the assumption of a major caregiving role by grandparents. Grandparents
appear to be regarded in the same way as other carers of people with disabilities, and
while they have much in common with other carers in that the hands-on caring demands
are the same, the differences are equally clear: they are in their older years and the
future looms much closer than that of the child for whom they care. Grandparent caregivers therefore have a unique set of experiences and needs.

One aspect of these is the relationship with the parent of the grandchild. Moreover,
stresses associated with the relationship with the grandchild's parent are also a part
of the experience of caregiving in this situation. When the needs of the child are
linked to parental substance abuse and addiction, Hayslip and Kaminski (2005, p.
263) report that many grandparents express disappointment in their own child for
creating the situation. They found one in three grandparents actually resented their
child and felt taken for granted. 'Impaired intergenerational relationships, unre-
solved conflicts, financial, educational and health factors, and geographical distance' are all factors identified by Katz and Kessel (2002, p. 116) as characterizing
the relationships between grandparent caregivers and their children. Those who
have healthy relationships with their child report feeling less resentful and bur-
dened. By contrast, the grandparents who are less involved in caregiving roles are
more likely to have a history of little involvement and negative pre-existing relationships with the parent (Mirfin-Veitch et al. 1997). Some families clearly have stronger
social bonds and are able to offer unconditional love and support, while others are
more distant.

Becoming a caregiver of a child as a grandparent is also linked to weakened wider social networks. This is associated with conflict between the expected life-course experienced by the peers of caregivers and the caregiving demands of grand-parents. The need to meet the practical demands of caregiving means grandparents become occupied in activities that lead them to become disengaged from their age peers. 'Many grandmothers give up working outside of the home to raise a grand-child, losing income and the less tangible benefits of employment,' such as social connectedness outside of the home (Hayslip and Kaminski 2005, p. 263). Janicki et al. (2000), report grandparent caregivers feeling shunned by their own peers who have long since relinquished caregiving responsibilities and show little willingness to help them out with their caregiving responsibilities. As in other caregiving situations, grandparents find it difficult to leave their grandchild alone or with someone else, and they therefore face restrictions on their ability to go out, with or without the child, and this has a significant impact on their ability to maintain social connectedness. Isolation from their peers and having limited times for themselves and their own pursuits is a common experience. Friendships with those in similar cohorts suffer (Miller et al. 2012). Spending time with friends and other family members becomes difficult because of caring responsibilities. The increased isolation weakens the chances of relief or support through informal avenues.

8.6.3   Caring for Children with Disability

Becoming a caregiver of a child with a disability presents particular demands. Not only are grandparents older and more likely to be less fit than younger parents, in many cases they will not have had experience of caring for someone with a dis-ability. In addition to the normal tasks of caring, grandparent caregivers often have to deal with disrupted sleep, manage difficult behaviours, deal with the physical challenges of caring and negotiate and advocate for the child in outside organisa-tions such as schools or other care centres. Kolomer et al. (2002) report that such grandparents are likely to receive less social support, yet they face higher levels of role strain and financial difficulty.

A constant concern is the wellbeing of the child and anxiety about the ability to care and advocate for the child into adulthood. Janicki et al. (2000, p. 49) found that grandparent caregivers felt challenged by the responsibilities of caring, 'fearing that they will be perceived as inadequate.' They often felt overwhelmed by the child's disabilities, and their days were fraught given the lack of support they had in the role. Grandparent caregivers also express concern about how they are perceived in the role, this reflecting worries that they may be seen as not being capable. This is tied to their age and to feeling overwhelmed in a role that did not fit with what soci-ety expected of an older person.

Disruptions to sleep compound the physical challenges and contribute to the feeling of being overwhelmed by the level of need and responsibility for the grandchild (Burton 1992). The negative consequences of caregiving, for example, emotional depression, physical injury and fatigue, all tend to be exacerbated by such inexperience. As Minkler and Fuller-Thomson (1999) observe, care-providing grandparents are frequently reminded of their own functional limitations and other personal restrictions as a consequence of their child care roles, thus making them more aware of what they cannot do (Seltzer and Kraus 1994). A non-caregiving grandparent who has trouble climbing stairs, for example, faces the issue far less often than a custodial grandparent who has no choice but to take the stairs many times each day, often carrying a child (Seeman 2009, p. 287).

In a 1992 study of the physical and emotional health of 75 grandmothers caring for children born to drug-addicted mothers, Minkler and colleagues found that 51 % of the grandmothers reported feeling emotionally depressed. Half said they could not get going and that they were totally exhausted; a third reported feeling lonely. But despite their own health problems, the grandparents wanted keep the children with them, and were willing to deny their own symptoms and needs, lest it result in the removal of the grandchild. Burnette (2000) in her study of Latino caregivers found a higher incidence of depression among caregiving grandparents than non-caregiving grandparents. Both studies point to the intensely overwhelming emotions experienced by grandparents: fear, anxiety, and isolation, the more intense when they considered their future and the future of the children whom they cared for. As Strawbridge et al. (1997) say, the children suffering developmental and emotional difficulties from the circumstances leading up to grandparent care (Pruchno 1999) as well as the main disability, will adversely affect the grandparents' health and wellbeing. Studies showing grandparental health problems come from Fuller-Thompson et al. (1997, p. 1385) who observe that grandparents reported '4 out of 5 limitations of activities of daily living.' In a later study (Fuller-Thompson and Minkler 2000), they showed too there is a greater risk of emotional burnout and depression for grandparent caregivers than for non-caregivers.

The burden of caring for children who require an unusually high degree of supervision or special care has been found to contribute to grandparents neglecting their own health care needs as we have seen (McCallion and Janicki 2000, p. 29). However, they tend to downplay problems with their own health and present a positive picture of themselves to ensure they are not perceived as incapable – to give the impression they are capable.

8.7 Reconnections

Grandparent caregivers share similar experiences with caregivers at other stages of their lifecycle. What is important here, though, is the way the age of the individuals concerned and their passage through life in their later years influences their experience of care. Grandparents who become caregivers, particularly those left to carry out the care role alone, do face social disconnectedness, this being evident in the lower levels of formal care support they receive and the role strain they experience.

The growing incidence of caregiving in this situation has led to new questions about the legal rights of grandparents as primary caregivers. Many have found they have responsibility without authority, and even though they may act effectively as legal guardians, they have little authority to plan for the child's future or request and receive formal support and services. There are also important financial questions associated with caring for a child with a disability. Without legal recognition, many are unable to access public assistance. Becoming a primary caregiver at this stage of life also raises questions about how to negotiate the normal social role expectations of older people in retirement.

While the experience of caregiving is demanding, stressful and socially isolating, it is also described as rewarding. Many describe it as emotionally satisfying, providing for greater intimacy and love. In their studies in the early 1990s, Minkler et al. (1992) and Kramer (1997) commented that grandparents said they drew strength from the knowledge that they were holding their family together and maintaining the family's identity. Grandparent caregivers find meaning through their caregiving, they experience satisfaction, personal growth and improved relationships. Dunne and Kettler (2008, p. 333) add that the role of primary carer of grandchildren gives the grandparents positive psychological experiences, knowing that their grandchildren are safe and secure.

Positive experiences of caregiving, both for the caregiver and the child, are more likely in environments where there is a good degree of social support. This can take the form of respite through informal supports from other family members, and as many grandparent carers say, they need respite and a break from caregiving duties. Apart from needing the space and time to recover from caregiving duties, grandparents also might need that to pick up on the lives they would have lived, and what their peers live. Greater recognition by formal service providers, be they social service providers, the schools sector, or the health sector, targeted support groups, financial assistance, and greater legislative recognition are all needed to support grandparents in the caregiving role.

8.8 Summary

This chapter has addressed those caregivers who find themselves in situations where their caregiving responsibilities are again at odds with normatively defined social role expectations. In the case of the young carers, this is undertaking adult responsibilities which would normally be considered beyond their capabilities. In the case of the grandparents, they are reprising the role of parents, substitute parents, or surrogate parents. Situations where children are carers of parents or other adults challenge the norms of childhood and adulthood. The motivations are clear in both areas. The differences between each of these situations and other caregiving situations are obvious: young carers are at the early stages of their life course and less likely to have access to the supports and services they need; grandparent carers are at the other end of the life course and are also less likely to have access to networks of support for the care of young children. Family affections, strength, viability and connections ensure that caregiving will take place despite current societal expectations and despite society's expectations. Policy initiatives to strengthen support networks within families, and to link these family caregivers to wider social networks and formal care services, have much potential to facilitate these expressions of family care.

Discussion Suggestions

Should children be involved in caregiving in this way?

What policies have potential to contribute to the wellbeing of young caregivers?

Is this an appropriate role for grandparents?

If so, what supports do you think they need?

Further Reading

Aldridge, J., & Becker, S. (1993). *Children who care: Inside the world of young carers.* Nottingham: Loughborough University: Young Carers Research Group.

Barnardo's, (2006). *Hidden lives.* London: Barnardo's.

Cass, B. (2007). Exploring social care: Applying a new construct to young carers and grandparent carers. *Australian Journal of Social Issues, 42*(2), 241–254.

Dearden, C., & Becker, S. (2000). *Growing up caring: Vulnerability transition to adulthood-young carers' experiences.* York: Joseph Rowntree Foundation.

McCallion, P., & Janicki, M. (Eds.). (2000). *Grandparents as carers of children with disabilities: Facing the challenges.* New York: Haworth Press Inc.

References: Young Carers

Ahmad, W. (Ed.). (2000). *Ethnicity, disability and chronic illness.* Buckingham: Open University Press.

Aldridge, J., & Becker, S. (1993). *Children who care: Inside the world of young carers.* Nottingham: Loughborough University: Young Carers Research Group.

Aldridge, J., & Becker, S. (1994). *My child, my carer: The parents' perspective.* Nottingham: Loughborough University: Young Carers Research Group.

Aldridge, J., & Becker, S. (2003). *Children caring for parents with mental illness, perspectives of young carers, parents and professionals.* Bristol: The Policy Press.

Aries, P. (1962). *Centuries of childhood.* New York: Vintage Books.

Banks, P., Cogan, N., Riddell, S., Deeley, S., Hill, M., & Tisdall, K. (2002). Does the covert nature of caring prohibit the development of effective services for young carers? *British Journal of Guidance and Counselling, 30*(3), 229–246.

Becker, S. (2007). Global perspectives on Children's unpaid caregiving in the family: Research and Policy on young Carers in the U.K., Australia, the U.S.A. and sub-Saharan Africa. *Global Social Policy, 7*(1), 23–50.

Becker, S., Aldridge, J., & Dearden, C. (1998). *Young carers and their families.* Oxford: Blackwell Science.

Bibby, A., & Becker, S. (2000). *Young carers in their own words*. London: Calouste Gulbenkian Foundation.

Butler, R., & Parr, H. (1999). *Mind and body spaces: Geographies of illness*. London: Routledge.

Carers Australia. (2009). Bring it: Young carers forum. *Carers Australia*. http://www.youngcarers. net.au/forum/

Cass, B., Smyth, C., Hill, T., Blaxland, M. & Hamilton, M. (2009). *Young carers in Australia: understanding the advantages and disadvantages of their caregiving* (Social Policy Research Paper No. 38). Australian Government, Department of Families, Housing, Community Services and Indigenous Affairs.

Charles, G., Stainton, T., & Marshall, S. (2008). Young carers: An invisible population. *Relational Child and Youth Care Practice, 22*(1), 5–12.

Charles, G., Stainton, T., & Marshall, S. (2009). Young carers: Mature before their time. *Reclaiming Children and Youth, 18*(2), 38–41.

Dearden, C., & Becker, S. (1995). *Young carers – The facts*. Sutton: Reed Business Publishing.

Dearden, C., & Becker, S. (2000). *Growing up caring: Vulnerability transition to adulthood-young carers' experiences*. York: Joseph Rowntree Foundation

Dearden, C., & Becker, S. (2002). *Young carers and education*. London: Carers U.K.

Dearden, C., Becker, S., & Aldridge, J. (1994). *Partners in caring: A briefing for professionals about young carers*. Leicestershire: Loughborough University: Young Carers Research Group, in association with Carers National Association.

Fallon, K. (1990, January 4). An involuntary workforce. *Community Care*, 12–13.

Fares, J. & Raju, D. (2007). *Child labor across the developing world: Patterns and correlations* (World Bank Policy Research Working Paper No. 4119).

Frank, J. (2002). *Making it work: Good practice with young carers and their families*. London: The Children's Society.

Frank, J., Tatum, C., & Tucker, S. (1999). *On small shoulders: Learning from the experiences of former young carers*. London: The Children's Society.

Franklin, B. (2002). *The new handbook of children's rights*. London: Routledge.

Gays, M. (2000). *Young carers in the ACT*. In: AIFS conference paper, www.aifs.gov.au/conferences/aifs7/gays.html

Grossman, F. K. (1972). *Brothers and sisters of retarded children: An exploratory study*. Syracuse: Syracuse University Press.

Hill, T., Thomson, C., & Cass, B. (2011). Young carers: Location, education and employment disadvantage. *Australian Journal of Labour Economics, 14*(2), 173–198.

Hunt, G., Levine, E., & Naiditch, L. (2005). *Young caregivers in the U.S.* National Alliance for Caregiving in Collaboration with United Hospital Fund.

International Labour Organisation (1999). *Conventions and recommendations on child labour*. http://www.ilo.org/ipec/facts/ILOconventionsonchildlabour/lang--en/index.htm

Liddiard, P., Tatum, C., & Tucker, S. (1997). *Young carers research project: Study of the common experiences of young carers in two different communities*. Milton Keynes: The Open University.

Lunn, T. (1990). *A new awareness: Community care* ("Inside" supplement). A Leeds Survey, Leeds City Council, Dept of Social Services, Leeds.

McDonald, J., Cumming, J., & Dew, K. (2009). An exploratory study of young carers and their families. *Kotuitui: New Zealand Journal of Social Science, 4*, 115–120.

Moore, T., McArthur, M., & Morrow, R. (2005). Attendance, achievement and participation: young carers' experiences of school in Australia. *Australian Journal of Education, 53*(1), 5–18.

Morrow, R. (2005). *A profile of known young carers and identification and snapshot of the ones who are hidden*. Perth: Curtin University of Technology.

Robson, E. (2003). Invisible carers: Young people in Zimbabwe's home-based healthcare. *Area, 32*(1), 59–69.

Robson, E. (2004). Hidden child workers: Young carers in Zimbabwe. *Antipode, 36*(2), 227–248.

Seeman, M. (2009). The changing role of mother of the mentally Ill: From Schizophrenogenic mother to multigenerational caregiver. *Psychiatry: Interpersonal and Biological Processes, 72*(3), 284–294.

Stables, J., & Smith, F. (1999). 'Caught in the Cinderella Trap': Narratives of disabled parents and young carers. In R. Butler & H. Parr (Eds.), *Mind and body spaces: Geographies of illness* (pp. 253–266). London: Routledge.

Thomas, N., Stainton, T., Jackson, S., Cheung, W., Doubtfire, S., & Webb, A. (2003). Your friends don't understand': Invisibility and unmet need in the lives of 'young carers. *Child & Family Social Work, 8*(1), 36–48.

Warren, J. (2007). Young carers: Conventional or exaggerated involvement in domestic and caring tasks. *Children & Society, 21*, 136–146.

References – Grandparents as Caregivers

Burnette, D. (2000). Latino grandparents rearing grandchildren with special needs effect on depressive symptomatology. *Journal of Gerontological Social Work, 33*, 1–16.

Burton, L. M. (1992). Black grandparents rearing children of drug-addicted parents. *The Gerontologist, 32*(4), 744–751.

Burton, L., & Bengtson, V. (1985). Black grandmothers: Issues of timing and continuity of roles. In V. Bengtson & J. Robertson (Eds.), *Grandparenthood* (pp. 61–77). Thousand Oaks: Sage.

Cass, B. (2007). Exploring social care: Applying a new construct to young carers and grandparent carers. *Australian Journal of Social Issues, 42*(2), 241–254.

Dearden, C., & Becker, S. (2004). *Young carers in the United Kingdom: The 2004 report.* Leicestershire: Loughborough University.

Dunne, E., & Kettler, L. (2008). Grandparents raising grandchildren in Australia; Exploring psychological health and grandparent's experience of providing kinship care. *International Journal of Social Welfare, 17*(4), 333–345.

Fuller-Thomson, E., & Minkler, M. (2000). African American grandparents raising grandchildren: A national profile of demographic and health characteristics. *Health & Social Work, 25*, 109–118.

Fuller-Thomson, E., Minkler, M., & Driver, D. (1997). A profile of grandparents raising grandchildren. *The Gerontologist, 37*(3), 406–411.

Grossman, F. K. (1972). *Brothers and sisters of retarded children: An exploratory study.* Syracuse: Syracuse University Press.

Hayslip, B., & Kaminski, P. (2005). Grandparents raising their grandchildren: A review of the literature and suggestions for practice. *The Gerontologist, 45*(2), 262–269.

Hayslip, Y. B., & Patrick, J. H. (Eds.). (2006). *Custodial grandparenting; Individual, cultural, and ethnic diversity.* New York: Springer.

Hill, T., Thomson, C., & Cass, B. (2011). Young carers: Location, education and employment disadvantage. *Australian Journal of Labour Economics, 14*(2), 173–198.

Janicki, M., McCallion, P., Grant-Griffin, L., & Kolomer, S. (2000). Grandparent caregivers: Characteristics of the grandparents and the children with disabilities they care for. *Journal of Gerontological Social Work, 33*(3), 35–56.

Katz, S., & Kessell, L. (2002). Grandparents of children with developmental disabilities: Perceptions, beliefs, and involvement in their care. *Issues in Comprehensive Paediatric Nursing, 25*(2), 113–128.

Kolomer, S., McCallion, P., & Janicki, M. (2002). African-American grandmother carers of children with disabilities: Predictors of depressive symptoms. *Journal of Gerontological Social Work, 37*(3/4), 45–63.

Kramer, B. J. (1997). Gain in the caregiving experience: Where are we? What next? *The Gerontologist, 3*, 218–232.

Lunn, T. (1990, February 22). A new awareness. *Community Care* ("Inside" supplement), viii.

Miller, E., Buys, L., & Woodbridge, S. (2012). Impact of disability on families: Grandparents perspectives. *Journal of Intellectual Disability Research, 59*(1), 102–110.

Minkler, M., & Fuller-Thompson, E. (1999). The health of grandparents raising grandchildren: Results of a national study. *American Journal of Public Health, 89*(9), 1384–1389.

Minkler, M., & Roe, K. M. (1993a). *Grandmothers as caregivers: Raising children of the crack cocaine epidemic.* Newbury Park: Sage.

Minkler, M., & Roe, K. M. (1993b). Community interventions to support grandparent caregivers. *The Gerontologist, 33,* 807–811.

Minkler, M., Roe, K. M., & Price, M. (1992). The physical and emotional health of grandmothers raising grandchildren in the crack cocaine epidemic. *The Gerontologist, 32*(5), 752–761.

Mirfin-Veitch, B., Bray, A., & Watson, M. (1997). 'We're just that sort of family': Intergenerational relationships in families including children with disabilities. *Family Relations, 46,* 305–311.

Pruchno, R. (1999). Raising grandchildren: The experiences of black and white grandmothers. *The Gerontologist, 39*(2), 209–221.

Seeman, M. V. (2009). The changing role of mother of the mentally Ill: From Schizophrenogenic mother to multigenerational caregiver. *Psychiatry, 72*(3), 284–294.

Seltzer, M. M., & Krauss, M. W. (1994). Aging parents with coresident adult children: The impact of lifelong caregiving. In M. Seltzer, M. Krauss, & M. Janicki (Eds.), *Life course perspectives on adulthood and old age* (pp. 3–18). Washington, DC: American Association on Mental Retardation.

Shore, J. R., & Hayslip, B. (1994). Custodial grandparenting: Implications for children's development. In A. E. Gottfried & A. W. Gottfried (Eds.), *Redefining families: Implications for children's development.* New York: Plenum Press.

Strawbridge, W. J., Wallhagen, M. I., Sherma, S. J., & Kaplan, G. A. (1997). New burdens or more of the same? Comparing grandparent, spouse, and adult-child caregivers. *The Gerontologist, 37,* 505–510.

Chapter 9
Recognising and Supporting Informal Care

9.1   Introduction

Our aim has been to raise the visibility of informal care and its contribution in contemporary social care systems, and to promote a greater appreciation of the experience of informal caregivers. The goal has been to provide an account of situations where members of our communities and families are called upon to provide support that goes beyond accepted family caring norms. We have focused on a number of informal caregiving situations and the experience of caregivers within them. That experience is shaped by the unique demands of the care situation, their access to social capital resources, and the support provided through formal care services.

   Care is a fundamental expression of family and community, and takes different forms through the life course. When individuals develop multiple, complex needs, non-professional family members play a critical role in providing a wide range of care tasks, but typically without recognition or entitlement to support themselves. Becoming a caregiver is increasingly an inevitable part of the life cycle and a likely life transition for family members. One aspect of that experience that seems clear to us, as we reflect on our own collective research and on the insights obtained from much of the contemporary scholarship on informal caregiving, is the notion that informal caregivers are united by shared experiences. We have used the notion of the rites of passage to frame the way we see those shared experiences. We have, thus, sought to capture the dynamics of caregiving and have explored elements of this process in a number of discrete situations: caregiving during infancy; for adults who acquire a disability through accidents of illness; for older people; and caregiving by young carers and grandparent carers. Each situation has a life course dimension that influences the experience of the caregiver. While the focus has been on chronic disability in a number of life course stages, the insights have potential to inform other caregiving situations. Informal caregivers share experiences of change and it is these that bring the diverse elements of informal caregiving together. Such shared experiences result in an enduring personal transformation that leads to a recognizable, but not always socially valued, identity as a caregiver.

P. Barrett et al., *Family Care and Social Capital: Transitions in Informal Care*,
DOI 10.1007/978-94-007-6872-7_9, © Springer Science+Business Media Dordrecht 2014

We have also sought to recognize explicitly the context of informal care in the terms of the concept of social capital. Social capital can be conceptualized in a number of ways relevant to informal caregiving, and we have considered what this might mean in a variety of caregiving contexts. Social capital can be thought of as a resource for people with disability, and our concern is with how that resource can be nurtured and supported. It can also be thought of as encompassing the capacity of informal caregivers to care, i.e., the immediate social capital that can be brought to bear on a situation of need. Thinking of social capital in this way allows recognition of the how it might be either boosted or diminished. When boosted, both the caregiver and the person with disability gain the benefits of socially connected care. When diminished or 'leached', caregivers come to share in the reduced circumstances of those they care for.

Social capital also refers to the capacity of caregivers to negotiate the bridges that connect social networks as they advocate for those they care for, and for other caregivers, both individually and collectively. As informal caregivers gain knowledge and expertise through the caregiving process, as they build bridges between health service professionals, care agencies and community groups, their capacity to contribute to this form of social capital grows. Informal, family care work is a resource for society and it complements social care systems. Social capital also represents the wider societal or community capacity to provide care.

We suggest, therefore, that we can gain a better understanding of the situation of informal caregivers by focusing on key points within the caregiving process, points which are characterized by experiences of separation and liminality, and considering the potential for reconnection. Recognising this community of shared experience has potential to inform policy development and practice guidelines. This is intended to encourage practitioners and policy makers to become more conversant with key issues in informal care situations and more willing to recognize and include informal caregivers in decision making.

Our approach has been informed by a range of disciplines including: social work and policy studies (Barrett and Hale) and occupational therapy (Butler). What follows is a review of our account of the dynamic experience of caregiving, an account which recognizes the risk of liminality and the hope of reconnection. We conclude by reflecting on the contribution of informal care to social capital, and the need for policy to support family carers.

9.2   Caring Across the Life Course

In Chaps. 4, 5, 6, 7 and 8 we have outlined key aspects of the experience of caregivers, drawing upon research into the transition processes in caregiving. While each chapter has had a different focus, addressing different stages of caregiving across the life course, it is also possible to see many commonalities in caregiving. It is clear that becoming a caregiver represents a major life change, one that can be examined in terms of the points of separation, the subsequent experience of liminality, and processes associated with reconnection. We have drawn on stages in the rites of passage concept given its usefulness in accommodating the variety of caregiving situations, and we have begun to reflect on just what is involved in achieving reconnection for family members who become informal caregivers.

Informal caregivers do tend to have an ambivalent social position and reconnection does involve both practical support so caregivers are not alone in their responsibility for the life of another, and a search for meaning in that new role. By suggesting the social position of informal caregivers is ambivalent, we want to draw attention to the lack of social value given to the role within the broader public sphere. From many caregiver comments there is a sense that the work of informal caregivers is underappreciated within health and social care systems and by the formal care sector, and under-acknowledged in policies for their support.

Each chapter identifies moments of separation. Depending on the nature of the disabling impairment or illness, some occur suddenly, some occur more slowly. The separation stage demarcates the boundaries between the current, expected and anticipated life of the family member and the realization that taking on a caregiving role will lead to significant change, a biographical disruption. Liminality also implies search for meaning in a new situation where pre-existing norms and ways-of-being are suspended. It is also a period when informal caregivers search for new knowledge and skills in the art of caring for a loved one, and new ways of living in this new social role. It is a time when the anticipated future gives way to uncertainty and the need for adjustment.

In Chap. 3 we summarized many of the spatial and temporal changes that occur, and these were illustrated in Chaps. 4, 5, 6, 7, and 8. The impact of these changes for the home life of caregivers and for the organization of daily life was illustrated in different caregiving situations. Becoming an informal caregiver also has significant implications for the way external spaces outside the home and the wider community are negotiated. For many people with disabilities, movement outside of the home is a movement within a foreign territory. Each new foray needs negotiation and new relationships, each needs caregiver input and strong advocacy on behalf of the disabled child or adult.

9.3 The Promise of Reconnection

The rites of passage framework for analysis implies reconnection, but reconnection is not assured and many caregiver lives could be described as an experience of ongoing liminality. Many have the responsibility for care without the authority, when formal care services are involved. The liminal experience is therefore reinforced by the lack of a wide social appreciation for the role.

We argue there needs to be greater recognition of the contribution made by informal caregivers by acknowledgement by health and welfare professionals and by policy makers that informal care warrants support. To reiterate, reconnection implies a social context and means not being alone but being reintegrated into the wider community and in sharing the burden of care. It implies finding positive meaning in the caregiver role and the support to sustain that. It involves an assurance in the resourcefulness of oneself in meeting care work demands, as well as assurance in the resourcefulness of others, be they formal care services or members of a social network, to be helped in helping the person with disability.

Reconnecting implies an ability to deploy resources, be they personal, social, political or financial, to move beyond liminal experiences. Reconnection is finding one's feet as a caregiver and being recognized and valued in that role. Reconnected caregivers are supported in their caring through, for example, opportunities for respite care, and they may be linked with formal support systems. Social recognition of the needs of carers implies being included in discussions with the cared-for person and professionals. It should mean that carers needs are assessed and the means provided to have them met. Carers need to feel valued and supported in their role, not as a way of substituting for formal care, but in support of their love, affection and duty to help the person in need. Social recognition implies the formal care sector accepts their knowledge and expertise and uses them to improve formal care practice and policies.

Reconnected care, however, does not mean a lack of change. Informal caregivers will be thrust back into states of liminality as they are forced to negotiate and renegotiate new developments in the cared-for person's condition or in their own response to it. Informal caregiving involves responding to 'multi-layered issues over time' and experiences of grappling with them 'again and again' (Edelson 2000, p. 50). For parents of children with disabilities, for example, the feelings of grief and loss will resurface throughout the child's life, for example at times when the parents realise that typical milestones such as college, marriage, grandchildren will be impossible. Learning to balance conflicting feelings is lifelong and often harder than losing a loved one altogether.

9.4 Social Capital

In Chap. 1 we acknowledge the emergence of five broad approaches to the study of care. Fine (2007) proposes these as 'parallel literatures, each indicative of a coherent, but in many ways quite distinct set of interests and concerns (p. 140)'. They addressed the ethic of care; social policy traditions; care in the health professions; care in the literature of work-life balance; and demographic approaches to care. At the end of this book we put forward the argument that the concept of social capital provides a bridge that makes these distinct sets of literature permeable and comprehensible to each other. Social capital is a construct that acts in similar ways to the construct of 'culture' in bringing together a number of otherwise competing discourses (Portes 1998). It is capable of weaving different literatures and providing a constant thread. The contribution of social capital to each of these fields is outlined here.

The ethic of care literature lends itself to the perspective of care as the embodiment of social capital. This approach speaks to the way that care can be categorized as work or labour in its own right. Social capital is embodied in the person of the carer who is able to take responsibility and to discharge the work of care in a competent manner (Tronto 1993). Bourdieu (1986) could identify the hazard that such embodied labour presented, since it was precisely such a form of social capital that could be euphemized and overlooked. His early essays on social capital described this form of labour and brought it into a philosophical discourse that could be extended to economic capital. The literature from care ethics has therefore been able to articulate care as a labour time. There is very little literature that speaks to the issue of direct payments to family carers. However, a philosophical stance that values the labour of care as a form of social capital resource seems to come close to making an argument for such payments.

The ethics of care literature is also a place where the relationship between carer and care-recipient can be acknowledged. One of the key aspects of competent care is the necessity to include responsivity to the disabled individual (Tronto 1993). However, such a focus seems to position the person in need of care always as a recipient, while the carer is forever positioned as donor. Social capital offers a way of problematizing the linear relationship between donor and recipient. For example, there are many ways in which care-recipients can be conceptualized as donors of social capital as well as recipients (Prilleltensky 2004). They may care for others because they are parents themselves, but also they may care for others simply by telling their story or acting in ways that are responsive to others. It is also the case that carers can move in and out of disability states, as well as acting as carers. The carer may at various times look after one person, but require to be cared for at others.

The use of the concept of donor and recipient within social capital can illuminate some of the power issues that arise within the relationship between carer and care-recipient. These dynamics can be difficult to describe in terms of relationships based on familial ties of affection. Social capital provides a perspective that suggests care may be given within the context of affection and intimacy, but equally suggests that these are not necessary conditions. Therefore, care is not precluded when these ties are not present. Social capital acts as a reminder of the feminist insight that power inheres in the capacity to command care. The 'power' of a dependent individual would otherwise be rendered invisible. Some of that power comes in the instant of recognition: when one person sees the need of another, the first step to care has been taken. However, this draws attention to the power issues related to who recognises a particular need and therefore acts on that recognition. The move towards community care within a neoliberal context could be interpreted as a deliberate act of blindness in relation to the dependency needs in society. The power dynamic in such a situation is essentially exploitative and not ethically supportable.

Care in the social policy literature has been more directly informed by a concern with the health outcomes of carers. There is ample evidence that the burden of care falls unequally on women and this literature has been instrumental in delineating the negative social capital inhering in care labour. Negative social capital is described by Portes (2000) as that situation where giving comes at too great a cost for some individuals or communities and results in the overall loss of resources. This occurs within cultural narratives of care where communities can become dysfunctional through customs that require large amounts of hospitality that are not adequately recompensed. The concept is bedded into accounts of care through the work of Kittay (1999) who draws, who draws attention to the plight of carers of those with severe disability who cannot reciprocate. Most social policy seems to be focused on removing this negative social capital, rather than in finding ways of enhancing the positive aspects of social capital. These solutions tend to be articulated within frameworks of the provision of social benefits or allowances to carers.

The approach to care taken by health professionals provides some interesting comparisons with informal care across a number of parameters. Increasingly, it seems that competent and articulate family carers respond to the efforts of health professionals with a sense of disappointment. Over and over, carer narratives describe how they learned that the solutions to their problems were not going to come from health professionals. The lack of regard seems to be mutual, and an anti-family bias can often be seen in the discourse of health professionals when they face complex disability situations. This antagonism runs parallel to disability discourse that critiques health professionals as colonisers of the experience of disability (Oliver 1993). Non-traditional approaches to health care seem to offer hope of a more comprehensive service to family carers.

In New Zealand a strongly family centered approach has arisen within the context of indigenous health care (Ministry of Health 2009). The Whanau Ora approach identifies the individualistic approach of most current healthcare approaches as inimical to the health of families. Although it is early days, the Whanau Ora approach offers ways in which healthcare systems can begin to strengthen the social capital available within informal care systems. There are some promising indications that flexible and creative use of funding used to strengthen the family can be more effective than more extended traditional interventions targeting the individual with disability.

At a less systematic level a strongly family-centered approach has also spontaneously arisen within non-indigenous groups. For example, families have begun to initiate micro enterprises and circles of support across the world. These include the experience of the CAPRE group at a small village in Nova Scotia, Canada, who have developed a range of micro businesses around their young people with disability; the PLAN group in Vancouver who focus on circles of support; and family collectives in New Zealand. These have been initiated by families asking questions about what will happen to their loved ones after they are gone, and refusing to accept the provision of programmes by health professionals as the only solution. These families generally do not ask for funding, but they focus on using their own resources in terms of social capital. There is a strong focus on building sustainable solutions, which seems to be the characteristic of families who have become strong in the sense of the social capital in which they are embedded.

The literature on work-life balance has been important in describing the role of informal care at a demographic level. This points, in various ways, to the equivalence of informal care with values such as GDP. The focus on finding ways of counting the labour of carers in various ways is a clear articulation of the social capital embedded within it. Such approaches are usually associated with the development of allowances for family care in general, in the form of benefits and parental leave, etc. In terms of the argument in this book, however, the economic valuing of care labour is an important addition to a perspective the makes the labour associated with care clearly visible. Care movements have followed the lead in providing figures for the kind of government funding that is saved by informal care across the sector (Carers UK 2010).

Another important component of this literature on work-life balance has been the increasing awareness of discriminatory practices affecting carers, which add to their burden (Clements 2009). Paid employment is one of the ways in which social capital is built, particularly elements of bridging social capital. Just as it is difficult for people with disability, it is often also very difficult for carers to obtain the degree of flexibility that enables them to maintain and pursue their own employment.

The other side of paid employment for women has been the way that it has removed a huge pool of potential carers from the equation. It is no coincidence that the discourse of social capital has arisen at a time and place where the labour of carers has never been less available. The emergence of social capital as a construct remembers this absent army and also, at some level, it acknowledges the work that continues to be done by women in non-western countries. The value of social capital is that it enables a discourse along lines of labour, rather than drawing it along more emotive gender lines.

The final literature is another demographic approach, this time addressing the wave of older people advancing with the ageing of the baby boomer generation (Cornwall and Davey 2004). In terms of social capital resources, it seems likely that this group will find ways of going into old age in ways that reflect innovative approaches. For example there are an increasing number of 'Timebank' initiatives, where carers provide care to other carers. In some places the government has under-written the timebank ideal, for instance in Japan, where old people have been encouraged to care for older people in return for the promise that they will be cared for in their turn. This is one way of actualizing the social capital that inheres in the labour time of carers.

Overall there appears to be three broad approaches to social capital that weave through these different literatures: (a) the social capital that is embodied in the individual carer; (b) social capital as a resource that is made available through the social networks of the carer; and (c) negative social capital that leads to the loss of resources from the carer.

9.5 Social Capital and the Need for Responsive Policy

We have attempted to take account of the context of caregiving, seeing personal interrelationships as nested within wider kin networks and linked with wider professional formal care networks. Informal care is both an expression of social capital and an activity that builds social capital. It is both an indicator of resources of mutual support within social networks and it has the effect of adding to the stock of social resources. This is most evident in the way caregivers develop links with the disability community and through this often become involved in mutual support as they reach out to assist the new caregivers. They develop skills in advocating for the child as they deal with health professionals. Carers become partners in care.

The challenge for decision makers is to develop policy which recognizes the contribution of social capital to meeting the needs of people with disability and to promote policies which build it up. We have seen that the vulnerability of people with disability to social exclusion is shared by their informal caregivers. In this regard, therefore, the efforts to identify and claim the legitimate rights of people with disabilities are relevant for informal caregivers. For people with disability, these include the right to individual choice, the right to autonomy in decision-making, and the right to control over services (Bigby et al. 2007). For people with disability such change has reinforced the development of consumer-driven models and the independent living movement. This perspective of autonomy and citizenship rights has emphasized a model of support which focuses on participation and inclusion. It is a call for change from 'other-defined' needs and wants to 'self-defined' needs and wants and towards personal control. We suggest these initiatives are equally relevant for informal caregivers.

Specifically, we recommend greater attention be given to caregiver needs at the time of assessment. It requires, as Hirst (2005) suggests, the promotion of early and regular health checks of caregivers' physical, emotional and psychological needs. Assessing the family carer's willingness, ability and capacity to carry out the work formalises the role and is a way of socially valuing and equipping caregivers. This role fitting will increase the likelihood of successful reconnected care work. Employment is an important means of sustaining the connectedness of the informal caregiver and improving the family finances. Policies to enable informal caregivers to reconcile their care demands with paid employment are therefore critical.

Facilitating the development of social capital implies strengthening the capacity of informal caregivers and caregiver groups to forge links with other organisations and in promoting community development initiatives. Supporting informal community networks is important – making available community meeting places and community groups, be they play groups, exercise groups, book groups, gardening groups or walking groups.

Researchers have potential to contribute to the development of strategies that will enhance the lives of carers and care-recipients. There is a need for ongoing research into the interface between formal and informal care. Too little attention has been paid to informal caregiving in terms of the management of services. Informal carers have said that their homes can be like 'a railway station' (Hale 2006) as professionals visit the care-recipient. Family caregivers are often left on the periphery as attention is directed towards the care-recipient, and there is a case for research that will lead to new models of care management that incorporate the family caregiver more fully. The notion that public assistance for family and informal carers will somehow weaken the inclination to take care of those in need is still pervasive in many areas. But informal care plays a critical role in our health and social service systems. There is a need for greater research into strategies that will lead to care-friendly communities – where family and informal caregivers are not unduly disadvantaged for carrying through with their inclination to help a loved one who is in need.

Informal caregiving needs to be recognised as a public health issue and additional resources to support carers and to prevent ill health made available. Socially valuing informal care will in many circumstances mean providing some kind of recompense to caregivers through payments and other forms of support.

In sum, Kittay et al.'s (2005) comments on shared characteristics of caring point to its significance:

> All caring, therefore, is at once intensely personal and inextricably social, symbolic, and meaningful. It is both deeply emotional and a rational, pragmatic, and practical endeavor. It is a practice that comprises certain fundamental moral virtues and human goods. It can be done well or badly; in a way that enriches or alienates, dignifies or humiliates either caregiver or the one cared for. Above all, caring is a practice that effects both the person receiving care and those providing it, the ethics of caregiving pertain to carer and care-recipient alike, and caring brings into being (or rests on) a relationship that has crucial cultural and ethical meanings (p. 444).

Caring is both a personal expression and an act with wider social significance. It is both emotional and rational, it affects the cared-for person and the caregiver. It is a relationship that has crucial social significance and it needs to be recognized as such.

Discussion Suggestions

Why is social capital important for family and informal caregivers?

Do you agree with Kittay's idea of doulia, with the implication that the community should be open to supporting the caregiver? If so, what form might this support take?

What are the pathways to building social capital and what are the blocks?

References

Bigby, C., Fyffe, C., & Ozanne, E. (2007). *Planning and support for people with intellectual disability. Issues for case managers and other practitioners.* London: Jessica Kingsley.

Bourdieu, P. (1986). *The forms of capital.* New York: Greenwood Press.

Carers UK. (2010). *Tipping point for care: Time for a new social contract.* www.carersuk.org

Clements, L. (2009). *Carers and their rights: The law relating to carers.* London: Carers UK.

Cornwall, J., & Davey, J. (2004). *Impact of population ageing in New Zealand on the demand for health and disability support services, and workforce implications.* Wellington: Ministry of Health.

Edelson, M. (2000). *My journey with Jake: A memoir of parenting and disability.* Toronto: Between the Lines.

Fine, M. (2007). *A caring society: Caring and the dilemmas of human services in the 21st century.* Basingstoke: Palgrave Macmillan.

Hale, B. (2006). *The meaning of home as it becomes a place for care – The emergence of a new life stage for frail older people?* Ph.D. Thesis for the University of Otago, Dunedin, New Zealand.

Hirst, M. (2005). Carer distress: A prospective, population-based study. *Social Science & Medicine, 61*(3), 697–708.

Kittay, E., Jennings, B., & Wasunna, A. (2005). Dependency, difference and the global ethic of longterm care. *The Journal of Political Philosophy, 13*(4), 443–469.

Ministry of Health. (2009). *Whanau Ora tool*. Wellington: New Zealand Ministry of Health.

Oliver, M. (1993). Re-defining disability: A challenge to research. In J. Swain, V. Finkelstein, S. French, & M. Oliver (Eds.), *Disabling barriers – Enabling environments*. London: Sage.

Portes, A. (1998). Social capital: Its origins and applications in modern sociology. *Annual Review of Sociology, 24*, 1–12.

Portes, A. (2000). The two meanings of social capital. *Sociological Forum, 15*(1), 1–12.

Prilleltensky, O. (2004). My child is not my carer: Mothers with physical disability and the well-being of children. *Disability & Society, 19*(3), 209–223.

Tronto, J. C. (1993). *Moral boundaries: A political argument for an ethic of care*. New York: Routledge.

Afterword

Carers New Zealand congratulates the authors of *Family Care and Social Capital: Voices of Informal Carers* for developing this thoughtful, comprehensive resource.

Though we can all expect to give or receive family care during our lives, it remains a private and often invisible role, one we humans have always undertaken for those we love or feel a duty toward, and one that is thus easily taken for granted.

Shedding light on this private world of caring has taken many years, through the work of carer peak bodies internationally, governments, not for profit and community organisations, and through the development of provoking research and resources like this one.

Historically caring is something families have done without fanfare for those with health, disability, or age-related needs. Today's carers are demanding more. In New Zealand, nine carers and adult disabled family members took a human rights case against the Government, arguing that to not pay family carers for the same work as those employed in caring jobs is discriminatory. After successive defeats, the Crown has stopped appealing these decisions and is at last exploring payment options for family carers. New Zealand's payment policy will be the first of its kind in the world, one that will be watched closely by other nations.

This year a new International Alliance of Carer Organizations meets for the first time in Dublin after years of planning by carer peak bodies from North America, Europe, Australia, and New Zealand. Initial goals will be to pursue United Nations and World Health Organization recognition for the world's population of family caregivers, and to provide a foundation that will allow us to collaboratively achieve key outcomes for carers.

As Baroness Pitkeathley often says, this is work that will never be done. Scholarly works like this publication, the efforts of the global carer movement, progressive government decision-making, and the evolution of progressive societies worldwide, are all steps toward ensuring that the hidden, often uncelebrated role of caring will be appropriately recognised and supported.

While much remains to be done for carers, and for those who work with and support them, it is also important to reflect on the significant progress that has been achieved for carers over the years.

P. Barrett et al., *Family Care and Social Capital: Transitions in Informal Care*, 159
DOI 10.1007/978-94-007-6872-7, © Springer Science+Business Media Dordrecht 2014

This book is another stepping stone in the journey to understand the impacts of caring, and how to ensure more thoughtful support for carers, whose work underpins every country's health and social systems.

Laurie Hilsgen

Laurie Hilsgen
CEO, Carers NZ
Secretariat, NZ Carers Alliance of 45 national not for profits

Author Index

P. Barrett et al., *Family Care and Social Capital: Transitions in Informal Care*, 161
DOI 10.1007/978-94-007-6872-7, © Springer Science+Business Media Dordrecht 2014

Subject Index

P. Barrett et al., *Family Care and Social Capital: Transitions in Informal Care*,
DOI 10.1007/978-94-007-6872-7, © Springer Science+Business Media Dordrecht 2014

Printed by Printforce, the Netherlands